OXFORD WORLD'S CLASSICS

DIALOGUES AND
THE NATURAL HISTORY

DAVID HUME (1711–76) was born and educated in Edinburgh. His philosophical writings, notably *A Treatise of Human Nature* (1739 and 1740), *An Enquiry concerning Human Understanding* (1748), and *An Enquiry concerning the Principles of Morals* (1751), were underestimated in his lifetime but have established him since as the greatest philosopher to have written in the English language. By contrast his immense *History of England* (1754–62), together with his essays, brought literary fame and wealth before his death.

His account of the natural causes of the phenomenon of religion, given in *The Natural History of Religion* (1757), and his profoundly critical and seminal examination, in the *Dialogues concerning Natural Religion* (1779), of the reasons usually advanced for belief in God— both reproduced here—together constitute the most formidable attack upon the rationality of belief in God ever mounted by a philosopher.

In the course of a life in which, by his own declaration, 'love of literary fame' was his ruling passion, Hume also contrived to distinguish himself as a tutor, as secretary to the commander of two British military expeditions, as librarian of the Advocates' Library and, in the 1760s, as a diplomat and senior civil servant. His brief autobiography, written a few weeks before his death, is included in this volume.

J. C. A. GASKIN is a graduate of Oxford University and a Fellow of Trinity College, Dublin where he was also Professor of Naturalistic Philosophy. His *Hume's Philosophy of Religion* (2nd edn., 1988) is widely regarded as the primary philosophical examination of all the main issues. He is also author of *The Quest for Eternity* and *Varieties of Unbelief*, and has edited Hobbes's *Elements of Law* and *Leviathan* for Oxford World's Classics. He was made a Doctor of Letters by the University of Dublin in 1997.

OXFORD WORLD'S CLASSICS

For almost 100 years Oxford World's Classics have brought readers closer to the world's great literature. Now with over 700 titles—from the 4,000-year-old myths of Mesopotamia to the twentieth century's greatest novels—the series makes available lesser-known as well as celebrated writing.

The pocket-sized hardbacks of the early years contained introductions by Virginia Woolf, T. S. Eliot, Graham Greene, and other literary figures which enriched the experience of reading. Today the series is recognized for its fine scholarship and reliability in texts that span world literature, drama and poetry, religion, philosophy and politics. Each edition includes perceptive commentary and essential background information to meet the changing needs of readers.

OXFORD WORLD'S CLASSICS

DAVID HUME

Principal Writings on Religion
including
Dialogues Concerning Natural Religion
and
The Natural History of Religion

Edited with an Introduction and Notes by
J. C. A. GASKIN

Oxford   New York
OXFORD UNIVERSITY PRESS

Oxford University Press, Great Clarendon Street, Oxford OX2 6DP
Oxford New York
Athens Auckland Bangkok Bogotá Buenos Aires Calcutta
Cape Town Chennai Dar es Salaam Delhi Florence Hong Kong Istanbul
Karachi Kuala Lumpur Madrid Melbourne Mexico City Mumbai
Nairobi Paris São Paulo Singapore Taipei Tokyo Toronto Warsaw
and associated companies in Berlin Ibadan

Oxford is a registered trade mark of Oxford University Press

Editorial material © J. C. A. Gaskin 1993

First published as a World's Classics paperback 1993
Reissued as an Oxford World's Classics paperback 1998

British Library Cataloguing in Publication Data
Data available

Library of Congress Cataloging in Publication Data
Hume, David, 1711–1776.
[Dialogues concerning natural religion]
Dialogues concerning natural religion; and, The natural history
of religion / David Hume; edited with an introduction by J. C. A. Gaskin.
p. cm.—(Oxford world's classics)
Dialogues concerning natural religion originally published: 1779;
The natural history of religion originally published: 1757.
Includes bibliographical references and index.
1. Natural theology—Early works to 1800. 2. Religion—Philosophy—
Early works to 1800. I. Gaskin, J. C. A. (John Charles Addison)
II. Hume, David, 1711–1776. Natural history of religion. 1993.
III. Title: Dialogues concerning natural religion.
IV. Title: Natural history of religion. V. Series.
B1493.D52 1993 210—dc20 93–18246
ISBN 0–19–283876–8

1 3 5 7 9 10 8 6 4 2

Printed in Great Britain by
Cox & Wyman, Reading, Berkshire

PREFACE

SINCE its first publication in 1779, there have been at least fourteen editions in English of the *Dialogues concerning Natural Religion*. Collected editions of Hume's works apart, *The Natural History of Religion* has not fared as well although, since 1963, it has appeared on four occasions bound in with the *Dialogues*. Apart from a few uncritical (and not always reliable) reprintings of the texts, the usual editorial strategy has been to surround what Hume wrote, especially in the *Dialogues*, with a vast bulk of interpretation and argument about what Hume really meant or believed.

The purposes of the present edition are more direct. They are to provide the reader with a reliable text and an editorial apparatus which will facilitate understanding without directing the interpretation or deciding the outcome of Hume's arguments in advance of his own words.

Accordingly, the Introduction gives an account of the overall structure of Hume's critique of religion and some indication of the problems of interpretation (not their solutions). The part-by-part abstracts of the *Dialogues* and *Natural History* are to assist in the locating of subjects, or in returning to a particular area of interest at the conclusion of a read. The volume concludes with an index of classical persons referred to in Hume's texts. Its purpose is to save numerous minor explanatory notes.

I am grateful to a number of colleagues who have looked at parts of what I have written or advised me about points of detail. I am also obliged to the Arts and Social Sciences Benefactions Fund of Dublin University for enabling me to avoid any personal embranglement with the digital twitching required to operate modern word processing machinery.

J. C. A. GASKIN

September 1992

CONTENTS

INTRODUCTION

HUME on religion may be read as biography, as literature or as philosophy. As biography, it may be examined for evidence about Hume's 'real' beliefs concerning religion. (He was brought up a Presbyterian, denied being a deist, expressed surprise that anyone should be an atheist, and yet seemed to undermine religious belief at almost every point.) The biographical question is undeniably fascinating but to give it primacy is to belittle and unduly personalize what he wrote. As literature, Hume's contribution to eighteenth-century prose is stylish: conspicuous for its memorable rhetorical exclamations, its ability to express a complex thought in brief compass, its irony and its occasional passion or dry self-deprecation. But it is as philosophy that Hume's writings attain classic status. In metaphysics, morality, and politics as well as in religion, he displays an extraordinary ability to peel away layers of familiar words that seem to convey sense and do not, and to expose the poverty of basic assumptions that look like truth and wisdom and are not.

Why then have Hume's principal writings on religion not previously appeared in the World's Classics Series? Part of the answer is that general interest in the philosophy of religion has grown hugely only in recent years, and Hume has come to be recognized as the founder of the subject in its modern form.

Another part of the answer is that the *Dialogues concerning Natural Religion* in particular were for a long time underestimated by the philosophical and theological establishments in Britain, possibly, one suspects, as a subconscious defence against the harm they were capable of inflicting upon conventional religious apologetics. Thus, for example, William Paley's *Evidences of Christianity* (1794) and *Natural Theology* (1802) had in effect been refuted by Hume in the *Dialogues* (1779) and elsewhere before they were even written; but Paley, not Hume, was the standard reading on religion for students throughout the nineteenth century and into the twentieth. Even when the balance changed in Hume's favour, under the influence of Logical Positivism in the 1930s and philosophical analysis in the post-war decades, the fashion was still to discuss a single argument or section of Hume's work in isolation from the rest.

But this will no longer do. Hume's writings on religion are not the piecemeal criticisms of a clever but careless sceptic. They are, as a number of books published since 1961 have shown,[1] a systematic critique of the whole subject by a philosophical genius who was also a moderate sceptic: one who looked at the world with a cool and consistent recognition of the very limited possibilities of real knowledge about 'remote and abstruce' subjects. Hume's writings on religion make up a whole, and need to be read as a whole.

Reason and Religion

Most successful religions contain two elements: an element of general and public information which, it is held, would be evident to anyone who looked at the facts of the world or the relevant arguments, quite apart from any privileged information; and an element of special information in the form of disclosed mysteries or revelations given uniquely to the initiate or to the person whose teaching the initiate is following. In Christianity these elements have conventionally been distinguished as 'natural religion', now more commonly called 'natural theology', and as 'revealed religion' or simply 'revelation'. But the terms 'natural religion' and 'revelation' have reference beyond Christianity, and two different conclusions that may be drawn from the arguments of natural religion, combined or not combined with different revelations, distinguish theism from deism, and one theistic religion from another.

Theism is the belief that (*a*) one and only one all-powerful God exists, (*b*) that this single God created the universe and is the ultimate reason for or explanation of all that is, *and also* (*c*) that God remains active and everywhere present ('immanent') in his creation, sustaining it in being, answering prayers, causing miracles on special occasions, and revealing himself and his purposes to mankind both in special revelations (e.g. through Abraham or Jesus or Mahomet) and in the general human experience of the divine.

[1] See entries under Flew, Gaskin, and Penelhum on p. xxix.

In this sense Judaism, Christianity, and Islam are all theistic religions although they differ radically in what they accept as a special revelation. All three religions accept the truth of (*a*) and (*b*) willy-nilly as a necessary prerequisite to (*c*), but equally each of them, to a greater or lesser extent at different times (and Christianity normally and almost from the beginning), holds that (*a*) and (*b*) are *reasonable* beliefs because they are supported by the arguments and evidence set out in natural religion.

These arguments are for the most part exceedingly ancient. Their roots are in Greek philosophical monotheism, particularly in the writings of Xenophon (reporting Socrates), Plato, Aristotle under certain interpretations and, in late and full summary form, in Cicero's *De Natura Deorum* (*Concerning the Nature of the Gods*). They were absorbed into early Christianity and, in English theological and philosophical writing of the late seventeenth century and throughout Hume's lifetime, the designations 'argument *a posteriori*' and 'argument *a priori*' referred to the two most widely employed of the arguments.

The argument *a posteriori* (literally 'from afterwards') is what we now loosely call the 'design argument': the argument that the natural order and/or purposes discernible in the world show that it has been the creation of a being with vast intelligence. The argument *a priori* (literally 'from before') is in fact several arguments approximating to what, since Kant, has generally been called the 'cosmological argument' (but again there are several). These are arguments of the form: 'the causal sequences of the universe *must* have a first cause', or 'the contingent things which are the universe *must* be held in being by an entity which necessarily exists', and so on.

Hume attacks both types of argument systematically—the argument *a priori* by implication in *A Treatise of Human Nature*, more directly in *An Enquiry concerning Human Understanding* (note particularly the last section), and explicitly in Part IX of the *Dialogues*; the argument *a posteriori* in Section XI of the *Enquiry* and virtually throughout the *Dialogues*.

But the claimed reasonableness of Christian theism is not exhausted by its appeal to natural religion in support of the basic theistic beliefs (*a*) and (*b*). It was additionally claimed—and these claims were codified and repeated by John Locke, Samuel Clarke,

and many others at or shortly before the beginning of the eighteenth century—that it was reasonable to believe the special revelation of God's nature and purposes contained in the Bible, and
particularly in the New Testament, on two grounds. One was that
the events of the New Testament fulfilled the prophecies of the
Old. The other was that the doctrines contained in the New Testament were authenticated by the performance of miracles. The latter
argument was more important and is as follows.

Granted both that the power of performing miracles (i.e. bringing about events impossible within the natural order) could only be
conferred upon a man by God, and that God would not confer such
a power upon those misrepresenting him, then any man who performed miracles gave evidence in so doing that he had authority
from God to deliver a revelation, and hence that the revelation was
true. The seeds of this argument appear to be embedded in the
Gospels themselves in more than one place (e.g. 1 John 3: 2). The
argument was both fashionable among the orthodox and under
attack from various deistic writers in the first half of the eighteenth
century. Hume replies to it in Section X of *An Enquiry concerning
Human Understanding* ('Of Miracles'), arguing, among other
things, that it is more probable that the historical records are in
some way inaccurate than that the miracles they relate actually
took place. In this instance Hume and the critics of the 'argument
from miracles' were remarkably effective. They opened the way
for nineteenth-century textual criticism which treated the books of
the Bible as normal historical documents and, as Soame Jenyns
observed as early as 1776, miracles and prophecies 'must now
depend for much of their credibility on the truth of that religion,
whose credibility they were at first intended to support'.[2]

But rational theism, Christian or otherwise, with its appeals to
arguments in support of its basic beliefs (*a*) and (*b*) (and, in the
Christian case, with its further appeals to special evidence in support of the historical revelation) was not the only rationalization of
religion current in the eighteenth century.

Deism is a philosophical view of religious belief which accepts
(*a*) and (*b*) on (and only on) the basis of the arguments and evidence produced in their favour, but rejects (*c*) in general and the

---

[2] Quoted in E. C. Mossner, *The Life of David Hume* (Edinburgh, 1954), 294.

notion of a special revelation in particular. It thus technically avoids atheism while rejecting the Christian or any other particular revelation of an immanent God. The Deity is indeed the Great Architect of the Universe, but is not busy in a minute part of it answering prayers, performing miracles, dictating laws to the patriarch of an ancient tribe, or advising the leaders of a modern cult.

As a critical philosophical position, deism had a considerable influence in England and France during the whole of Hume's lifetime,[3] and the reasons why Hume strenuously rejected the appellation 'deist' need to be understood. In the first place, the term was bandied about by the orthodox as a reproach—like calling someone an atheist in a devoutly religious community only not quite as serious. In the second place, whatever Hume really believed about religion, his comprehensive critical analysis of the arguments and evidence of natural religion was even more a rejection of deism than it was of rational theism. If the *evidence* for (*a*) and (*b*) is defective, the theist still has something to cling on to in (*c*), even if it is only some version of 'blind faith' in the revelation, augmented by personal 'religious experience'; and since acceptance of (*c*) presupposes the truth of (*a*) and (*b*), theism as belief may survive the destruction of its rational basis. The deist, on the other hand, having already rejected (*c*) on whatever grounds, has nothing left but atheism if the arguments for accepting (*a*) and (*b*) are null and void.

Hume would not admit to being an atheist for at least two reasons. One was because of the social inconveniences attached. As it was, he was twice rejected for professorial chairs at Scottish universities on account of his 'infidelity', and was on several occasions threatened with ostracization or even prosecution on account of his publications despite his evident care to keep his most critical views at several removes from himself. (Note the *reported* views of the Epicurean in Section XI of the *Enquiry*, and the literary form of the *Dialogues* which distances what is said from the author.) The second reason was, as we shall see, because

---

[3] Note for instance the rise and prevalence of Freemasonry in the eighteenth century and the deistic language of its rituals. A masterful survey of the whole scene of thought, including the controversy concerning miracles but excluding Freemasonry, is still provided by Sir Leslie Stephen's *History of English Thought in the Eighteenth Century*, originally published in 1876.

any conclusion as confident and positive as atheism would have been inconsistent with the scepticism expressed by Hume in his philosophical works.

In short: the reasonableness of Christianity depended upon the arguments of natural religion (arguments shared by other theistic religions *and* by philosophical deism) and upon revelation, itself held to be authenticated by prophecy and miracles. Hume mounts a large-scale and immensely effective attack upon natural religion in the *Enquiry* and *Dialogues*, and a brief but seminal attack upon the credentials of revelation in Section X of the *Enquiry*. The *Dialogues* and the section of the *Enquiry* specifically concerned with natural religion are reproduced in full in the present volume. Section X of the *Enquiry*, everywhere available in countless re-printings, anthologies, and collections of essays on miracles, is not.

The Scope of Hume's Critique

Hume's philosophical critique of religion does not stop short at an examination of the specific arguments and evidence adduced in its favour. He also deploys in his main works on general philosophy, *A Treatise of Human Nature* and the first *Enquiry*, particularly in the later, a species of 'mitigated scepticism' which is inconsistent with any positive assertion about God's nature, existence, or non-existence. The matter is historically and philosophically compli-cated and needs to be elucidated in the light of a full reading of the *Enquiry* and of some other contemporary and secondary literature.[4] But, in barest outline, it is as follows:

Pyrrhonism, the most notorious species of ancient scepticism (sometimes distinguished by Hume as 'excessive' scepticism) set out to destroy all claims to real knowledge and all philosophical, religious and practical certainties. The main surviving source for such scepticism, the works of Sextus Empiricus (second century AD), first became generally available in modern Europe in a Latin

[4] The most discerning work on the subject is Terence Penelhum, *God and Skepticism* (Dordrecht, 1983), but see also Richard H. Popkin, *The History of Skepticism from Erasmus to Spinoza* (Berkeley, Calif., 1979). For a scholarly philosophical examination of classical scepticism, see J. Barnes and J. Annas, *The Modes of Scepticism* (Cambridge, 1985), and for Hume's scepticism in particular, see J. C. A. Gaskin, *Hume's Philosophy of Religion*, 2nd edn. (London, 1988), chs. 5–7.

version published in Paris in 1562. Its influence was remarkable—
conspicuously in Montaigne's famous *Apology for Raimond Sebon*
(1580), in Descartes's search for what could not be doubted, in the
writings of Pascal and Malebranche, and in some of the entries in
Bayle's celebrated *Dictionary* (the first version of which appeared
in 1696). As a young man, Hume inherited the Pyrrhonian tradition
and found that, philosophically and psychologically, it could attain
almost frighteningly nihilistic proportions. As he exclaims towards
the conclusion of Book I of the *Treatise*, 'I am ready to reject all
belief and reasoning, and can look upon no opinion even as more
probable or likely than another.'

But nine years later, in the first *Enquiry*, he develops, and in the
final section explicitly affirms, another species of scepticism which
is ultimately derived from the Academy—the teaching institution
set up by Plato—in the period when it was known as the 'New
Academy' and was dominated by Carneades (*c*.214–129 BC) and
his successors. In its ancient form, Academic Scepticism both
sharply criticized philosophical dogmas of the sort being purveyed
by the Stoics and Epicureans,[5] and also attempted to distinguish (as
Pyrrhonism did not distinguish) between claims to probable
knowledge that we must accept as a basis for action and life, and
claims to philosophical or religious certainties which on investigation can be seen to be entirely ungraspable. Such Academic
Scepticism was passed on from Carneades, via Clitomachus and
Philo of Larissa (*c*.160–80 BC), to Cicero (106–43 BC), and is
particularly evident in the latter's *Academica*, a work well known
to Hume.

In the *Enquiry*, Hume differentiates between 'Pyrrhonian or
excessive scepticism' which doubts everything and cannot in practice be sustained by any living man, and 'a more *mitigated* scep-

---

[5] Of these three great schools of Hellenistic philosophy, the Stoics and Epicureans were 'dogmatic', i.e. they asserted a positive account of the nature of the
universe and of man's place in it. Scepticism—both Pyrrhonian and Academic
—was negative and critical. Epicureanism provided a scandalously materialistic
alternative to Christianity, to which Hume adverts in both Section XI of the first
Enquiry and Part VIII of the *Dialogues* where he appears to deplore, while actually using, Epicurean ideas. Stoicism is both a complex metaphysic of reality
and a noble ethical system. It plays little explicit part in Hume's writings on
religion, although some comment on its psychological failings can be found in
the *Dialogues*, Part I.

ticism or *academic* philosophy' which recognizes an essential difference between, on the one hand, the natural assumptions of common life which all of us unthinkingly adopt and must follow whether we think about them or not, and, on the other hand, abstruse philosophical conclusions in metaphysics and religion which we do not have to adopt or follow. The former, the 'natural instincts' of common life, are and have to remian immune to sceptical destruction. They include, according to Hume, belief that past experience is a reliable guide to future experience, and belief that an external world exists continuously and independently of our individual perception of it. But abstruse philosophy and theology have no such immunity. Their conclusions are remote from common life and experience, and sceptical doubts and objections are entirely appropriate to claims about the existence of beings 'above' or 'beyond' this world, to accounts of the ultimate origin of the universe or the 'constitution of spirits'. We cannot, according to Hume in Section VII of the *Enquiry*, reach *any* certainty or warranted conclusion about such matters: 'Our line [i.e. our understanding] is too short to fathom such immense abysses'.

Thus Hume's philosophical programme—particularly apparent in the first and last sections of the *Enquiry*—commends a form of scepticism that concerns precisely the sort of things about which religion pronounces with greatest confidence: the nature of God and other spirits, the immortal or after-life existence of human persons and the ultimate origin of things. Hume thus not only criticizes natural religion on its own terms. He also sets up a whole way of looking at human knowledge which would make the conclusions of natural religion untenable and all confident religious pronouncements (and, for that matter, confident atheism) suspect *per se*.

But if theistic belief is supported by such thin reasoning, and if much of religion otherwise is 'mere superstition', why is religion so common in the world? Because, Hume answers in *The Natural History of Religion*, there is a distinction between the reasons for a belief and the causes of it.[6] A belief may have widely established

---

[6] Very roughly, and not in terms Hume uses, the *causes* of a belief are explanations of the occurrence of the belief which refer to particular environmental, physical, or cultural conditions, or to the individual history of the believer, without commenting on the truth or falsity of the belief and without

causes which keep it in being quite independently of the reasons alleged for holding it, and this, Hume argues, is the case with religion. Men are almost always, almost everywhere, afraid of the influences upon their lives which they cannot predict or control, and these they call gods and seek to propitiate with worship and sacrifice. From this initial analysis Hume continues in the *Natural History* with his account of the causes and consequences of the phenomenon of religion.

But even if religion is unsupported by good evidence, and even if its occurrence can be explained by the operation of natural causes, surely, someone will claim (and Kant in the *Critique of Practical Reason* did claim), it should still be cherished because belief in the divine and in an afterlife are essential practical conditions for morality? No, Hume argues in parts of the *Enquiry*, towards the end of both the *Dialogues* and the *Natural History*, and in the essay 'Of Suicide'. In the first place, fear of God and the expectations of an afterlife have less day-to-day effect upon our conduct than is generally supposed. In the second place, religions do positive harm. They invent mortal sins like suicide which have no natural depravity, and they create 'frivolous merits' which partake of no natural good, like abstaining from certain foods or attending ceremonies. Moreover, as parts of Hume's magisterial *History of England* illustrate, religions result in cruel persecutions, bigotry, strife between sects or between sects and the civil power, and the hunting down of unorthodox opinions.

But is there any real secular alternative to religiously based morality, however imperfect that may in practice be? According to Hume, in *An Enquiry concerning the Principles of Morals*, there is. It is a social and utilitarian morality based upon human needs and human nature. Hume never explicitly says it is superior to and can replace religious morality, but his account makes no reference whatever to divine sanctions or fiats, and the implication is clear.

So, taking as a whole his writings on or related to religion, Hume maintains that religion is supported by weak or spurious arguments; that it has ascertainable natural causes; that it is unneces-

being able to commend the belief as true (or false) to anyone not subject to the conditions described. *Reasons* for a belief are explanations which commend the truth of the belief, irrespective of causal explanations, by appeal to common norms of rationality.

sary for morality; and that it has damaging effects upon human life and society.

Dialogues *and* Natural History: *Composition and Complementarity*

In 'My Own Life' Hume mentions all his major works except the *Dialogues*. But the evidence in letters is very helpful and shows that at least the first four parts of the work, possibly all of it with the exception of Part XII, had been written by early 1751. In the 1750s the manuscript was circulated among chosen friends who advised him not to publish as its criticisms of natural religion would augment the complaints of those who regarded him as a mischievous infidel. The manuscript was revised in various points of detail about 1761 and again in 1776 when Hume knew he was approaching death. The main features of these revisions, apparent in the extant manuscript, are recorded in the present edition.

In 1776 the evidence of Hume's will and of surviving letters shows him making anxious provisions for the posthumous publication of the *Dialogues*. He had two fair copies made of the manuscript. In his will (4 January 1776), he left all his manuscripts to Adam Smith 'desiring him to publish my Dialogues concerning Natural Religion'. In a letter (3 May 1776) he declared, 'If I live a few Years longer, I shall publish them myself.' But he remained worried by the possibility that Adam Smith might find publication 'improper' on account of his 'situation'; and, finally, he added a codicil to his will on 7 August (he died on the 25th) laying a duty on his nephew, young David Hume, to publish the *Dialogues* if they 'be not publishd within two Years and a half of my Death'. Hume's nephew performed his duty in 1779 in an edition without comment or embellishment but remarkably true to Hume's final authorized manuscript intentions.

In one of his last letters, dated 8 June 1776, Hume wrote of the *Dialogues*: 'Some of my Friends flatter me, that it is the best thing I ever wrote. I have hitherto forborne to publish it, because I was of late desirous to live quietly, and keep remote from all Clamour . . .' The judgement of his friends was not flattery. For twenty-five years Hume had kept out of public view a work of great profundity and compelling philosophical sophistication: the culmination of his critique of the rationality of religion and of belief in God.

The Natural History of Religion, on the other hand, was published in 1757, reasonably soon after its composition, as one of *Four Dissertations*. (The other three, as published, do not concern religion.)[7] It is first mentioned in Hume's correspondence in a letter of June 1755 to his publisher Andrew Millar. Hume there remarks 'There are four short Dissertations, which I have kept some years by me', and he mentions one of them 'where there is a good deal of Literature', i.e. the footnotes, references, quotations, and so on which distinguish the *Natural History*. The inference is that the *Natural History*, like the *Dialogues*, was probably written between Hume's return from Turin at the beginning of 1749 and the start of his serious work on the *History of England* in early 1752.

The *Dialogues* and the *Natural History* are thus connected, both by the period of Hume's life from which they emerge and by the complementarity of their subject matter. The former deals with religion's foundation in reason, the latter with its 'origin in human nature', its causes and consequences. The only problem for the reader is that Hume introduces the *Natural History* by granting what he evidently questions at great depth in the *Dialogues*. He writes in the Introduction: 'The whole frame of nature bespeaks an intelligent author; and no rational enquirer can, after serious reflection, suspend his belief a moment with regard to the primary principles of genuine Theism and Religion.'

There is indeed a problem in discerning Hume's real position at the end of the *Dialogues*, and this concession in the *Natural History* is part of that problem; but for ordinary reading purposes it is as if Hume is saying: for the time being we need not bother about the rationality of religious belief (a delicate and dangerous issue) since we are dealing with the causes and origins which make it an

---

[7] The original four dissertations mentioned in Hume's letter did not include 'Of Suicide' and 'Of the Immortality of the Soul', which were concerned with religion and were added to fill up the space left by Hume's removal of an unsatisfactory dissertation on geometry. They were set up in print before Hume 'repented' and had them replaced by the interesting but inoffensive dissertation, 'Of the Standard of Taste'. It is probable that Hume repented as a result of threats to him or his publisher that they would attract prosecution. A good account of the whole matter is in an article by E. C. Mossner, *Modern Philology* (1950), 35–57.

almost universal phenomenon irrespective of its foundation in reason. Rationality is another problem, reserved for full treatment one day in the *Dialogues*, although already given a preliminary run in Section XI of the *Enquiry*, and to be recalled even at the end of the *Natural History* itself.

The Dialogues: Actors and Originals

Five persons are named in the *Dialogues*: Pamphilus, the auditor and reporter of what is said; Hermippus, the person whom he addresses; and the three speakers: Cleanthes, the advocate of the 'argument *a posteriori*'; Demea, the defender of the 'argument *a priori*' who also appeals to 'mysticism'; and Philo, the sceptical critic.

It is certainly true that Hume owes much to Cicero's dialogues in *De Natura Deorum* (*Concerning the Nature of the Gods*), that Cicero's characters represent the particular philosophical schools of Epicureanism, Stoicism, and Academic Scepticism, and that some of their arguments influence what Hume's characters have to say. But in no sense are Hume's characters representative of these schools. What is more, their particular arguments relate them in no way to the best known bearers of their names in antiquity. Cleanthes' arguments in the *Dialogues* are not those associated with Cleanthes the early Stoic and author of the 'Hymn to Zeus'. Hume's Philo is not Philo of Alexandria, the Hellenistic Jew who sought for a synthesis of Greek philosophy and Jewish religion; and there is no Demea of any philosophical consequence recorded in antiquity. Indeed it could easily be that Hume simply chose the names for most of his characters at random, or as a result of chancing to note a group of names together in one of his favourite classical authors. In Lucian's *Dialogues of the Courtesans*, three fictional characters—Pamphilus 'a young man', Philo 'a ship owner', and Demea 'a general'—are mentioned on the same page. But, having said that Hume's speakers do not represent ancient philosophical schools or persons, a significant link can be traced between Hume's Philo and philosophical influences on Cicero.

In *De Natura Deorum*, Cicero introduces three speakers: Velleius an Epicurean, Balbus a Stoic, and Cotta the Academic Sceptic and critic (like Hume's Philo) of both the others. But Cotta, a real person and friend of Cicero's, and Cicero himself were both taught by Philo of Larissa who had been one of the sceptical heads of the New Academy, and it is entirely reasonable to suppose that in using the name 'Philo' for his sceptic Hume intended his readers to sense the association with Academic Scepticism. There is, moreover, a connection via Cicero between Hume's Cleanthes and the real Stoic Cleanthes. In Cicero's work, Cotta attacks the Stoic Balbus, one of whose heroes is the real Cleanthes. In Hume's work, Philo attacks an invented Cleanthes. Both the real and the invented Cleanthes represent positive or 'dogmatic' accounts of religion against sceptical objections.

But the debt to Cicero and Greek philosophy runs deeper than these erudite connections. *De Natura Deorum* is Hume's philosophical and literary model. There is a similar attempt to set out contrasting positions fairly , a similar clash between two positive theses (in Cicero, Velleius and Balbus; in Hume, Demea and Cleanthes) and a negative critic (Cotta and Philo respectively), and Hume introduces and concludes the *Dialogues* in a manner clearly borrowed from Cicero. More importantly, not only are some of Cicero's thoughts and arguments re-used by Hume, but Hume's mitigated scepticism derives, as has already been pointed out, from the Academic Scepticism evident in both *De Natura Deorum* and Cicero's *Academica*. There is even clear evidence in Cicero of the anti-Pyrrhonian arguments which Hume takes over and develops into his view that 'natural instincts' must be immune to scepticism if we are to live at all. In places, Hume's and Cicero's words are strikingly similar.[8]

But the more obvious question to most readers is whether Cleanthes, Demea, and Philo represent any of Hume's near contemporaries. In a literal sense they do not. To an unusual extent, Hume's intellectual home is the humanism of the great classical

---

[8] Note, for example, *Academica*, ii. 31: '. . . those who assert that nothing can be grasped deprive us of these things that are the very tools and equipment of life, or rather overthrow the whole of life from its foundations and deprive the animate creature itself of the mind that animates it . . .' See also ii. 99: 'For it is contrary to nature for nothing to be probable, and entails that entire subversion of life of which you, Lucillus, were speaking.' And ii. 104: '. . . we hold that he who restrains himself from assent about all things nevertheless does move and act . . .' Cf. *Dialogues*, Part I, and the first *Enquiry*, Section XII, Part i.

authors rather than what he came to regard as the narrow and life-contorting dogmas of Christianity. Nevertheless it would be surprising if his characters expressed no element of the contemporary views with which Hume would have been familiar as an educated and well-read man. In one place, the contemporary element is acknowledged.

Demea's thesis concerning the 'argument *a priori*' in Part IX is Samuel Clarke's from his Boyle Lectures of 1704 and 1705. What is more, wherever Demea commits himself to the view that God's existence can be proved *a priori*, he is expressing himself in a manner which Hume and his readers would readily associate with Clarke or other rationalists, such as William Wollaston in *The Religion of Nature Delineated* (1722) or, somewhat less readily, their now better known contemporary Leibniz. But Demea also expresses views (which are not Clarke's) about the adorable mystery of God and about God's incomprehensible attributes. They are more like the religiously inclined excessive sceptic who argues that, because nothing whatever can be known with certainty, therefore there is as much warrant for believing in God as for believing—for example—that water quenches thirst.

Such extreme fideism (recognition of the incapacity of the intellect to attain knowledge of the divine and hence reliance on faith alone) might seem psychologically unrealistic combined with Demea's rationalism. But people do indeed combine both. Pascal in the seventeenth century is an obvious example.

Cleanthes on the other hand has more to say than Demea and is more consistent in what he says. In very general terms, he represents the empirical, *a posteriori* arguments and probable conclusions that are typically, but by no means uniquely, expressed by Joseph Butler in *The Analogy of Religion* (1736, and numerous later editions). In keeping with such quasi-empiricism, Cleanthes deploys the design argument and tries to solve the problem of evil; but also, in accord with Hume's own arguments in *A Treatise of Human Nature* and elsewhere, he opposes Demea's appeal to the argument *a priori*.

If Philo is indebted to any near contemporary of Hume's, it is most evidently and specifically to some of the entries in Bayle's *Dictionary*, and these are indicated in the notes to the present text. But despite traceable debts to the sceptical tradition, it is to Hume himself that one must look for most of Philo's arguments. What Philo's *conclusions* really are, and whether Hume himself would have endorsed them, are questions yet to be answered.

The Dialogues: *Argument and Enigma*

The problem is that throughout the *Dialogues* Philo articulates with great subtlety and originality critical positions which one would readily associate with Hume. He, like Hume, urges a suspension of judgement because the whole subject of God's nature is beyond our possible understanding. Philo, like Hume, defends mitigated scepticism and questions the supposed dependence of morality on religion. Above all, he, like Hume's sceptical friend in Section XI of the *Enquiry*, conducts a sustained and powerful critique of the inference from the world as it is to God as he is supposed to be. Then at the beginning of Part XII Philo suddenly admits he has been amusing himself with his objections: 'a purpose, an intention, or design strikes everywhere the most careless, the most stupid thinker.' As an academic colleague of mine remarked about Hume, having just read the *Dialogues* for the first time, 'What does the dashed fellow actually *believe* in the end?'

The consensus of opinion about who *speaks* for Hume has always pointed to Philo and still clearly does so. No one character exclusively expresses the author's arguments and opinions but, as Hume himself remarks in a letter (see below, p. 25), 'I coud have supported naturally enough [the character of Philo]'. But that need not imply that the other characters express weak philosophical positions or never say anything that their author would find convincing or important. The model for Hume is Cicero with his balanced presentation of opposed positions, not Plato with (generally) his version of Socrates backed up by yes-men and opposed by the philosophically naïve who are doomed to confusion. But this still does not cope with Philo's 'retraction' and the final interpretation of the *Dialogues*. Philo may speak for Hume, but what does Philo *say*?

The agreed facts are these: Philo is the dramatically dominant speaker in the *Dialogues* and this becomes particularly evident towards the end. Philo, whether a 'careless' sceptic or not, articulates arguments which sound consistent with what Hume writes elsewhere, and are of such importance that they are still regularly taken into account in modern discussions of the philosophy of religion, despite Cleanthes' strong objections to them. Philo gives up these arguments at the start of Part XII and repeats his retraction three pages later: 'Here then the existence of a Deity is plainly ascertained by reason.' But in Part XII Philo also subjects this retraction to certain qualifications. The question is: what is left of the retraction when the qualifications are taken into account? There is no short and decisive answer.

One possibility is that nothing is left to be ascertained by reason concerning the nature of the Deity (the question with which the *Dialogues* commenced), and the existence of the Deity (the question everyone accepted as answered at the start) is a matter of virtually contentless assent: that mitigated scepticism and fideism are brought together by a proper acknowledgement of the limits of our understanding; that the difference between them becomes 'merely verbal'; and hence that it is what we do, whether we worship or occupy our lives with other practical matters, not what we really understand to be the case, that differentiates atheist and theist.

Another possible answer is that we so easily perceive order in the world and so naturally associate it with design, that the 'argument *a posteriori*' tends to survive the systematic destruction of its rational basis, a destruction which is anyway never *entirely* conclusive like the refutation of an *a priori* argument. The result of this is assent to the possible existence of *some* creative deity. But argument from world to god, as Philo contends throughout, tells us almost nothing about this deity. Such a virtually contentless affirmation accords with an early letter (30 June 1743) in which Hume remarked that he had an objection 'to everything we commonly call Religion, except the Practice of Morality, and the Assent of the Understanding to the Proposition *that* God *exists*'.

Part of Hume's greatness is that he leaves us thinking about profound issues, not accepting or resisting conclusions behind which he has put his own personal authority. As Cicero remarks at the beginning of *De Natura Deorum*:

Those however who seek to learn my personal opinion on the various questions show an unreasonable degree of curiosity. In discussion it is not so much weight of authority as force of argument that should be demanded. Indeed the authority of those who profess to teach is often a positive hindrance to those who desire to learn; they cease to employ their own judgement, and take what they perceive to be the verdict of their chosen master as settling the question. (Loeb, 13.)

Hume either offers us no decisive verdict concerning his vast and awesome subject, or he offers one which is so complex that readers must grapple with the arguments for themselves and not be too disappointed if they find the outcome ambiguous or hesitant.

Causes and Consequences of Religion: The Natural History

It is immediately evident that the style and content of the *Natural History* is more literary than the *Dialogues*. The *Dialogues* are controlled argument in conversational form. There are scarcely any footnote references to authorities, and only well-known persons or schools of philosophy are named or appealed to in the text. In contrast, the *Natural History* is packed with detailed evidence drawn from classical sources. It is a work of scholarship from which general factual conclusions emerge. It is about the origins of religion in human nature, the causes that produce the phenomenon of religion in human society, the effects of religion upon human life and conduct, and the cyclical variation between polytheism, when the gods become too absurdly anthropomorphic to be credible, and monotheism, when God becomes inaccessibly remote without the aid of intermediaries. It is concerned with the effects of different species of religion upon tolerance, upon morality and upon what society finds admirable. In brief, it is a work on the psychology, anthropology, history, and social outcomes of religion. But its implications are more critical of religion than this description would lead us to expect.

Despite Hume's several repetitions of the assurance given in his Introduction that 'The whole frame of nature bespeaks an intelligent author', it is almost impossible to avoid the impression that he is saying that the phenomenon of religion is unattractive. It originates in fear of unknown influences upon human society. It thrives in situations of fearful dread and ignorance of the future. Monotheism, in contrast to ancient polytheism, is intolerant. Monotheism introduces unnatural and destructive species of virtue into human

affairs. The worship of a being supposed to be supremely powerful, conjoined with the excuse that 'the gods have maxims of
justice peculiar to themselves', results in intellectual dishonesty
and moral double-dealing. In effect (though not in declared intention), monotheism 'as it has commonly been found in the world'
has resulted in more actual human sacrifices to God—religious
wars and disorders, and the killing of heretics—than ever was
demanded by such few and very ancient cults as explicitly required
human sacrifice.

This is all somewhat worrying for the believer, especially when
we are led in the *Natural History* to the conclusion, first, that these
odious results spring from beliefs whose causes we can identify
(and thus presumably resist), and, finally, that the real content of
the beliefs is so confused and obscure that 'Doubt, uncertainty,
suspence of judgment appear the only result of our most accurate
scrutiny': a conclusion similarly reached by Hume at the end of the
Dialogues and in the final section of the *Enquiry*; a conclusion
which surely is his own.

A NOTE ON THE TEXTS

THE five items gathered together in this collection of Hume's principal writings on religion do not have uniform publishing histories.

In two cases, *An Enquiry concerning Human Understanding* and *The Natural History of Religion*, the manuscripts no longer exist. Numerous editions were however corrected and seen through the press by Hume himself. The last of these, *Essays and Treatises on Several Subjects*, 2 vols. (London, 1777), is (subject to trivial and obvious corrections) the copy text for the present volume.

In the *Natural History* Hume's highly attenuated and sometimes inadequate footnote references are silently expanded or corrected by the present editor. Translations and other interpolations within these footnotes are indicated by square brackets. The translations are taken from the Loeb editions of the classics wherever possible. Following the convention adopted by Hume himself, long and discursive notes are gathered at the end of the *Natural History* but signalled in the text by a footnote.

In two cases, the brief autobiography 'My Own Life' and the *Dialogues concerning Natural Religion*, the manuscripts are still extant. They were specifically destined by Hume for publication, and were indeed published in 1777 and 1779 respectively.

In the present edition, 'My Own Life' is the text of the 1777 printing, revised in the light of a re-examination of the manuscript in the National Library of Scotland. The text now follows Hume's punctuation exactly. His manuscript alterations are also noted where they are of any interest.

The *Dialogues* is Kemp Smith's text from his Oxford, 1935 edition, together with his account of the important manuscript variations. Smith has done an abidingly good job here in recording variations which have philosophical, literary, or biographical significance and in ignoring trivial alterations and minute corrections.

The private letter of 1751 was never intended by Hume for publication and it seems appropriate to differentiate it from those that were by printing what Hume actually wrote: elisions, odd spellings, quaint capital letters, etc. The text is from Vol. i of

J. Y. T. Greig's fine edition of *The Letters of David Hume*, 2 vols. (Oxford, 1932; repr. New York and London, 1983).

Throughout the volume the present editor's explanatory notes are signalled by asterisks in the text. They are listed by page references at the back of the volume. The sixty or so classical sources, philosophers, historians, etc. referred to by Hume are grouped in an index of such names at the end of the volume and are not separately dealt with in the explanatory notes.

SELECT BIBLIOGRAPHY

Editions

The three principal editions of the *Dialogues* surround the text with much editorial interpretation: ed. N. Kemp Smith (Oxford, 1935 and Edinburgh, 1947); ed. Nelson Pike (New York, 1970); ed. Stanley Tweyman (London and New York, 1991). Kemp Smith's edition contains ancillary material of abiding importance. In *The Natural History of Religion and Dialogues concerning Natural Religion*, ed. A. Wayne Colver and J. V. Price (Oxford, 1976), the editors have been at enormous pains to trace references and to note variations but the text itself is, as a consequence, somewhat difficult to read straightforwardly as literature or philosophy. A number of other printings of the *Dialogues* exist but have lazy or negligible editorial input.

Books about Hume on Religion

A. G. N. Flew, *Hume's Philosophy of Belief* (London, 1961), concerns mainly the first *Enquiry* but two chapters are about Hume on religion. J. C. A. Gaskin, *Hume's Philosophy of Religion*, 2nd edn. (London, 1988), is the only full-scale philosophical analysis of all Hume's work on religion. *Hume's Philosophy of Religion*, [no editor given] (Winston-Salem, NC, 1986) is an uninspiring collection of four essays rescued by an excellent contribution by D. F. Norton, 'Hume, Atheism, and the Autonomy of Morals'. S. Tweyman, *Scepticism and Belief in Hume's Dialogues concerning Natural Religion* (Dordrecht, 1986) is a commentary on and interpretation of the *Dialogues*. See also K. E. Yandell, *The Inexplicable Mystery* (Philadelphia, 1990).

Books relating Hume on Religion to the History of Ideas

R. M. Burns, *The Great Debate on Miracles* (Lewisburg, Pa., 1981) concerns miracles, but is interesting in general for understanding Hume's attack on religion. One of those rare books that combines historical scholarship with real philosophical insights is

T. Penelhum, *God and Skepticism* (Dordrecht, 1983). For other interesting studies, see: R. H. Hurlbutt, *Hume, Newton and the Design Argument* (Lincoln, Nebr., 1965); A. Jeffner, *Butler and Hume on Religion* (Stockholm, 1966); P. Jones, *Hume's Sentiments: Their Ciceronian and French Context* (Edinburgh, 1982); and R. H. Popkin, *The High Road to Pyrrhonism* (San Diego, Calif., 1980).

The standard modern biography of Hume is E. C. Mossner's *David Hume* (Edinburgh, 1954; Oxford, 1970 and 1980).

CHRONOLOGY

1711   Birth of David Hume (originally Home) in Edinburgh on 26 April.

1711–22   Boyhood at Ninewells, the family house in Scotland, about ten miles from Berwick upon Tweed.

1714   Accession of George 1 establishes the Hanoverian succession.

1715   Jacobite Rebellion.

1723   Matriculates at Edinburgh University where he remains until 1725 or 1726 without taking a degree.

1726–34   Studies Law, reads extensively, and attempts a career in banking at Bristol.

1734–7   Lives in France, first at Rheims and then at La Fleche, writing the *Treatise*.

1739–40   *A Treatise of Human Nature* published.

1741–2   First edition of *Essays, Moral and Political* published.

1744–5   Fails to obtain the Chair of Moral Philosophy at Edinburgh.

1745   Becomes tutor to the Marquess of Annandale for a year.

1745   Jacobite Rebellion: Hume in London and not in sympathy with the cause.

1748   Appointed secretary to General St Clair on diplomatic missions to Vienna and Turin.

1748   *Philosophical Essays concerning Human Understanding* (later entitled *An Enquiry concerning Human Understanding*) published.

1751   *An Enquiry concerning the Principles of Morals*.

1751   Works on manuscript of *Dialogues concerning Natural Religion*.

1752   Fails to obtain the Chair of Moral Philosophy at Glasgow.

1752   *Political Discourses* published.

1752–7   Appointed Keeper of the Advocates' Library, Edinburgh.

Principal Writings on Religion

including

Dialogues concerning
Natural Religion

and

The Natural History
of Religion

MY OWN LIFE

It is difficult for a man to speak long of himself without vanity: therefore, I shall be short. It may be thought an instance of vanity that I pretend at all to write my life; but this Narrative shall contain little more than the History of my Writings; as, indeed, almost all my life has been spent in literary pursuits and occupations. The first success of most of my writings was not such as to be an object of vanity.

I was born the 26th of April 1711, old style, at Edinburgh. I was of a good family, both by father and mother: my father's family is a branch of the Earl of Home's, or Hume's; and my ancestors had been proprietors of the estate, which my brother possesses, for several generations. My mother was daughter of Sir David Falconer, President of the College of Justice: the title of Lord Halkerton came by succession to her brother.

My family, however, was not rich, and being myself a younger brother, my patrimony, according to the mode of my country, was of course very slender. My father, who passed for a man of parts, died when I was an infant; leaving me, with an elder brother and a sister, under the care of our mother, a woman of singular merit, who, though young and handsome, devoted herself entirely to the rearing and educating of her children. I passed through the ordinary course of education with success, and was seized very early with a passion for literature, which has been the ruling passion of my life, and the great source of my enjoyments. My studious disposition, my sobriety, and my industry, gave my family a notion that the law was a proper profession for me; but I found an unsurmountable aversion to everything but the pursuits of philosophy and general learning; and while they fancied I was poring upon Voet and Vinnius, Cicero and Virgil were the authors which I was secretly devouring.

My very slender fortune, however, being unsuitable to this plan of life, and my health being a little broken by my ardent application, I was tempted, or rather forced, to make a very feeble trial for entering into a more active scene of life. In 1734, I went to Bristol, with some recommendations to eminent merchants, but in a few months found that scene totally unsuitable to me. I went over to France, with a view of prosecuting my studies in a country retreat; and I there laid that plan of life, which I have steadily and success-fully pursued: I resolved to make a very rigid frugality supply my deficiency of fortune, to maintain unimpaired my independency, and to regard every object as contemptible, except the improve-ment of my talents in literature.

During my retreat in France, first at Reims, but chiefly at La Fleche in Anjou, I composed my *Treatise of Human Nature*. After passing three years very agreeably in that country, I came over to London in 1737. In the end of 1738, I published my Treatise; and immediately went down to my mother and my brother, who lived at his country house,[1] and was employing himself very judiciously and successfully in the improvement of his fortune.

Never literary attempt was more unfortunate than my Treatise of Human Nature. It fell *dead-born from the press*; without reaching such distinction, as even to excite a murmur among the zealots. But being naturally of a cheerful and sanguine temper, I very soon recovered the blow, and prosecuted with great ardour my studies in the country. In 1742, I printed at Edinburgh the first part of my Essays: the work was favourably received, and soon made me entirely forget my former disappointment. I continued with my mother and brother in the country; and in that time, recovered the knowledge of the Greek language, which I had too much neglected in my early youth.

In 1745, I received a letter from the Marquis of Annandale, inviting me to come and live with him in England: I found also, that the friends and family of that young nobleman, were desirous of putting him under my care and direction: For the state of his mind and health required it. I lived with him a twelvemonth: My appointments during that time made a considerable accession to my small fortune. I then received an invitation from General St. Clair to attend him as a secretary to his expedition, which was at first meant against Canada, but ended in an incursion on the coast of France: Next year, to wit 1747, I received an invitation from the General to attend him in the same station in his military embassy to the courts of Vienna and Turin. I there wore the uniform of an

---

[1] [Hume first wrote 'seat' then changed to 'house'.]

officer; and was introduced at these courts as aid-de-camp to the general, along with Sir Harry Erskine and Captain Grant, now General Grant. These two years were almost the only interruptions which my studies have received during the course of my life: I passed them agreeably and in good company: and my appointments, with my frugality, had made me reach a fortune, which I called independent, though most of my friends were inclined to smile when I said so: in short, I was now master of near a thousand pounds.

I had always entertained a notion, that my want of success in publishing the Treatise of Human Nature, had proceeded more from the manner than the matter; and that I had been guilty of a very usual indiscretion, in going to the press too early. I therefore cast the first part of that work anew in the Enquiry concerning Human Understanding, which was published while I was at Turin. But this piece was at first little more successful than the Treatise of Human Nature. On my return from Italy, I had the mortification to find all England in a ferment on account of Dr. Middleton's Free Enquiry; while my performance was entirely overlooked and neglected. A new edition, which had been published at London of my Essays, moral and political, met not with a much better reception.

Such is the force of natural temper, that these disappointments made little or no impression on me. I went down in 1749 and lived two years with my brother at his country-house:[1] for my mother was now dead. I there composed the second part of my Essays, which I called Political Discourses; and also my Enquiry concerning the Principles of Morals, which is another part of my Treatise, that I cast anew. Meanwhile, my bookseller, A. Millar, informed me, that my former publications (all but the unfortunate Treatise) were beginning to be the subject of conversation, that the sale of them was gradually increasing, and that new editions were demanded. Answers, by Reverends and Right Reverends, came out two or three in a year: And I found by Dr. Warburton's railing that the books were beginning to be esteemed in good company. However, I had fixed a resolution, which I inflexibly maintained, never to reply to any body; and not being very irascible in my

---

[1] [Hume first wrote 'seat' then changed to 'house'.]

temper, I have easily kept myself clear of all literary squabbles. These symptoms of a rising reputation gave me encouragement as I was ever more disposed to see the favourable than unfavourable side of things; a turn of mind, which it is more happy to possess than to be born to an estate of ten thousand a year.

In 1751, I removed from the country to the town; the true scene for a man of letters. In 1752, were published at Edinburgh, where I then lived, my Political Discourses, the only work of mine that was successful on the first publication: It was well received abroad and at home. In the same year was published at London my Enquiry concerning the Principles of Morals, which, in my own opinion (who ought not to judge on that subject) is of all my writings, historical, philosophical, or literary, incomparably the best: It came unnoticed and unobserved into the world.

In 1752, the Faculty of Advocates chose me their Librarian, an office from which I received little or no emolument, but which gave me the command of a large library. I then formed the plan of writing the History of England; but being frightened with the notion of continuing a narrative, through a period of 1700 years, I commenced with the accession of the House of Stuart; an epoch, when, I thought, the misrepresentations of faction began chiefly to take place. I was, I own, sanguine in my expectations of the success of this work. I thought, that, I was the only historian, that had at once neglected present power, interest, and authority, and the cry of popular prejudices; and as the subject was suited to every capacity, I expected proportional applause: But miserable was my disappointment: I was assailed by one cry of reproach, disapprobation, and even detestation: English, Scotch, and Irish; Whig and Tory; churchman and sectary, freethinker and religionist; patriot and courtier united in their rage against the man, who had presumed to shed a generous tear for the fate of Charles I, and the Earl of Strafford: and after the first ebullitions of this fury were over, what was still more mortifying, the book seemed to sink into oblivion. Mr. Millar told me, that in a twelve-month he sold only forty-five copies of it. I scarcely indeed heard of one man in the three kingdoms, considerable for rank or letters, that could endure the book. I must only except the primate of England, Dr. Herring, and the primate of Ireland, Dr. Stone; which seem two odd exceptions. These dignified prelates separately sent me messages not to be discouraged.

I was, however, I confess, discouraged; and had not the war been at that time breaking out between France and England, I had certainly retired to some provincial town of the former kingdom, have changed my name, and never more have returned to my native country. But as this scheme was not now practicable, and the subsequent volume was considerably advanced, I resolved to pick up courage and to persevere.

In this interval I published at London, my Natural History of Religion along with some other small pieces: Its public entry was rather obscure, except only that Dr. Hurd wrote a pamphlet against it, with all the illiberal petulance, arrogance, and scurrility, which distinguishes the Warburtonian school. This pamphlet gave me some consolation for the otherwise indifferent reception of my performance.

In 1756, two years after the fall of the first volume, was published the second volume of my History, containing the period from the death of Charles I, till the Revolution. This performance happened to give less displeasure to the Whigs, and was better received. It not only rose itself; but helped to buoy up its unfortunate brother.

But though I had been taught by experience, that the Whig party were in possession of bestowing all places, both in the state and in literature, I was so little inclined to yield to their senseless clamour, that in above a hundred alterations, which farther study, reading, or reflection engaged me to make in the reigns of the two first Stuarts, I have made all of them invariably to the Tory side. It is ridiculous to consider the English constitution before that period as a regular plan of liberty.

In 1759 I published my History of the House of Tudor. The clamour against this performance was almost equal to that against the History of the two first Stuarts. The reign of Elizabeth was particularly obnoxious. But I was now callous against the impressions of public folly; and continued very peaceably and contentedly in my retreat at Edinburgh, to finish, in two volumes, the more early part of the English History; which I gave to the public in 1761 with tolerable, and but tolerable success.

But notwithstanding this variety of winds and seasons, to which my writings had been exposed, they had still been making such advances, that the copy money, given me by the booksellers, much exceeded anything formerly known in England: I was become not only independent, but opulent. I retired to my native country of Scotland, determined never more to set my foot out of it; and retaining the satisfaction of never having preferred a request to one great man, or even making advances of friendship to any of them. As I was now turned of fifty, I thought of passing all the rest of my life in this philosophical manner; when I received in 1763 an invitation from the Earl of Hertford, with whom I was not in the least acquainted, to attend him on his embassy to Paris, with a near prospect of being appointed secretary to the embassy, and, in the meanwhile, of performing the functions of that office. This offer, however inviting, I at first declined; both because I was reluctant to begin connexions with the great, and because I was afraid that the civilities and gay company of Paris would prove disagreeable to a person of my age and humour: But on his lordship's repeating the invitation, I accepted of it. I have every reason, both of pleasure and interest, to think myself happy in my connexions with that nobleman; as well as afterwards, with his brother, General Conway.

Those who have not seen the strange effects of modes, will never imagine the reception I met with at Paris, from men and women of all ranks and stations. The more I recoiled from their excessive civilities, the more I was loaded with them.[1] There is, however, a real satisfaction in living at Paris from the great number of sensible, knowing, and polite company with which that city abounds above all places in the universe. I thought once of settling there for life.

I was appointed secretary to the embassy, and in summer 1765, Lord Hertford left me being appointed Lord Lieutenant of[2] Ireland. I was *chargé d'affaires*, till the arrival of the Duke of Richmond towards the end of the year. In the beginning of 1766, I left Paris and next summer, went to Edinburgh, with the same view as formerly of burying myself in a philosophical retreat. I returned to that place, not richer, but with much more money, and a much larger income, by means of Lord Hertford's friendship, than I left it; and I was desirous of trying what superfluity could produce, as

---

[1] [Hume has written and then struck out: 'Dr. Sterne told me, that he saw I was [wording too heavily scored to be legible] torn in the same manner that he himself had been in London; but he added, that his vogue lasted only one winter.]

[2] [Hume first wrote 'on taking posession [*sic*] of'.]

I had formerly made an experiment of a competency. But in 1767, I received from Mr. Conway an invitation to be under-secretary; and this invitation both the character of the person, and my connexions with Lord Hertford, prevented me from declining. I returned to Edinburgh in 1769, very opulent (for I possessed a revenue of 1000 l. a year) healthy, and though somewhat stricken in years, with the prospect of enjoying long my ease, and of seeing the increase of my reputation.

In spring 1775, I was struck with a disorder in my bowels, which at first gave me no alarm, but has since, as I apprehend it, become mortal and incurable. I now reckon upon a speedy dissolution. I have suffered very little pain from my disorder; and what is more strange, have, notwithstanding the great decline of my person; never suffered a moment's abatement of my spirits: Insomuch, that were I to name the period of my life which I should most choose to pass over again I might be tempted to point to this later period. I possess the same ardour as ever in study, and the same gaiety in company. I consider besides, that a man of sixty-five, by dying, cuts off only a few years of infirmities: And though I see many symptoms of my literary reputation's breaking out at last with additional lustre, I know, that I had but few years to enjoy it. It is difficult to be more detached from life than I am at present.

To conclude historically with my own character—I am, or rather was (for that is the style, I must now use in speaking of myself; which emboldens me the more to speak my sentiments) I was, I say, a man of mild dispositions, of command of temper, of an open, social, and cheerful humour, capable of attachment, but little susceptible of enmity, and of great moderation in all my passions. Even my love of literary fame, my ruling passion, never soured my humour, notwithstanding my frequent disappointments. My company was not unacceptable to the young and careless, as well as to the studious and literary: and as I took a particular pleasure in the company of modest women, I had no reason to be displeased with the reception I met with from them. In a word, though most men any wise eminent, have found reason to complain of calumny, I never was touched, or even attacked by her baleful tooth: And though I wantonly exposed myself to the rage of both civil and religious factions, they seemed to be disarmed in my behalf of their wonted fury: My friends never had occasion to vindicate any one circumstance of my character and conduct: Not but that the zealots, we may well suppose, would have been glad to invent and propagate any story to my disadvantage, but they could never find any which, they thought, would wear the face of probability. I cannot say, there is no vanity in making this funeral oration of myself; but I hope it is not a misplaced one; and this is a matter of fact which is easily cleared and ascertained.

April 18, 1776.

AN ENQUIRY CONCERNING
HUMAN UNDERSTANDING
Section XI

OF A PARTICULAR PROVIDENCE* AND
OF A FUTURE STATE

I WAS lately engaged in conversation with a friend who loves sceptical paradoxes; where, though he advanced many principles, of which I can by no means approve, yet as they seem to be curious, and to bear some relation to the chain of reasoning carried on throughout this enquiry, I shall here copy them from my memory as accurately as I can, in order to submit them to the judgement of the reader.

Our conversation began with my admiring the singular good fortune of philosophy, which, as it requires entire liberty above all other privileges, and chiefly flourishes from the free opposition of sentiments and argumentation, received its first birth in an age and country of freedom and toleration, and was never cramped, even in its most extravagant principles, by any creeds, confessions, or penal statutes. For, except the banishment of Protagoras,* and the death of Socrates,* which last event proceeded partly from other motives, there are scarcely any instances to be met with, in ancient history, of this bigotted jealousy, with which the present age is so much infested. Epicurus* lived at Athens to an advanced age, in peace and tranquillity: Epicureans[1] were even admitted to receive the sacerdotal character, and to officiate at the altar, in the most sacred rites of the established religion: And the public encouragement[2] of pensions and salaries was afforded equally, by the wisest of all the Roman emperors,[3] to the professors of every sect of phi-

[1] Lucian, *The Carousal or The Lapiths* [Loeb, i. 421].

[2] Lucian, *The Eunuch* [Loeb, v. 333. Lucian mentions that Stoics, Platonists, and Epicureans were paid 'a matter of ten thousand drachmas a year for instructing boys'].

[3] See Lucian, *ibid.*, and Dio Cassius, *Roman History*, Book LXXII [Loeb, ix. 55: 'When Marcus Aurelius [AD 121–80, Emperor 161–81] had come to Athens . . . for the benefit of the whole world he established teachers at Athens in every branch of knowledge, granting these teachers an annual salary'].

losophy. How requisite such kind of treatment was to philosophy, in her early youth, will easily be conceived, if we reflect, that, even at present, when she may be supposed more hardy and robust, she bears with much difficulty the inclemency of the seasons, and those harsh winds of calumny and persecution, which blow upon her.

You admire, says my friend, as the singular good fortune of philosophy, what seems to result from the natural course of things, and to be unavoidable in every age and nation. This pertinacious bigotry, of which you complain, as so fatal to philosophy, is really her offspring, who, after allying with superstition, separates himself entirely from the interest of his parent, and becomes her most inveterate enemy and persecutor. Speculative dogmas of religion, the present occasions of such furious dispute, could not possibly be conceived or admitted in the early ages of the world; when mankind, being wholly illiterate, formed an idea of religion more suitable to their weak apprehension, and composed their sacred tenets of such tales chiefly as were the objects of traditional belief, more than of argument or disputation.* After the first alarm, therefore, was over, which arose from the new paradoxes and principles of the philosophers; these teachers seem ever after, during the ages of antiquity, to have lived in great harmony with the established superstition, and to have made a fair partition of mankind between them; the former claiming all the learned and wise, the latter possessing all the vulgar and illiterate.

It seems then, say I, that you leave politics entirely out of the question, and never suppose, that a wise magistrate can justly be jealous of certain tenets of philosophy, such as those of Epicurus, which, denying a divine existence, and consequently a providence and a future state, seem to loosen, in a great measure, the ties of morality, and may be supposed, for that reason, pernicious to the peace of civil society.

I know, replied he, that in fact these persecutions never, in any age, proceeded from calm reason, or from experience of the pernicious consequences of philosophy; but arose entirely from passion and prejudice. But what if I should advance farther, and assert, that if Epicurus had been accused before the people, by any of the *sycophants* or informers of those days, he could easily have defended his cause, and proved his principles of philosophy to be as salutary as those of his adversaries, who endeavoured, with such zeal, to expose him to the public hatred and jealousy?

I wish, said I, you would try your eloquence upon so extraordinary a topic, and make a speech for Epicurus, which might satisfy, not the mob of Athens, if you will allow that ancient and polite city to have contained any mob, but the more philosophical part of his audience, such as might be supposed capable of comprehending his arguments.

The matter would not be difficult, upon such conditions, replied he: And if you please, I shall suppose myself Epicurus for a moment, and make you stand for the Athenian people, and shall deliver you such an harangue as will fill all the urn with white beans, and leave not a black one to gratify the malice of my adversaries.*

Very well: Pray proceed upon these suppositions.

I come hither, O ye Athenians, to justify in your assembly what I maintained in my school, and I find myself impeached by furious antagonists, instead of reasoning with calm and dispassionate enquirers. Your deliberations, which of right should be directed to questions of public good, and the interest of the commonwealth, are diverted to the disquisitions of speculative philosophy; and these magnificent, but perhaps fruitless enquiries, take place of your more familiar but more useful occupations. But so far as in me lies, I will prevent this abuse. We shall not here dispute concerning the origin and government of worlds. We shall only enquire how far such questions concern the public interest. And if I can persuade you, that they are entirely indifferent to the peace of society and security of government, I hope that you will presently send us back to our schools, there to examine, at leisure, the question the most sublime, but at the same time, the most speculative of all philosophy.

The religious philosophers, not satisfied with the tradition of your forefathers, and doctrine of your priests (in which I willingly acquiesce), indulge a rash curiosity, in trying how far they can establish religion upon the principles of reason;* and they thereby excite, instead of satisfying, the doubts, which naturally arise from a diligent and scrutinous enquiry. They paint, in the most magnificent colours, the order, beauty, and wise arrangement of the universe; and then ask, if such a glorious display of intelligence could proceed from the fortuitous concourse of atoms, or if chance could produce what the greatest genius can never sufficiently admire.* I shall not examine the justness of this argument. I shall allow it to be as solid as my antagonists and accusers can desire. It is sufficient, if I can prove, from this very reasoning, that the question is entirely speculative, and that, when, in my philosophical disquisitions, I deny a providence and a future state, I undermine not the foundations of society, but advance principles, which they themselves, upon their own topics, if they argue consistently, must allow to be solid and satisfactory.

You then, who are my accusers, have acknowledged, that the chief or sole argument for a divine existence (which I never questioned) is derived from the order of nature; where there appear such marks of intelligence and design, that you think it extravagant to assign for its cause, either chance, or the blind and unguided force* of matter. You allow, that this is an argument drawn from effects to causes. From the order of the work, you infer, that there must have been project and forethought in the workman. If you cannot make out this point, you allow, that your conclusion fails; and you pretend not to establish the conclusion in a greater latitude than the phenomena of nature will justify. These are your concessions. I desire you to mark the consequences.

When we infer any particular cause from an effect, we must proportion the one to the other, and can never be allowed to ascribe to the cause any qualities, but what are exactly sufficient to produce the effect. A body of ten ounces raised in any scale may serve as a proof, that the counterbalancing weight exceeds ten ounces; but can never afford a reason that it exceeds a hundred. If the cause, assigned for any effect, be not sufficient to produce it, we must either reject that cause, or add to it such qualities as will give it a just proportion to the effect. But if we ascribe to it farther qualities, or affirm it capable of producing other effects, we can only indulge the licence of conjecture, and arbitrarily suppose the existence of qualities and energies, without reason or authority.

The same rule holds, whether the cause assigned be brute unconscious matter, or a rational intelligent being. If the cause be known only by the effect, we never ought to ascribe to it any qualities, beyond what are precisely requisite to produce the effect: Nor can we, by any rules of just reasoning, return back from the cause, and infer other effects from it, beyond those by which alone it is known to us. No one, merely from the sight of one of Zeuxis's* pictures, could know, that he was also a statuary or architect, and was an artist no less skilful in stone and marble than in colours. The talents and taste, displayed in the particular work before us; these we may safely conclude the workman to be possessed of. The cause must be proportioned to the effect; and if we exactly and precisely proportion it, we shall never find in it any qualities, that point farther, or afford an inference concerning any other design or performance. Such qualities must be somewhat beyond what is merely requisite for producing the effect, which we examine.

Allowing, therefore, the gods to be the authors of the existence or order of the universe; it follows, that they possess that precise degree of power, intelligence, and benevolence, which appears in their workmanship; but nothing farther can ever be proved, except we call in the assistance of exaggeration and flattery to supply the defects of argument and reasoning. So far as the traces of any attributes, at present, appear, so far may we conclude these attributes to exist. The supposition of farther attributes is mere hypothesis; much more the supposition, that, in distant regions of space or periods of time, there has been, or will be, a more magnificent display of these attributes, and a scheme of administration more suitable to such imaginary virtues. We can never be allowed to mount up from the universe, the effect, to Jupiter,* the cause; and then descend downwards, to infer any new effect from that cause; as if the present effects alone were not entirely worthy of the glorious attributes, which we ascribe to that deity. The knowledge of the cause being derived solely from the effect, they must be exactly adjusted to each other; and the one can never refer to anything farther, or be the foundation of any new inference and conclusion.

You find certain phenomena in nature. You seek a cause or author. You imagine that you have found him. You afterwards become so enamoured of this offspring of your brain, that you imagine it impossible, but he must produce something greater and more perfect than the present scene of things, which is so full of ill and disorder. You forget, that this superlative intelligence and benevolence are entirely imaginary, or, at least, without any foundation in reason; and that you have no ground to ascribe to him any qualities, but what you see he has actually exerted and displayed in his productions. Let your gods, therefore, O philosophers, be suited to the present appearances of nature: and presume not to alter these appearances by arbitrary suppositions, in order to suit them to the attributes, which you so fondly ascribe to your deities.

When priests and poets, supported by your authority, O Athenians, talk of a golden or silver age, which preceded the present state of vice and misery, I hear them with attention and with reverence. But when philosophers, who pretend to neglect authority, and to cultivate reason, hold the same discourse, I pay them not, I own, the same obsequious submission and pious deference. I ask; who carried them into the celestial regions, who admitted them into the councils of the gods, who opened to them the book of fate, that they thus rashly affirm, that their deities have executed, or will execute, any purpose beyond what has actually appeared? If they tell me, that they have mounted on the steps or by the gradual ascent of reason, and by drawing inferences from effects to causes, I still insist, that they have aided the ascent of reason by the wings of imagination; otherwise they could not thus change their manner of inference, and argue from causes to effects; presuming, that a more perfect production than the present world would be more suitable to such perfect beings as the gods, and forgetting that they have no reason to ascribe to these celestial beings any perfection or any attribute, but what can be found in the present world.*

Hence all the fruitless industry to account for the ill appearances of nature, and save the honour of the gods; while we must acknowledge the reality of that evil and disorder, with which the world so much abounds. The obstinate and intractable qualities of matter, we are told, or the observance of general laws, or some such reason, is the sole cause, which controlled the power and benevolence of Jupiter, and obliged him to create mankind and every sensible creature so imperfect and so unhappy.* These attributes then, are, it seems, beforehand, taken for granted, in their greatest latitude. And upon that supposition, I own that such conjectures may, perhaps, be admitted as plausible solutions of the ill phenomena. But still I ask; Why take these attributes for granted, or why ascribe to the cause any qualities but what actually appear in the effect? Why torture your brain to justify the course of nature upon suppositions, which, for aught you know, may be entirely imaginary, and of which there are to be found no traces in the course of nature?

The religious hypothesis,* therefore, must be considered only as a particular method of accounting for the visible phenomena of the universe: but no just reasoner will ever presume to infer from it any single fact, and alter or add to the phenomena, in any single particular. If you think, that the appearances of things prove such causes, it is allowable for you to draw an inference concerning the existence of these causes. In such complicated and sublime subjects, every one should be indulged in the liberty of conjecture and argument. But here you ought to rest. If you come backward, and arguing from your inferred causes, conclude, that any other fact has existed, or will exist, in the course of nature, which may serve as a fuller display of particular attributes; I must admonish you, that you have departed from the method of reasoning, attached to the present subject, and have certainly added something to the attributes of the cause, beyond what appears in the effect; otherwise you could never, with tolerable sense or propriety, add anything to the effect, in order to render it more worthy of the cause.

Where, then, is the odiousness of that doctrine, which I teach in my school, or rather, which I examine in my gardens? Or what do you find in this whole question, wherein the security of good morals, or the peace and order of society, is in the least concerned?

I deny a providence, you say, and supreme governor of the world, who guides the course of events, and punishes the vicious with infamy and disappointment, and rewards the virtuous with honour and success, in all their undertakings. But surely, I deny not the course itself of events, which lies open to every one's inquiry and examination. I acknowledge, that, in the present order of things, virtue is attended with more peace of mind than vice, and meets with a more favourable reception from the world. I am sensible, that, according to the past experience of mankind, friendship is the chief joy of human life, and moderation the only source of tranquillity and happiness. I never balance between the virtuous and the vicious course of life; but am sensible, that, to a well-disposed mind, every advantage is on the side of the former. And what can you say more, allowing all your suppositions and reasonings? You tell me, indeed, that this disposition of things proceeds from intelligence and design. But whatever it proceeds from, the disposition itself, on which depends our happiness or misery, and consequently our conduct and deportment in life is still the same. It is still open for me, as well as you, to regulate my behaviour, by my experience of past events. And if you affirm, that, while a divine providence is allowed, and a supreme distributive justice in the universe, I ought to expect some more particular reward of the good, and punishment of the bad, beyond the ordinary course of events; I here find the same fallacy, which I have before endeavoured to detect. You persist in imagining, that, if we grant that divine existence, for which you so earnestly contend, you may safely infer consequences from it, and add something to the experienced order of nature, by arguing from the attributes which you ascribe to your gods. You seem not to remember, that all your reasonings on this subject can only be drawn from effects to causes; and that every argument, deduced from causes to effects, must of necessity be a gross sophism; since it is impossible for you to know anything of the cause, but what you have antecedently, not inferred, but discovered to the full, in the effect.

But what must a philosopher think of those vain reasoners, who, instead of regarding the present scene of things as the sole object of their contemplation, so far reverse the whole course of nature, as to render this life merely a passage to something farther; a porch, which leads to a greater, and vastly different building; a prologue, which serves only to introduce the piece, and give it more grace and propriety? Whence, do you think, can such philosophers derive their idea of the gods? From their own conceit and imagination surely. For if they derived it from the present phenomena, it would never point to anything farther, but must be exactly adjusted to them. That the divinity may *possibly* be endowed with attributes, which we have never seen exerted; may be governed by principles of action, which we cannot discover to be satisfied: all this will freely be allowed. But still this is mere *possibility* and hypothesis. We never can have reason to *infer* any attributes, or any principles of action in him, but so far as we know them to have been exerted and satisfied.

Are there any marks of a distributive justice in the world? If you answer in the affirmative, I conclude, that, since justice here exerts itself, it is satisfied. If you reply in the negative, I conclude, that you have then no reason to ascribe justice, in our sense of it, to the gods. If you hold a medium between affirmation and negation, by saying, that the justice of the gods, at present, exerts itself in part, but not in its full extent; I answer, that you have no reason to give it any particular extent, but only so far as you see it, *at present*, exert itself.

Thus I bring the dispute, O Athenians, to a short issue with my antagonists. The course of nature lies open to my contemplation as well as to theirs. The experienced train of events is the great standard, by which we all regulate our conduct. Nothing else can be appealed to in the field, or in the senate. Nothing else ought ever to be heard of in the school, or in the closet.* In vain would our limited understanding break through those boundaries, which are too narrow for our fond imagination. While we argue from the course of nature, and infer a particular intelligent cause, which first bestowed, and still preserves order in the universe, we embrace a principle, which is both uncertain and useless. It is uncertain; because the subject lies entirely beyond the reach of human experience. It is useless; because our knowledge of this cause being derived entirely from the course of nature, we can never, according to the rules of just reasoning, return back from the cause with any new inference, or making additions to the common and experienced course of nature, establish any new principles of conduct and behaviour.

I observe (said I, finding he had finished his harangue) that you neglect not the artifice of the demagogues of old; and as you were pleased to make me stand for the people, you insinuate yourself into my favour by embracing those principles, to which, you know, I have always expressed a particular attachment. But allowing you to make experience (as indeed I think you ought) the only standard of our judgement concerning this, and all other questions of fact; I doubt not but, from the very same experience, to which you appeal, it may be possible to refute this reasoning, which you have put into the mouth of Epicurus. If you saw, for instance, a half-finished building, surrounded with heaps of brick and stone and mortar, and all the instruments of masonry; could you not *infer* from the effect, that it was a work of design and contrivance? And could you not return again, from this inferred cause, to infer new additions to the effect, and conclude, that the building would soon be finished, and receive all the further improvements, which art could bestow upon it? If you saw upon the sea-shore the print of one human foot, you would conclude, that a man had passed that way, and that he had also left the traces of the other foot, though effaced by the rolling of the sands or inundation of the waters. Why then do you refuse to admit the same method of reasoning with regard to the order of nature? Consider the world and the present life only as an imperfect building, from which you can infer a superior intelligence; and arguing from that superior intelligence, which can leave nothing imperfect; why may you not infer a more finished scheme or plan, which will receive its completion in some distant point of space or time? Are not these methods of reasoning exactly similar? And under what pretence can you embrace the one, while you reject the other?

The infinite difference of the subjects, replied he, is a sufficient foundation for this difference in my conclusions. In works of *human* art* and contrivance, it is allowable to advance from the effect to the cause, and returning back from the cause, to form new inferences concerning the effect, and examine the alterations, which it has probably undergone, or may still undergo. But what is the foundation of this method of reasoning? Plainly this; that man is a being, whom we know by experience, whose motives and designs we are acquainted with, and whose projects and inclinations have a certain connexion and coherence, according to the laws which nature has established for the government of such a creature. When, therefore, we find, that any work has proceeded from the skill and industry of man; as we are otherwise acquainted with the nature of the animal, we can draw a hundred inferences concerning what may be expected from him; and these inferences will all be founded in experience and observation. But did we know man only from the single work or production which we examine, it were impossible for us to argue in this manner; because our knowledge of all the qualities, which we ascribe to him, being in that case derived from the production, it is impossible they could point to anything farther, or be the foundation of any new inference. The print of a foot in the sand can only prove, when considered alone, that there was some figure adapted to it, by which it was produced: but the print of a human foot proves likewise, from our other experience, that there was probably another foot, which also left its impression, though effaced by time or other accidents. Here we mount from the effect to the cause; and descending again from the cause, infer alterations in the effect; but this is not a continuation of the same simple chain of reasoning. We comprehend in this case a hundred other experiences and observations, concerning the *usual* figure and members of that species of animal, without which this method of argument must be considered as fallacious and sophistical.

The case is not the same with our reasonings from the works of nature. The Deity is known to us only by his productions, and is a single being in the universe, not comprehended under any species or genus, from whose experienced attributes or qualities, we can, by analogy, infer any attribute or quality in him. As the universe shews wisdom and goodness, we infer wisdom and goodness. As it shews a particular degree of these perfections, we infer a particular degree of them, precisely adapted to the effect which we examine. But farther attributes or farther degrees of the same attributes, we can never be authorised to infer or suppose, by any rules of just reasoning. Now, without some such licence of supposition, it is impossible for us to argue from the cause, or infer any alteration in the effect, beyond what has immediately fallen under our observation. Greater good produced by this Being must still prove a greater degree of goodness: a more impartial distribution of rewards and punishments must proceed from a greater regard to justice and equity. Every supposed addition to the works of nature makes an addition to the attributes of the Author of nature; and consequently, being entirely unsupported by any reason or argument, can never be admitted but as mere conjecture and hypothesis.[1]

---

[1] In general, it may, I think, be established as a maxim, that where any cause is known only by its particular effects, it must be impossible to infer any new effects from that cause; since the qualities, which are requisite to produce these new effects along with the former, must either be different, or superior, or of more extensive operation, than those which simply produced the effect, whence alone the cause is supposed to be known to us. We can never, therefore, have any reason to suppose the existence of these qualities. To say, that the new effects proceed only from a continuation of the same energy, which is already known from the first effects, will not remove the difficulty. For even granting this to be the case (which can seldom be supposed), the very continuation and exertion of a like energy (for it is impossible it can be absolutely the same), I say, this exertion of a like energy, in a different period of space and time, is a very

The great source of our mistake in this subject, and of the unbounded licence of conjecture, which we indulge, is, that we tacitly consider ourselves, as in the place of the Supreme Being, and conclude, that he will, on every occasion, observe the same conduct, which we ourselves, in his situation, would have embraced as reasonable and eligible. But, besides that the ordinary course of nature may convince us, that almost everything is regulated by principles and maxims very different from ours; besides this, I say, it must evidently appear contrary to all rules of analogy to reason, from the intentions and projects of men, to those of a Being so different, and so much superior. In human nature, there is a certain experienced coherence of designs and inclinations; so that when, from any fact, we have discovered one intention of any man, it may often be reasonable, from experience, to infer another, and draw a long chain of conclusions concerning his past or future conduct. But this method of reasoning can never have place with regard to a Being, so remote and incomprehensible, who bears much less analogy* to any other being in the universe than the sun to a waxen taper, and who discovers himself only by some faint traces or outlines, beyond which we have no authority to ascribe to him any attribute or perfection. What we imagine to be a superior perfection, may really be a defect. Or were it ever so much a perfection, the ascribing of it to the Supreme Being, where it appears not to have been really exerted, to the full, in his works, savours more of flattery and panegyric, than of just reasoning and sound philosophy. All the philosophy, therefore, in the world, and all the religion, which is nothing but a species of philosophy, will never be able to carry us beyond the usual course of experience, or give us measures of conduct and behaviour different from those which are furnished by reflections on common life. No new fact can ever be inferred from the religious hypothesis; no event foreseen or foretold; no reward or punishment expected or dreaded, beyond what is already known by practice and observation. So that my apology for Epicurus will still appear solid and satisfactory;

---

arbitrary supposition, and what there cannot possibly be any traces of in the effects, from which all our knowledge of the cause is originally derived. Let the *inferred* cause be exactly proportioned (as it should be) to the known effect; and it is impossible that it can possess any qualities, from which new or different effects can be *inferred*.

nor have the political interests of society any connexion with the philosophical disputes concerning metaphysics and religion.

There is still one circumstance, replied I, which you seem to have overlooked. Though I should allow your premises, I must deny your conclusion. You conclude, that religious doctrines and reasonings *can* have no influence on life, because they *ought* to have no influence; never considering, that men reason not in the same manner you do, but draw many consequences from the belief of a divine Existence, and suppose that the Deity will inflict punishments on vice, and bestow rewards on virtue, beyond what appear in the ordinary course of nature. Whether this reasoning of theirs be just or not, is no matter. Its influence on their life and conduct must still be the same. And, those, who attempt to disabuse them of such prejudices, may, for aught I know, be good reasoners, but I cannot allow them to be good citizens and politicians; since they free men from one restraint upon their passions, and make the infringement of the laws of society, in one respect, more easy and secure.

After all, I may, perhaps, agree to your general conclusion in favour of liberty, though upon different premises from those, on which you endeavour to found it. I think, that the state ought to tolerate every principle of philosophy; nor is there an instance, that any government has suffered in its political interests by such indulgence. There is no enthusiasm* among philosophers; their doctrines are not very alluring to the people; and no restraint can be put upon their reasonings, but what must be of dangerous consequence to the sciences, and even to the state, by paving the way for persecution and oppression in points, where the generality of mankind are more deeply interested and concerned.

But there occurs to me (continued I) with regard to your main topic, a difficulty, which I shall just propose to you without insisting on it; lest it lead into reasonings of too nice and delicate a nature. In a word, I much doubt whether it be possible for a cause to be known only by its effect (as you have all along supposed) or to be of so singular and particular a nature as to have no parallel and no similarity with any other cause or object, that has ever fallen under our observation. It is only when two *species* of objects are found to be constantly conjoined, that we can infer the one from the other; and were an effect presented, which was entirely singular, and could not be comprehended under any known *species*, I do not see, that we could form any conjecture or inference at all concerning its cause. If experience and observation and analogy be, indeed, the only guides which we can reasonably follow in inferences of this nature; both the effect and cause must bear a similarity and resemblance to other effects and causes, which we know, and which we have found, in many instances, to be conjoined with each other. I leave it to your own reflection to pursue the consequences of this principle. I shall just observe, that, as the antagonists of Epicurus always suppose the universe, an effect quite singular and unparalleled, to be the proof of a Deity, a cause no less singular and unparalleled; your reasonings, upon that supposition, seem, at least, to merit our attention. There is, I own, some difficulty, how we can ever return from the cause to the effect, and, reasoning from our ideas of the former, infer any alteration on the later, or any addition to it.

A LETTER CONCERNING
THE DIALOGUES,
10 March 1751

To Gilbert Elliot   Ninewells,
of Minto   near Berwick.

Dear Sir

You wou'd perceive by the Sample I have given you, that I make Cleanthes the Hero of the Dialogue. Whatever you can think of, to strengthen that Side of the Argument, will be most acceptable to me. Any Propensity you imagine I have to the other Side, crept in upon me against my Will: And tis not long ago that I burn'd an old Manuscript Book, wrote before I was twenty; which contain'd, Page after Page, the gradual Progress of my Thoughts on that head. It begun with an anxious Search after Arguments, to confirm the common Opinion: Doubts stole in, dissipated, return'd, were again dissipated, return'd again; and it was a perpetual Struggle of a restless Imagination against Inclination, perhaps against Reason.

I have often thought, that the best way of composing a Dialogue, wou'd be for two Persons that are of different Opinions about any Question of Importance, to write alternately the different Parts of the Discourse, & reply to each other. By this Means, that vulgar Error woud be avoided, of putting nothing but Nonsense into the Mouth of the Adversary: And at the same time, a Variety of Character & Genius being upheld, woud make the whole look more natural & unaffected. Had it been my good Fortune to live near you, I shou'd have taken on me the Character of Philo, in the Dialogue, which you'll own I coud have supported naturally enough: And you woud not have been averse to that of Cleanthes.* I believe, too, we coud both of us have kept our Temper very well; only, you have not reach'd an absolute philosophical Indifference on these Points. What Danger can ever come from ingenious Reasoning & Enquiry? The worst speculative Sceptic ever I knew, was a much better Man than the best superstitious Devotee & Bigot. I must inform you, too, that this was the way of thinking of the Antients on this Subject. If a Man made Profession of Philosophy, whatever his Sect was, they always expected to find more Regularity in his Life and Manners, than in those of the ignorant & illiterate. There is a remarkable Passage of Appian to this Purpose. That Historian observes, that notwithstanding the establish'd Prepossession in Favour of Learning, yet some Philosophers, who have been trusted with absolute Power, have very much abus'd it; and he instances in Critias, the most violent of the Thirty, & Ariston, who govern'd Athens in the time of Sylla. But I find, upon Enquiry, that Critias was a profest Atheist, & Ariston an Epicurean, which is little or nothing different:* And yet Appian wonders at their Corruption, as much as if they had been Stoics or Platonists. A modern Zealot woud have thought that Corruption unavoidable.

I cou'd wish that Cleanthes' Argument coud be so analys'd, as to be render'd quite formal & regular. The Propensity of the Mind towards it, unless that Propensity were as strong & universal as that to believe in our Senses & Experience, will still, I am afraid, be esteem'd a suspicious Foundation. Tis here I wish for your Assistance. We must endeavour to prove that this Propensity is somewhat different from our Inclination to find our own Figures in the Clouds, our Face in the Moon, our Passions & Sentiments even in inanimate Matter. Such an Inclination may, & ought to be controul'd, & can never be a legitimate Ground of Assent.

The Instances I have chosen for Cleanthes are, I hope, tolerably happy, & the Confusion in which I represent the Sceptic seems natural. But si quid novisti rectius, &c.*

You ask me, If the idea of Cause & Effect is nothing but Vicinity, (you shoud have said constant Vicinity, or regular Conjunction), I woud gladly know *whence is that farther Idea of Causation against which you argue*?* This Question is pertinent; but I hope I have answer'd it. We feel, after the constant Conjunction, an easy Transition from one Idea to the other, or a Connexion in the Imagination. And as it is usual for us to transfer our own Feelings to the Objects on which they are dependent, we attach the internal Sentiment to the external Objects. If no single Instances of Cause & Effect appear to have any Connexion, but only repeated similar ones, you will find yourself oblig'd to have Recourse to this Theory.

I am sorry our Correspondence shou'd lead us into these abstract

Speculations. I have thought, & read, & compos'd very little on such Questions of late. Morals, Politics, & Literature have employ'd all my Time; but still the other Topics I must think more curious, important, entertaining, & useful, than any Geometry that is deeper than Euclid. If in order to answer the Doubts started, new Principles of Philosophy must be laid; are not these Doubts themselves very useful? Are they not preferable to blind, & ignorant Assent? I hope I can answer my own Doubts: But if I coud not, is it to be wonder'd at? To give myself Airs, & speak magnificently, might I not observe, that Columbus did not conquer Empires & plant Colonies?

If I have not unravell'd the Knot so well, in these last Papers I sent you, as perhaps I did in the former, it has not, I assure you, proceeded from Want of good Will; but some Subjects are easier than others; At some Times one is happier in his Researches & Enquiries than at others. Still I have Recourse to the *si quid novisti rectius.* Not in order to pay you a Compliment, but from a real philosophical Doubt & Curiosity.

I do not pay Compliments, because I do not desire them. For this Reason, I am very well pleas'd you speak so coldly of my Petition.* I had, however, given Orders to have it printed, which perhaps may be executed: Tho' I believe I had better have left it alone. Not beause it will give Offence, but because it will not give Entertainment: Not because it may be call'd profane; but because it may perhaps be deservedly call'd dull. To tell the Truth, I was always so indifferent about Fortune, & especially now, that I am more advanc'd in Life, & am a little more at my Ease, suited to my extreme Frugality, that I neither fear nor hope any thing from any man, and am very indifferent either about Offence or Favour. Not only, I woud not sacrifice Truth & Reason to political Views, but scarce even a Jest. You may tell me that I ought to have revers'd the Order of these Points, & have put the Jest first: As it is usual for People to be the fondest of their Performances on Subjects on which they are least made to excel. And that, consequently, I woud give more to be thought a good Droll, than to have the Praises of Erudition, & Subtility, & Invention.—This malicious Insinuation, I will give no Answer to, but proceed with my Subject.

I find, however, I have no more to say on it, but to thank you for Strabo. If the Carrier who will deliver you this do not find you at home, you will please send the Book to his Quarters. His Name is Thomas Henderson, the Berwick Carrier. He leaves the Town on the Thursdays, about the Middle of the day; he puts up at James Henderson, Stabler, betwixt the Foot of Cant's Close & Blackfriars' Wynd.

After you have done with these Papers, please return them by the same Carrier. But there is no Hurry. On the contrary the longer you keep them, I shall still believe you are thinking the more seriously to execute what I desire of you. I am Dear Sir

Yours most sincerely
DAVID HUME.

P.S.

If you'll be persuaded to assist me in supporting Cleanthes, I fancy you need not take Matters any higher than Part 3. He allows, indeed, in Part 2, that all our Inference is founded on the Similitude of the Works of Nature to the usual Effects of Mind. Otherwise they must appear a mere Chaos. The only Difficulty is, why the other Dissimilitudes do not weaken the Argument. And indeed it woud seem from Experience & Feeling, that they do not weaken it so much as we might naturally expect. A Theory to solve this woud be very acceptable.

I hope you intend to be in this Country this Season. I am sorry to hear Mrs Murray has been ill. But I hope she is now better.

I make no Scruple to push you to write me something regular on this Subject. It will be a kind of Exercise to you; & improve your Style & Invention.

DIALOGUES CONCERNING
NATURAL RELIGION

PAMPHILUS TO HERMIPPUS

IT has been remarked, my HERMIPPUS, that, though the ancient philosophers conveyed most of their instruction in the form of dialogue, this method of composition has been little practised in later ages, and has seldom succeeded in the hands of those who have attempted it. Accurate and regular argument, indeed, such as is now expected of philosophical enquirers, naturally throws a man into the methodical and didactic manner; where he can immediately, without preparation, explain the point at which he aims; and thence proceed, without interruption, to deduce the proofs, on which it is established. To deliver a SYSTEM in conversation scarcely appears natural; and while the dialogue-writer desires, by departing from the direct style of composition, to give a freer air to his performance, and avoid the appearance of *author* and *reader*, he is apt to run into a worse inconvenience, and convey the image of *pedagogue* and *pupil*. Or if he carries on the dispute in the natural spirit of good company, by throwing in a variety of topics, and preserving a proper balance among the speakers; he often loses so much time in preparations and transitions, that the reader will scarcely think himself compensated, by all the graces of dialogue, for the order, brevity, and precision, which are sacrificed to them.

There are some subjects, however, to which dialogue-writing is peculiarly adapted, and where it is still preferable to the direct and simple method of composition.

Any point of doctrine, which is so *obvious*, that it scarcely admits of dispute, but at the same time so *important*, that it cannot be too often inculcated, seems to require some such method of handling it; where the novelty of the manner may compensate the triteness of the subject, where the vivacity of conversation may enforce the precept, and where the variety of lights, presented by various personages and characters, may appear neither tedious nor redundant.

Any question of philosophy, on the other hand, which is so *obscure* and *uncertain*, that human reason can reach no fixed determination with regard to it; if it should be treated at all; seems to lead us naturally into the style of dialogue and conversation. Reasonable men may be allowed to differ, where no one can reasonably be positive: Opposite sentiments, even without any decision, afford an agreeable amusement: And if the subject be curious and interesting, the book carries us, in a manner, into company; and unites the two greatest and purest pleasures of human life, study and society.

Happily, these circumstances are all to be found in the subject of NATURAL RELIGION.* What truth so obvious, so certain, as the *being* of a God, which the most ignorant ages have acknowledged, for which the most refined geniuses have ambitiously striven to produce new proofs and arguments? What truth so important as this, which is the ground of all our hopes, the surest foundation of morality, the firmest support of society, and the only principle which ought never to be a moment absent from our thoughts and meditations? But in treating of this obvious and important truth; what obscure questions occur, concerning the *nature* of that divine Being; his attributes, his decrees, his plan of providence? These have been always subjected to the disputations of men: Concerning these, human reason has not reached any certain determination: But these are topics so interesting, that we cannot restrain our restless enquiry with regard to them; though nothing but doubt, uncertainty and contradiction, have, as yet, been the result of our most accurate researches.

This I had lately occasion to observe, while I passed, as usual, part of the summer season with CLEANTHES, and was present at those conversations of his with PHILO and DEMEA, of which I gave you lately some imperfect account. Your curiosity, you then told me, was so excited, that I must of necessity enter into a more exact detail of their reasonings, and display those various systems which they advanced with regard to so delicate a subject as that of natural religion. The remarkable contrast in their characters still farther raised your expectations; while you opposed the accurate philosophical turn of CLEANTHES to the careless scepticism of PHILO, or compared either of their dispositions with the rigid inflexible orthodoxy of DEMEA. My youth rendered me a mere auditor of their disputes; and that curiosity, natural to the early season of life, has so deeply imprinted in my memory the whole chain and connection of their arguments, that, I hope, I shall not omit or confound any considerable part of them in the recital.

PART I

AFTER I joined the company, whom I found sitting in CLEANTHES's library, DEMEA paid CLEANTHES some compliments, on the great care which he took of my education, and on his unwearied perseverance and constancy in all his friendships. The father of PAMPHILUS, said he, was your intimate friend: The son is your pupil, and may indeed be regarded as your adopted son; were we to judge by the pains which you bestow in conveying to him every useful branch of literature and science. You are no more wanting, I am persuaded, in prudence than in industry. I shall, therefore, communicate to you a maxim, which I have observed with regard to my own children, that I may learn how far it agrees with your practice. The method I follow in their education is founded on the saying of an ancient, 'That students of philosophy ought first to learn logics, then ethics, next physics, last of all, of the nature of the Gods.'[1] This science of natural theology, according to him, being the most profound and abstruse of any, required the maturest judgment in its students; and none but a mind, enriched with all the other sciences, can safely be entrusted with it.

Are you so late, says PHILO, in teaching your children the principles of religion? Is there no danger of their neglecting or rejecting altogether, those opinions, of which they have heard so little during the whole course of their education? It is only as a science, replied DEMEA, subjected to human reasoning and disputation, that I postpone the study of natural theology. To season their minds with early piety is my chief care; and by continual precept and instruction, and I hope too, by example, I imprint deeply on their tender minds an habitual reverence for all the principles of religion. While they pass through every other science, I still remark the uncertainty of each part, the eternal disputations of men, the obscurity of all philosophy, and the strange, ridiculous conclusions, which some of the greatest geniuses have derived from the principles of mere human reason. Having thus tamed their mind to a proper submission and self-diffidence, I have no longer any scruple of opening to

[1] Chrysippus apud Plut. *de repug. Stoicorum* [ch. 9, 1035 *a*, *b*].

them the greatest mysteries of religion, nor apprehend any danger from that assuming arrogance of philosophy, which may lead them to reject the most established doctrines and opinions.

Your precaution, says PHILO, of seasoning your children's minds with early piety, is certainly very reasonable; and no more than is requisite, in this profane and irreligious age. But what I chiefly admire in your plan of education, is your method of drawing advantage from the very principles of philosophy and learning, which, by inspiring pride and self-sufficiency, have commonly, in all ages, been found so destructive to the principles of religion. The vulgar, indeed, we may remark, who are unacquainted with science and profound enquiry, observing the endless disputes of the learned, have commonly a thorough contempt for philosophy; and rivet themselves the faster, by that means, in the great points of theology, which have been taught them. Those who enter a little into study and enquiry, finding many appearances of evidence in doctrines the newest and most extraordinary, think nothing too difficult for human reason; and presumptuously breaking through all fences, profane the inmost sanctuaries of the temple. But CLEANTHES will, I hope, agree with me, that, after we have abandoned ignorance, the surest remedy, there is still one expedient left to prevent this profane liberty. Let DEMEA's principles be improved and cultivated: Let us become thoroughly sensible of the weakness, blindness, and narrow limits of human reason: Let us duly consider its uncertainty and needless contrarieties, even in subjects of common life and practice: Let the errors and deceits of our very senses be set before us; the insuperable difficulties, which attend first principles in all systems; the contradictions, which adhere to the very ideas of matter, cause and effect, extension, space, time, motion; and in a word, quantity of all kinds, the object of the only science, that can fairly pretend to any certainty or evidence. When these topics are displayed in their full light, as they are by some philosophers and almost all divines; who can retain such confidence in this frail faculty of reason as to pay any regard to its determinations in points so sublime, so abstruse, so remote from common life and experience?[1] When the coherence of the parts of a stone, or even that composition of parts, which renders it ex-

---

[1] [experience *for* practice.]

tended; when these familiar objects, I say, are so inexplicable,* and contain circumstances so repugnant and contradictory; with what assurance can we decide concerning the origin of worlds, or trace their history from eternity to eternity?

While PHILO pronounced these words, I could observe a smile in the countenances both of DEMEA and CLEANTHES. That of DEMEA seemed to imply an unreserved satisfaction in the doctrines delivered: But in CLEANTHES's features, I could distinguish an air of finesse;[1] as if he perceived some raillery or[2] artificial malice in the reasonings of PHILO.

You propose then, PHILO, said CLEANTHES, to erect religious faith on philosophical scepticism; and you think, that if certainty or evidence be expelled from every other subject of enquiry, it will all retire to these theological doctrines, and there acquire a superior force and authority. Whether your scepticism be as absolute and sincere as you pretend, we shall learn bye and bye, when the company breaks up: We shall then see, whether you go out at the door or the window; and whether you really doubt, if your body has gravity, or can be injured by its fall; according to popular opinion, derived from our fallacious senses and more fallacious experience. And this consideration, DEMEA, may, I think, fairly serve to abate our ill-will to this humourous[3] sect of the sceptics. If they be thoroughly in earnest, they will not long trouble the world with their doubts, cavils, and disputes: If they be only in jest, they are, perhaps, bad railliers, but can never be very dangerous, either to the state, to philosophy, or to religion.

In reality, PHILO, continued he, it seems certain, that though a man, in a flush of humour, after intense reflection on the many contradictions and imperfections of human reason, may entirely renounce all belief and opinion; it is impossible for him to persevere in this total scepticism, or make it appear in his conduct for a few hours. External objects press in upon him: Passions solicit him: His philosophical melancholy dissipates; and even the utmost violence upon his own temper will not be able, during any time, to preserve the poor appearance of scepticism. And for what reason impose on himself such a violence? This is a point in which it will

---

[1] [finesse *for* finesse and raillery.]   [2] [raillery or *added.*]
[3] [humourous *for* pleasant.]

be impossible for him ever to satisfy himself, consistently with his sceptical principles: So that upon the whole nothing could be more ridiculous than the principles of the ancient Pyrrhonians;* if in reality they endeavoured, as is pretended, to extend throughout,[1] the same scepticism, which they had learned from the declamations of their school,[2] and which they ought to have confined to them.

In this view, there appears a great resemblance between the sects of the Stoics* and Pyrrhonians, though perpetual antagonists: And both of them seem founded on this erroneous maxim, that what a man can perform sometimes, and in some dispositions, he can perform always, and in every disposition. When the mind, by Stoical reflections, is elevated into a sublime enthusiasm of virtue, and strongly smit with any *species* of honour or public good, the utmost bodily pain and sufferance will not prevail over[3] such a high sense of duty; and it is possible, perhaps, by its means, even to smile and exult in the midst of tortures. If this sometimes may be the case in fact and reality, much more may a philosopher, in his school, or even in his closet, work himself up to such an enthusiasm, and support in imagination the acutest pain or most calamitous event which he can possibly conceive. But how shall he support this enthusiasm itself? The bent of his mind relaxes,* and cannot be recalled at pleasure: Avocations lead him astray[4]: Misfortunes attack him unawares: And the *philosopher* sinks by degrees into the *plebeian*.

I allow of your comparison between the Stoics and Sceptics, replied Philo. But you may observe, at the same time, that though the mind cannot, in Stoicism, support the highest flights of philosophy, yet even when it sinks lower, it still retains somewhat of its former disposition; and the effects of the Stoic's reasoning will appear in his conduct in common life, and through the whole tenor of his actions. The ancient schools, particularly that of Zeno, produced examples of virtue and constancy which seem astonishing to present times.

---

[1] [extend throughout *for* introduce into common life.]
[2] [from the declamations of their school *for* from the sciences.]
[3] [not prevail over *for* make small impression in opposition to.]
[4] [lead him astray *for* call him aside.]

Vain Wisdom all and false Philosophy.
Yet with a pleasing sorcery could charm
Pain, for a while, or anguish, and excite
Fallacious Hope, or arm the obdurate breast
With stubborn Patience, as with triple steel.[1]

In like manner, if a man has accustomed himself to sceptical considerations on the uncertainty and narrow limits of reason, he will not entirely forget them when he turns his reflection on other subjects;[2] but in all his philosophical[3] principles and reasoning, I dare not say, in his common conduct,[4] he will be found different from those, who either never formed any opinions in the case, or have entertained sentiments more favourable to human reason.

To whatever length any one may push his speculative principles of scepticism, he must act, I own, and live, and converse like other men; and for this conduct he is not obliged to give any other reason than the absolute necessity he lies under of so doing. If he ever carries his speculations farther than this necessity constrains him, and philosophises, either on natural or moral subjects, he is allured by a certain pleasure and satisfaction, which he finds in employing himself after that manner. He considers besides, that every one, even in common life, is constrained to have more or less of this philosophy; that from our earliest infancy we make continual advances in forming more general principles of conduct and reasoning; that the larger experience we acquire, and the stronger reason we are endowed with, we always render our principles the more general and comprehensive; and that what we call *philosophy* is nothing but a more regular and methodical operation of the same kind. To philosophise on such subjects is nothing essentially different from reasoning on common life;* and we may only expect greater stability, if not greater truth, from our philosophy, on account of its exacter and more scrupulous method of proceeding.

But when we look beyond human affairs and the properties of the surrounding bodies: When we carry our speculations into the two eternities, before and after the present state of things; into the creation and formation of the universe; the existence and properties

---

[1] [*Paradise Lost*, ii.]

[2] [turns . . . subjects *for* leaves his closet.]

[3] [philosophical *added*.]

[4] [I dare not say, in his common conduct *added*.]

of spirits; the powers and operations of one universal spirit, exist-
ing without beginning and without end; omnipotent, omniscient,
immutable, infinite, and incomprehensible: We must be far
removed from the smallest tendency to scepticism not to be
apprehensive, that we have here got quite beyond the reach of
our faculties. So long as we confine our speculations to trade, or
morals, or politics, or criticism, we make appeàls, every moment,
to common sense and experience, which strengthen our philosophical conclusions, and remove (at least, in part) the suspicion,
which we so justly entertain with regard to every reasoning that is
very subtile and refined. But in theological reasonings, we have not
this advantage; while at the same time we are employed upon
objects, which, we must be sensible, are too large for our grasp,
and of all others, require most to be familiarised to our apprehension. We are like foreigners in a strange country, to whom
everything must seem suspicious, and who are in danger every
moment of transgressing against the laws and customs of the
people with whom they live and converse. We know not how far
we ought to trust our vulgar methods of reasoning in such a
subject; since, even in common life and in that province which is
peculiarly appropriated to them, we cannot account for them, and
are entirely guided by a kind of instinct or necessity in employing
them.[1]

All sceptics pretend, that, if reason be considered in an abstract
view, it furnishes invincible arguments against itself, and that we
could never retain any conviction or assurance, on any subject,[2]
were not the sceptical reasonings so refined and subtile, that they
are not able to counterpoise the more solid and more natural
arguments, derived from the senses and experience. But it is evident, whenever our arguments lose this advantage, and run wide of
common life, that the most refined scepticism comes to be upon a
footing with them, and is able to oppose and counterbalance them.
The one has no more weight than the other. The mind must remain

---

[1] [At the close of this paragraph Hume adds on the margin, and then scores
out, the following: 'A very small part of this great system, during a very small
time, is very imperfectly discovered to us: And do we thence pronounce decisively concerning the whole?' This passage, with slightly altered wording, is transferred by Hume to p. 51, where it is written on the margin.]

[2] [on any subject *for* even in the most common affairs of life.]

in suspense between them; and it is that very suspense or balance, which is the triumph of scepticism.*

But I observe, says CLEANTHES, with regard to you, PHILO, and all speculative sceptics, that your doctrine and practice are as much at variance in the most abstruse points of theory as in the conduct of common life. Wherever evidence discovers itself, you adhere to it, notwithstanding your pretended scepticism; and I can observe, too, some of your sect to be as decisive as those who make greater professions of certainty and assurance.[1] In reality, would not a man be ridiculous, who pretended to reject NEWTON's explication of the wonderful phenomenon of the rainbow,* because that explication gives a minute anatomy of the rays of light; a subject, forsooth, too refined for human comprehension? And what would you say to one, who having nothing particular to object to the arguments of COPERNICUS and GALILÆO* for the motion of the earth, should withhold his assent, on that general principle, that these subjects were too magnificent and remote to be explained by the narrow and fallacious reason of mankind?

There is indeed a kind of brutish and ignorant scepticism, as you well observed, which gives the vulgar a general prejudice against what they do not easily understand, and makes them reject every principle which requires elaborate reasoning to prove and establish it. This species of scepticism is fatal to knowledge, not to religion; since we find, that those who make greatest profession of it, give often their assent, not only to the great truths of theism, and natural theology,[2] but even to the most absurd tenets, which a traditional superstition has recommended to them. They firmly believe in witches; though they will not believe nor attend to the most simple proposition of Euclid. But the refined and philosophical sceptics fall into an inconsistence of an opposite nature. They push their researches into the most abstruse corners of science; and their assent attends them in every step, proportioned to the evidence which they meet with. They are even obliged to acknowledge, that the most abstruse and remote objects arc those which are best explained by philosophy. Light is in reality anatomized: The true system of the heavenly bodies is discovered and ascertained. But

---

[1] [assurance *for* dogmatism.]
[2] [theology *for* religion.]

the nourishment of bodies by food[1] is still an inexplicable mystery: The cohesion of the parts of matter is still incomprehensible. These sceptics, therefore, are obliged, in every question, to consider each particular evidence apart, and proportion their assent to the precise degree of evidence* which occurs. This is their practice in all natural, mathematical, moral, and political science. And why not the same, I ask, in the theological and religious? Why must conclusions of this nature be alone rejected on the general presumption of the insufficiency of human reason, without any particular discussion of the evidence? Is not such an unequal conduct a plain proof of prejudice and passion?

Our senses, you say, are fallacious, our understanding erroneous, our ideas even of the most familiar objects, extension, duration, motion, full of absurdities and contradictions. You defy me to solve the difficulties, or reconcile the repugnancies, which you discover in them. I have not capacity for so great an undertaking: I have not leisure for it: I perceive it to be superfluous. Your own conduct, in every circumstance, refutes your principles; and shows the firmest reliance on all the received maxims of science, morals, prudence, and behaviour.

I shall never assent to so harsh an opinion as that of a celebrated writer,[2] who says that the sceptics are not a sect of philosophers: They are only a sect of liars. I may, however, affirm (I hope without offence), that they are a sect of jesters or railliers. But for my part, whenever I find myself disposed to mirth and amusement, I shall certainly choose my entertainment of a less perplexing and abstruse nature. A comedy, a novel, or at most a history, seems a more natural recreation than such metaphysical subtilties and abstractions.

In vain would the sceptic make a distinction between science and common life, or between one science and another. The argu-

---

[1] [nourishment of bodies by food *for* falling of a stone.]

[2] *L'Art de penser*. [*La Logique ou l'art de penser*, by Antoine Arnauld (1612–94), published in 1662. The passage here referred to is in the *Premier discours* (1843 edition, p. 26): 'Personne ne douta jamais sérieusement qu'il y a une terre, un soleil et une lune, ni si le tout est plus grand que sa partie. On peut bien faire dire extérieurement à sa bouche qu'on en doute, parce que l'on peut mentir; mais on ne peut pas le faire dire à son esprit. Ainsi le Pyrrhonisme n'est pas une secte de gens qui soient persuadés de ce qu'ils disent, mais c'est une secte de menteurs.']

ments employed in all, if just, are of a similar nature, and contain the same force and evidence. Or if there be any difference among them, the advantage lies entirely on the side of theology and natural religion. Many principles of mechanics are founded on very abstruse reasoning; yet no man, who has any pretensions to science, even no speculative sceptic, pretends to entertain the least doubt with regard to them. The COPERNICAN system contains the most surprising paradox, and the most contrary to our natural conceptions, to appearances, and to our very senses:* Yet even monks and inquisitors are now constrained to withdraw their opposition to it. And shall PHILO, a man of so liberal a genius, and extensive knowledge, entertain any general undistinguished scruples with regard to the religious hypothesis, which is founded on the simplest and most obvious arguments, and, unless it meet with artificial obstacles, has such easy access and admission into the mind of man?

And here wè may observe, continued he, turning himself to-wards DEMEA, a pretty curious circumstance in the history of the sciences. After the union of philosophy with the popular religion,* upon the first establishment of Christianity, nothing was more usual, among all religious teachers, than declamations against reason, against the senses, against every principle, derived merely from human research and enquiry. All the topics of the ancient Academics[1]* were adopted by the Fathers; and thence propagated for several ages in every school and pulpit throughout Christen-dom. The Reformers* embraced the same principles of reasoning, or rather declamation; and all panegyrics on the excellency of faith were sure to be interlarded with some severe strokes of satire against natural reason. A celebrated prelate too,[2] of the Romish communion, a man of the most extensive learning, who wrote a demonstration of Christianity, has also composed a treatise, which contains all the cavils of the boldest and most determined PYRRHONISM. LOCKE* seems to have been the first Christian, who ventured openly to assert, that *faith* was nothing but a species of *reason*, that religion was only a branch of philosophy, and that a

---

[1] [and sceptics *omitted.*]

[2] Mons. Huet. [Peter Daniel Huet (1630–1721), Bishop of Avranches. The treatise here referred to, *Traité philosophique de la faiblesse de l'esprit humain*, was published posthumously in 1723. Cf. Mark Pattison's *Essays*, vol. i, p. 299.]

chain of arguments, similar to that which established any truth in morals, politics, or physics, was always employed in discovering all the principles of theology, natural and revealed. The ill use, which BAYLE* and other libertines made of the philosophical scepticism of the Fathers and first Reformers, still farther propagated the judicious sentiment of Mr. LOCKE: And it is now, in a manner, avowed, by all pretenders to reasoning and philosophy, that atheist and sceptic are almost synonymous. And as it is certain, that no man is in earnest, when he professes the latter principle; I would fain hope that there are as few, who seriously maintain the former.

Don't you remember, said PHILO, the excellent saying of Lord BACON* on this head? That a little philosophy, replied CLEANTHES, makes a man an atheist: A great deal converts him to religion. That is a very judicious remark too, said PHILO. But what I have in my eye is another passage, where, having mentioned DAVID's fool,* who said in his heart there is no God, this great philosopher observes, that the atheists now a days have a double share of folly: For they are not contented to say in their hearts there is no God, but they also utter that impiety with their lips, and are thereby guilty of multiplied indiscretion and imprudence. Such people, though they were ever so much in earnest, cannot, methinks, be very formidable.

But though you should rank me in this class of fools, I cannot forbear communicating a remark, that occurs to me from the history of the religious and irreligious scepticism with which you have entertained us. It appears to me, that there are strong symptoms of priestcraft in the whole progress of this affair. During ignorant ages, such as those which followed the dissolution of the ancient schools,* the priests perceived, that atheism, deism,* or heresy of any kind, could only proceed from the presumptuous questioning of received opinions, and from a belief that human reason was equal to everything. Education had then a mighty influence over the minds of men, and was almost equal in force to those suggestions of the senses and common understanding, by which the most determined sceptic must allow himself to be governed. But at present, when the influence of education is much diminished, and men, from a more open commerce of the world, have learned to compare the popular principles of different nations and ages, our sagacious divines have changed their whole system of philosophy, and talk the language of STOICS, PLATONISTS, and PERIPATETICS,* not that of PYRRHONIANS and ACADEMICS. If we distrust human reason, we have now no other principle to lead us into religion. Thus, sceptics in one age, dogmatists in another; whichever system best suits the purpose of these reverend gentlemen,[1] in giving them an ascendant over mankind, they are sure to make it their favourite principle, and established tenet.

It is very natural, said CLEANTHES, for men to embrace those principles, by which they find they can best defend their doctrines; nor need we have any recourse to priestcraft to account for so reasonable an expedient. And surely, nothing can afford a stronger presumption, that any set of principles are true, and ought to be embraced, than to observe, that they tend to the confirmation of true religion, and serve to confound the cavils of atheists, libertines, and freethinkers of all denominations.

---

[1] [these reverend gentlemen *for* the clergy.]

PART II

I MUST OWN, CLEANTHES, said DEMEA, that nothing can more surprise me, than the light, in which you have, all along, put this
argument. By the whole tenor of your discourse, one would imagine that you were maintaining the being of a God, against the
cavils of atheists and infidels; and were necessitated to become a
champion for that fundamental principle of all religion. But this, I
hope, is not by any means a question among us. No man; no man,
at least, of common sense, I am persuaded, ever entertained a
serious doubt with regard to a truth so certain and self-evident. The
question is not concerning the *being* but the *nature* of *God*. This, I
affirm, from the infirmities of human understanding, to be altogether incomprehensible and unknown to us. The essence of that
supreme mind, his attributes, the manner of his existence, the very
nature of his duration; these and every particular, which regards so
divine a Being, are mysterious to men. Finite, weak, and blind
creatures, we ought to humble ourselves in his august presence,
and, conscious of our frailties, adore in silence his infinite perfections, which eye hath not seen, ear hath not heard, neither hath it
entered into the heart of man to conceive them.* They are covered
in a deep cloud from human curiosity: It is profaneness to attempt
penetrating through these sacred obscurities: And next to the
impiety of denying his existence, is the temerity of prying into
his nature and essence, decrees and attributes.

But lest you should think, that my *piety* has here got the better of
my *philosophy*, I shall support my opinion, if it needs any support,
by a very great authority. I might cite all the divines almost, from
the foundation of Christianity, who have ever treated of this or any
other theological subject: But I shall confine myself, at present, to
one equally celebrated for piety and philosophy. It is Father
MALEBRANCHE,* who, I remember, thus expresses himself.[1] 'One
ought not so much (says he) to call God a spirit, in order to express
positively what he is, as in order to signify that he is not matter. He
is a Being infinitely perfect: Of this we cannot doubt. But in the

---

[1] *Recherche de la vérité, liv. 3*, chap. 9.

same manner as we ought not to imagine, even supposing him corporeal, that he is cloathed with a human body, as the ANTHROPOMORPHITES* asserted, under colour that that figure was the most perfect of any; so neither ought we to imagine, that the Spirit of God has human ideas, or bears *any* resemblance to our spirit; under colour that we know nothing more perfect than a human mind. We ought rather to believe, that as he comprehends the perfections of matter without being material . . . he comprehends also the perfections of created spirits, without being spirit, in the manner we conceive spirit: That his true name is, *He that is*, or in other words, Being without restriction, All Being, the Being infinite and universal.'

After so great an authority, DEMEA, replied PHILO, as that which you have produced, and a thousand more, which you might produce, it would appear ridiculous in me to add my sentiment, or express my approbation of your doctrine. But surely, where reasonable men treat these subjects, the question can never be concerning the *being*, but only the *nature* of the Deity. The former truth, as you well observe, is unquestionable and self-evident. Nothing exists without a cause; and the original cause of this universe (whatever it be)* we call God; and piously ascribe to him every species of perfection. Whoever scruples this fundamental truth deserves every punishment, which can be inflicted among philosophers, to wit, the greatest ridicule, contempt and disapprobation. But as all perfection is entirely relative, we ought never to imagine, that we comprehend the attributes of this divine Being, or to suppose, that his perfections have any analogy or likeness to the perfections of a human creature. Wisdom, thought, design, knowledge; these we justly ascribe to him; because these words are honourable among men, and we have no other language or other conceptions, by which we can express our adoration of him. But let us beware, lest we think, that our ideas any wise correspond to his perfections, or that his attributes have any resemblance to these qualities among men. He is infinitely superior to our limited view and comprehension; and is more the object of worship in the temple, than of disputation in the schools.

In reality, CLEANTHES, continued he, there is no need of having recourse to that affected scepticism, so displeasing to you, in order to come at this determination. Our ideas* reach no farther than our

experience: We have no experience of divine attributes and operations: I need not conclude my syllogism: You can draw the inference yourself. And it is a pleasure to me (and I hope to you too) that
just reasoning and sound piety here concur in the same conclusion,
and both of them establish the adorably mysterious and incomprehensible nature of the supreme Being.

Not to lose any time in circumlocutions, said CLEANTHES, ad-
dressing himself to DEMEA, much less in replying to the pious
declamations of PHILO; I shall briefly explain how I conceive this
matter. Look round the world: Contemplate the whole and every
part of it: You will find it to be nothing but one great machine,
subdivided into an infinite number of lesser machines, which again
admit of subdivisions, to a degree beyond what human senses and
faculties can trace and explain. All these various machines, and
even their most minute parts, are adjusted to each other with an
accuracy, which ravishes into admiration all men, who have ever
contemplated them. The curious adapting of means to ends,
throughout all nature, resembles exactly, though it much exceeds,
the productions of human contrivance; of human design, thought,
wisdom, and intelligence. Since therefore the effects resemble
each other, we are led to infer, by all the rules of analogy, that the
causes also resemble; and that the Author of nature is somewhat
similar to the mind of man; though possessed of much larger
faculties, proportioned to the grandeur of the work, which he has
executed. By this argument *a posteriori*, and by this argument
alone, do we prove at once the existence of a Deity, and his
similarity to human mind and intelligence.

I shall be so free, CLEANTHES, said DEMEA, as to tell you, that
from the beginning, I could not approve of your conclusion concerning the similarity of the Deity to men; still less can I approve
of the mediums, by which you endeavour to establish it. What! No
demonstration of the being of a God! No abstract arguments! No
proofs *a priori*!* Are these, which have hitherto been so much
insisted on by philosophers, all fallacy, all sophism? Can we reach
no farther in this subject than experience[1] and probability? I will
not say, that this is betraying the cause of a Deity: But surely, by
this affected candour, you give advantage to atheists, which they

[1] [moral evidence *substituted for* experience, and *then* experience *restored.*]

never could obtain, by the mere dint of argument and reasoning.

What I chiefly scruple in this subject, said PHILO, is not so much, that all religious arguments are by CLEANTHES reduced to experience, as that they appear not to be even the most certain and irrefragable of that inferior kind. That a stone will fall, that fire will burn, that the earth has solidity, we have observed a thousand and a thousand times; and when any new instance of this nature is presented, we draw without hesitation the accustomed inference. The exact similarity of the cases gives us a perfect assurance of a similar event; and a stronger evidence is never desired nor sought after. But wherever you depart, in the least, from the similarity of the cases, you diminish proportionably the evidence; and may at last bring it to a very weak *analogy*, which is confessedly liable to error and uncertainty. After having experienced the circulation of the blood in human creatures, we make no doubt that it takes place in Titius and Mævius: But from its circulation in frogs and fishes, it is only a presumption, though a strong one, from analogy, that it takes place in men and other animals. The analogical reasoning is much weaker, when we infer the circulation of the sap in vegetables from our experience that the blood circulates in animals; and those, who hastily followed that imperfect analogy, are found, by more accurate experiments, to have been mistaken.

If we see a house, CLEANTHES, we conclude, with the greatest certainty, that it had an architect or builder; because this is precisely that species of effect, which we have experienced to proceed from that species of cause. But surely you will not affirm, that the universe bears such a resemblance to a house, that we can with the same certainty infer a similar cause, or that the analogy is here entire and perfect. The dissimilitude is so striking, that the utmost you can here pretend to is a guess, a conjecture, a presumption concerning a similar cause; and how that pretension will be received in the world, I leave you to consider.

It would surely be very ill received, replied CLEANTHES; and I should be deservedly blamed and detested, did I allow, that the proofs of a Deity amounted to no more than a guess or conjecture. But is the whole adjustment of means to ends in a house and in the universe so slight a resemblance? The œconomy of final causes? The order, proportion, and arrangement of every part? Steps of a stair are plainly contrived, that human legs may use them in mounting; and this inference is certain and infallible. Human legs are also contrived for walking and mounting; and this inference, I allow, is not altogether so certain, because of the dissimilarity which you remark; but does it, therefore, deserve the name only of presumption or conjecture?

Good God! cried DEMEA, interrupting him, where are we? Zealous defenders of religion allow, that the proofs of a Deity fall short of perfect evidence! And you, PHILO, on whose assistance I depended, in proving the adorable mysteriousness of the divine nature, do you assent to all these extravagant opinions of CLEANTHES? For what other name can I give them? Or why spare my censure, when such principles are advanced, supported by such an authority, before so young a man as PAMPHILUS?

You seem not to apprehend, replied PHILO, that I argue with CLEANTHES in his own way; and by showing him the dangerous consequences of his tenets, hope at last to reduce him to our opinion. But what sticks most with you, I observe, is the representation which CLEANTHES has made of the argument *a posteriori*; and finding that that argument is likely to escape your hold and vanish into air, you think it so disguised, that you can scarcely believe it to be set in its true light. Now, however much I may dissent, in other respects, from the dangerous principles of CLEANTHES, I must allow, that he has fairly represented that argument; and I shall endeavour so to state the matter to you, that you will entertain no farther scruples with regard to it.

Were a man to abstract from every thing which he knows or has seen, he would be altogether incapable, merely from his own ideas, to determine what kind of scene the universe must be, or to give the preference to one state or situation of things above another. For as nothing, which he clearly conceives, could be esteemed impossible or implying a contradiction,* every chimera of his fancy would be upon an equal footing; nor could he assign any just reason, why he adheres to one idea or system, and rejects the others, which are equally possible.

Again; after he opens his eyes, and contemplates the world, as it really is, it would be impossible for him, at first, to assign the cause of any one event; much less, of the whole of things or of the universe. He might set his fancy a rambling; and she might bring him in an infinite variety of reports and representations. These would all be possible; but being all equally possible, he would never, of himself, give a satisfactory account for his preferring one of them to the rest. Experience alone can point out to him the true cause of any phenomenon.

Now according to this method of reasoning, DEMEA, it follows (and is, indeed, tacitly allowed by CLEANTHES himself) that order, arrangement, or the adjustment of final causes is not, of itself, any proof of design; but only so far as it has been experienced to procceed from that principle. For aught we can know *a priori*, matter may contain the source or spring of order originally, within itself, as well as mind does; and there is no more difficulty in conceiving, that the several elements, from an internal unknown cause, may fall into the most exquisite arrangement, than to conceive that their ideas, in the great, universal mind, from a like internal, unknown cause, fall into that arrangement. The equal possibility of both these suppositions is allowed. But by experience we find (according to CLEANTHES), that there is a difference between them. Throw several pieces of steel together, without shape or form; they will never arrange themselves so as to compose a watch: Stone, and mortar, and wood, without an architect, never erect a house. But the ideas in a human mind, we see, by an unknown, inexplicable œconomy, arrange themselves so as to form the plan of a watch or house. Experience, therefore, proves, that there is an original principle of order in mind, not in matter. From similar effects we infer similar causes. The adjustment of means to ends[1] is alike in the universe, as in a machine of human contrivance. The causes, therefore, must be resembling.

I was from the beginning scandalised, I must own, with this resemblance, which is asserted, between the Deity and human creatures; and must conceive it to imply such a degradation of the supreme Being as no sound theist could endure. With your assistance, therefore, DEMEA, I shall endeavour to defend what you justly call the adorable mysteriousness of the divine nature, and shall refute this reasoning of CLEANTHES; provided he allows, that I have made a fair representation of it.

When CLEANTHES had assented, PHILO, after a short pause, proceeded in the following manner.

---

[1] [means to ends *for* final causes.]

That all inferences, CLEANTHES, concerning fact, are founded on experience, and that all experimental reasonings are founded on the supposition, that similar causes prove similar effects, and similar effects similar causes; I shall not, at present, much dispute with you. But observe, I entreat you, with what extreme caution all just reasoners proceed in the transferring of experiments to similar cases. Unless the cases be exactly similar, they repose no perfect confidence in applying their past observation to any particular phenomenon. Every alteration of circumstances occasions a doubt concerning the event; and it requires new experiments to prove certainly, that the new circumstances are of no moment or importance. A change in bulk, situation, arrangement, age, disposition of the air, or surrounding bodies; any of these particulars may be attended with the most unexpected consequences: And unless the objects be quite familiar to us, it is the highest temerity to expect with assurance, after any of these changes, an event similar to that which before fell under our observation. The slow and deliberate steps of philosophers, here, if any where, are distinguished from the precipitate march of the vulgar, who, hurried on by the smallest similitude, are incapable of all discernment or consideration.

But can you think, CLEANTHES, that your usual phlegm* and philosophy have been preserved in so wide a step as you have taken, when you compared to the universe houses, ships, furniture, machines; and from their similarity in some circumstances inferred a similarity in their causes? Thought, design, intelligence, such as we discover in men and other animals, is no more than one of the springs and principles of the universe, as well as heat or cold, attraction or repulsion, and a hundred others, which fall under daily observation. It is an active cause, by which some particular parts of nature, we find, produce alterations on other parts. But can a conclusion, with any propriety, be transferred from parts to the whole? Does not the great disproportion bar all comparison and inference? From observing the growth of a hair, can we learn any thing concerning the generation of a man? Would the manner of a leaf's blowing,* even though perfectly known, afford us any instruction concerning the vegetation of a tree?

But allowing that we were to take the *operations* of one part of nature upon another for the foundation of our judgment concerning the *origin* of the whole (which never can be admitted); yet why select so minute, so weak, so bounded a principle as the reason and design of animals is found to be upon this planet? What peculiar privilege has this little agitation of the brain which we call thought,* that we must thus make it the model of the whole universe? Our partiality in our own favour does indeed present it on all occasions: But sound philosophy ought carefully to guard against so natural an illusion.

So far from admitting, continued PHILO, that the operations of a part can afford us any just conclusion concerning the origin of the whole, I will not allow any one part to form a rule for another part, if the latter be very remote from the former. Is there any reasonable ground to conclude, that the inhabitants of other planets possess thought, intelligence, reason, or any thing similar to these faculties in men? When nature has so extremely diversified her manner of operation in this small globe; can we imagine, that she incessantly copies herself throughout so immense a universe? And if thought, as we may well suppose, be confined merely to this narrow corner, and has even there so limited a sphere of action; with what propriety can we assign it for the original cause of all things? The narrow views of a peasant, who makes his domestic œconomy the rule for the government of kingdoms, is in comparison a pardonable sophism.

But were we ever so much assured, that a thought and reason, resembling the human, were to be found throughout the whole universe, and were its activity elsewhere vastly greater and more commanding than it appears in this globe: Yet I cannot see, why the operations of a world, constituted, arranged, adjusted, can with any propriety be extended to a world, which is in its embryo-state, and is advancing towards that constitution and arrangement. By observation, we know somewhat of the œconomy, action, and nourishment of a finished animal; but we must transfer with great caution that observation to the growth of a fœtus in the womb, and still more, to the formation of an animalcule* in the loins of its male parent. Nature, we find, even from our limited experience, possesses an infinite number of springs and principles, which incessantly discover themselves on every change of her position and situation. And what new and unknown principles would acturate her in so new and unknown a situation as that of the formation of a universe, we cannot, without the utmost temerity, pretend to determine.

[A very small part of this great system, during a very short time, is very imperfectly discovered to us: And do we thence pronounce decisively concerning the origin of the whole?][1]

Admirable conclusion! Stone, wood, brick, iron, brass, have not, at this time, in this minute globe of earth, an order or arrangement without human art and contrivance: Therefore the universe could not originally attain its order and arrangement, without something similar to human art. But is a part of nature a rule for another part very wide of the former? Is it a rule for the whole?[2] Is a very small part a rule for the universe? Is nature in one situation, a certain rule for[3] nature in another situation, vastly different from the former?

And can you blame me, CLEANTHES, if I here imitate the prudent reserve of SIMONIDES, who, according to the noted story,[4] being asked by HIERO, *What God was?* desired a day to think of it, and then two days more; and after that manner continually prolonged the term, without ever bringing in his definition or description? Could you even blame me, if I had answered at first, *that I did not know*, and was sensible that this subject lay vastly beyond the reach of my faculties? You might cry out sceptic and raillier as much as you pleased: But having found, in so many other subjects, much more familiar, the imperfections and even contradictions of human reason, I never should expect any success from its feeble conjectures, in a subject, so sublime, and so remote from the sphere of our observation. When two *species* of objects have always been observed to be conjoined together, I can *infer*, by custom, the existence of one wherever I *see* the existence of the other: And this I call an argument from experience.* But how this argument can have place, where the objects, as in the present case,[5] are single, individual, without parallel, or specific resemblance, may be difficult to explain. And will any man tell me with a serious countenance, that an orderly universe must arise from some thought and art, like the human; because we have experience of it? To ascertain this reasoning, it were requisite, that we had experience of the

---

[1] [This paragraph transferred from p. 37.]   [2] [whole *for* world.]
[3] [a certain rule for *for* precisely similar to.]
[4] [Cf. Cicero, *De Natura Deorum*, Bk. 1, 22.]
[5] [concerning the origin of the world *omitted.*]

origin of worlds; and it is not sufficient surely, that we have seen ships and cities arise from human art and contrivance. . . .

PHILO was proceeding in this vehement manner, somewhat between jest and earnest, as it appeared to me; when he observed some signs of impatience in CLEANTHES, and then immediately stopped short. What I had to suggest, said CLEANTHES, is only that you would not abuse terms, or make use of popular expressions to subvert philosophical reasonings. You know, that the vulgar often distinguish reason from experience, even where the question relates only to matter of fact and existence; though it is found, where that *reason* is properly analysed, that it is nothing but a species of experience. To prove by experience the origin of the universe from mind is not more contrary to common speech than to prove the motion of the earth from the same principle. And a caviller might raise all the same objections to the COPERNICAN system, which you have urged against my reasonings. Have you other earths, might he say, which you have seen to move? Have . . .

Yes! cried PHILO, interrupting him, we have other earths. Is not the moon another earth, which we see to turn round its centre? Is not Venus another earth, where we observe the same phenomenon? Are not the revolutions of the sun also a confirmation, from analogy, of the same theory? All the planets, are they not earths, which revolve about the sun? Are not the satellites moons, which move round Jupiter and Saturn, and along with these primary planets, round the sun? These analogies and resemblances, with others, which I have not mentioned, are the sole proofs of the COPERNICAN system: And to you it belongs to consider, whether you have any analogies of the same kind to support your theory.

In reality, CLEANTHES, continued he, the modern system of astronomy is now so much received by all enquirers, and has become so essential a part even of our earliest education, that we are not commonly very scrupulous in examining the reasons upon which it is founded. It is now become a matter of mere curiosity to study the first writers on that subject, who had the full force of prejudice to encounter, and were obliged to turn their arguments on every side, in order to render them popular and convincing. But if we peruse GALILÆO's famous Dialogues* concerning the system of the world, we shall find, that great genius, one of the sublimest that ever existed, first bent all his endeavours to prove, that there was no foundation for the distinction commonly made between elementary and celestial substances. The schools,* proceeding from the illusions of sense, had carried this distinction very far; and had established the latter substances to be ingenerable, incorruptible, unalterable, impassible; and had assigned all the opposite qualities to the former. But GALILÆO, beginning with the moon, proved its similarity in every particular to the earth; its convex figure, its natural darkness when not illuminated, its density, its distinction into solid and liquid, the variations of its phases, the mutual illuminations of the earth and moon, their mutual eclipses, the inequalities of the lunar surface, &c. After many instances of this kind, with regard to all the planets, men plainly saw, that these bodies became proper objects of experience; and that the similarity of their nature enabled us to extend the same arguments and phenomena from one to the other.

In this cautious proceeding of the astronomers, you may read your own condemnation, CLEANTHES; or rather may see, that the subject in which you are engaged exceeds all human reason and enquiry. Can you pretend to show any such similarity between the fabric of a house, and the generation of a universe? Have you ever seen nature in any such situation as resembles the first arrangement of the elements? Have worlds ever been formed under your eye? and have you had leisure to observe the whole progress of the phenomenon, from the first appearance of order to its final consummation? If you have, then cite your experience, and deliver your theory.

PART III

How the most absurd argument, replied CLEANTHES, in the hands of a man of ingenuity and invention, may acquire an air of[1] probability! Are you not aware, PHILO, that it became necessary for COPERNICUS and his first disciples to prove the similarity of the terrestrial and celestial matter; because several philosophers, blinded by old systems, and supported by some sensible appearances,[2] had denied this similarity? But that it is by no means necessary, that theists should prove the similarity of the works of nature to those of art; because this similarity is self-evident and undeniable? The same matter, a like form: What more is requisite to show[3] an analogy between their causes, and to ascertain the origin of all things from a divine purpose and intention? Your objections, I must freely tell you, are no better than the abstruse cavils of those philosophers, who denied motion; and ought to be refuted in the same manner, by illustrations, examples, and instances, rather than by serious argument and philosophy.

Suppose, therefore, that an articulate voice were heard in the clouds, much louder and more melodious than any which human art could ever reach: Suppose, that this voice were extended in the same instant over all nations, and spoke to each nation in its own language and dialect: Suppose, that the words delivered not only contain a just sense and meaning, but convey some instruction altogether worthy of a benevolent Being, superior to mankind: Could you possibly hesitate a moment concerning the cause of this voice? And must you not instantly ascribe it to some design or purpose? Yet I cannot see but all the same objections (if they merit that appellation) which lie against the system of theism, may also be produced against this inference.

Might you not say, that all conclusions concerning fact were founded on experience: That when we hear an articulate voice in the dark, and thence infer a man, it is only the resemblance of the effects, which leads us to conclude that there is a like resemblance

---

[1] [truth and *omitted*.]

[2] [some sensible appearances *for* the illusions of sense.]

[3] [show *for* prove.]

in the cause: But that this extraordinary voice, by its loudness, extent, and flexibility to all languages, bears so little analogy to any human voice, that we have no reason to suppose any analogy in their causes: And consequently, that a rational, wise, coherent speech proceeded, you knew not whence, from some accidental whistling of the winds, not from any divine reason or intelligence? You see clearly your own objections in these cavils; and I hope too, you see clearly, that they cannot possibly have more force in the one case than in the other.

But to bring the case still nearer the present one of the universe, I shall make two suppositions, which imply not any absurdity or impossibility. Suppose, that there is a natural, universal, invariable language, common to every individual of human race; and that books are natural productions, which perpetuate themselves in the same manner with animals and vegetables, by descent and propagation. Several expressions of our passions contain a universal language: All brute[1] animals have a natural speech, which, however limited, is very intelligible to their own species. And as there are infinitely fewer parts and less contrivance in the finest composition of eloquence, than in the coarsest organized body, the propagation of an *Iliad* or *Æneid* is an easier supposition than that of any plant or animal.

Suppose, therefore, that you enter into your library, thus peopled by natural[2] volumes, containing the most refined reason and most exquisite beauty: Could you possibly open one of them, and doubt, that its original cause bore the strongest analogy to mind and intelligence? When it reasons and discourses; when it expostulates, argues, and enforces its views and topics; when it applies sometimes to the pure intellect, sometimes to the affections; when it collects, disposes, and adorns every consideration suited to the subject: could you persist in asserting, that all this, at the bottom, had really no meaning, and that the first formation of this volume in the loins of its original[3] parent proceeded not from thought and design? Your obstinacy, I know, reaches not that degree of firmness: Even your sceptical play and wantonness would be abashed at so glaring an absurdity.

---

[1] [brute *added*.]   [2] [vegetating animal *omitted*.]
[3] [original *added*.]

But if there be any difference, PHILO, between this supposed case and the real one of the universe, it is all to the advantage of the latter. The anatomy of an animal affords many stronger instances of design than the perusal of LIVY or TACITUS.[1] And any objection which you start in the former case, by carrying me back to so unusual and extraordinary a scene as the first formation of worlds, the same objection has place on the supposition of our vegetating library. Choose, then, your party, PHILO, without ambiguity or evasion: Assert either that a rational volume is no proof of a rational cause, or admit of a similar cause to all the works of nature.

Let me here observe too, continued CLEANTHES, that this religious argument, instead of being weakened by that scepticism, so much affected by you, rather acquires force from it, and becomes more firm and undisputed. To exclude all argument or reasoning of every kind is either affectation or madness. The declared profession of every reasonable sceptic is only to reject abstruse, remote and refined arguments; to adhere to common sense and the plain instincts of nature; and to assent, wherever any reasons strike him with so full a force, that he cannot, without the greatest violence, prevent it. Now the arguments for natural religion are plainly of this kind; and nothing but the most perverse, obstinate metaphysics can reject them. Consider, anatomize the eye: Survey its structure and contrivance; and tell me, from your own feeling, if the idea of a contriver does not immediately flow in upon you with a force like that of sensation.* The most obvious conclusion surely is in favour of design; and it requires time, reflection and study, to summon up those frivolous, though abstruse, objections, which can support infidelity. Who can behold the male and female of each species, the correspondence of their parts and instincts, their passions and whole course of life before and after generation, but must be sensible, that the propagation of the species is intended by nature? Millions and millions of such instances present themselves through every part of the universe; and no language can convey a more intelligible, irresistible meaning, than the curious adjustment of final causes. To what degree, therefore, of blind dogmatism must one have attained, to reject such natural and such convincing arguments?

[1] [Livy or Tacitus *for* the Iliad.]

[¹Some beauties in writing we may meet with, which seem contrary to rules, and which gain the affections, and animate the imagination, in opposition to all the precepts of criticism, and to the authority of the established masters of art. And if the argument for theism be, as you pretend, contradictory to the principles of logic; its universal, its irresistible influence proves clearly, that there may be arguments of a like irregular nature. Whatever cavils may be urged; an orderly world, as well as a coherent, articulate speech, will still be received as an incontestable proof of design and intention.]

It sometimes happens, I own, that the religious arguments have not their due influence on an ignorant savage and barbarian; not because they are obscure and difficult, but because he never asks himself any question with regard to them. Whence arises the curious structure of an animal? From the copulation of its parents. And these whence? From *their* parents. A few removes set the objects at such a distance, that to him they are lost in darkness and confusion; nor is he actuated by any curiosity to trace them farther. But this is neither dogmatism nor scepticism, but stupidity; a state of mind very different from your sifting, inquisitive disposition, my ingenious friend. You can trace causes from effects: You can compare the most distant and remote objects: And your greatest errors proceed not from barrenness of thought and invention, but from too luxuriant a fertility, which suppresses your natural good sense, by a profusion of unnecessary scruples and objections.

Here I could observe, HERMIPPUS, that PHILO was a little embarrassed and confounded: But while he hesitated in delivering an answer, luckily for him, DEMEA broke in upon the discourse, and saved his countenance.

Your instance, CLEANTHES, said he, drawn from books and language, being familiar, has, I confess, so much more force on that account; but is there not some danger too in this very circumstance, and may it not render us presumptuous, by making us imagine we comprehend the Deity, and have some adequate idea of his nature and attributes? When I read a volume, I enter into the mind and intention of the author: I become him, in a manner, for the instant; and have an immediate feeling and conception of those ideas,

---

¹ [This paragraph in brackets is added on the last page of Part III, with marks to indicate point of insertion.]

which revolved in his imagination, while employed in that composition. But so near an approach we never surely can make to the Deity. His ways are not our ways. His attributes are perfect, but incomprehensible. And this volume of nature contains a great and inexplicable riddle, more than any intelligible discourse or reasoning.

The ancient PLATONISTS, you know, were the most religious and devout of all the pagan philosophers: Yet many of them, particularly PLOTINUS, expressly declare, that intellect or understanding is not to be ascribed to the Deity, and that our most perfect worship of him consists, not in acts of veneration, reverence, gratitude or love; but in a certain mysterious self-annihilation* or total extinction of all our faculties. These ideas are, perhaps, too far stretched; but still it must be acknowledged, that, by representing the Deity as so intelligible, and comprehensible, and so similar to a human mind,[1] we are guilty of the grossest and most narrow partiality, and make ourselves the model of the whole universe.

[2All the *sentiments* of the human mind, gratitude, resentment, love, friendship, approbation, blame, pity, emulation, envy, have a plain reference to the state and situation of man, and are calculated for preserving the existence, and promoting the activity of such a being in such circumstances. It seems therefore unreasonable to transfer such sentiments to a supreme existence, or to suppose him actuated by them; and the phenomena, besides, of the universe will not support us in such a theory. All our *ideas*, derived from the senses, are confessedly false and illusive; and cannot, therefore, be supposed to have place in a supreme intelligence: And as the ideas of internal sentiment, added to those of the external senses, compose the whole furniture of human understanding, we may conclude, that none of the *materials* of thought are in any respect similar in the human and in the divine intelligence. Now, as to the *manner* of thinking; how can we make any comparison between them, or suppose them any wise resembling? Our thought is fluctuating, uncertain, fleeting, successive, and compounded; and were we to remove these circumstances, we absolutely annihilate

[1] [and so similar to a human mind *added*.]

[2] [This concluding paragraph in brackets is added, with marks to indicate point of insertion, on lower part of the last page of Part III, and continued on an otherwise blank sheet.]

its essence, and it would, in such a case, be an abuse of terms to apply to it the name of thought or reason. At least, if it appear more pious and respectful (as it really is) still to retain these terms, when we mention the supreme Being, we ought to acknowledge, that their meaning, in that case, is totally incomprehensible; and that the infirmities of our nature do not permit us to reach any ideas, which in the least[1] correspond to the ineffable sublimity of the divine attributes.]

[1] [in the least *added*.]

PART IV

IT seems strange to me, said CLEANTHES, that you, DEMEA, who are so sincere in the cause of religion, should still maintain the mysterious, incomprehensible nature of the Deity, and should insist so strenuously, that he has no manner of likeness or resemblance to human creatures.[1] The Deity, I can readily allow, possesses many powers and attributes, of which we can have no comprehension: But if our ideas, so far as they go, be not just and adequate, and correspondent to his real nature, I know not what there is in this subject worth insisting on. Is the name, without any meaning, of such mighty importance? Or how do you MYSTICS, who maintain the absolute incomprehensibility of the Deity, differ from sceptics or atheists, who assert, that the first cause of All is unknown and unintelligible? Their temerity must be very great, if, after rejecting the production by a mind; I mean, a mind resembling the human (for I know of no other), they pretend to assign, with certainty, any other specific, intelligible cause: And their conscience must be very scrupulous indeed, if they refuse to call the universal, unknown cause a God or Deity; and to bestow on him as many sublime eulogies and unmeaning epithets, as you shall please to require of them.

Who could imagine, replied DEMEA, that CLEANTHES, the calm, philosophical CLEANTHES, would attempt to refute his antagonists, by affixing a nick-name to them; and like the common bigots and inquisitors of the age, have recourse to invective and declamation, instead of reasoning? Or does he not perceive, that these topics are easily retorted, and that *anthropomorphite* is an appellation as invidious, and implies as dangerous consequences, as the epithet of *mystic*, with which he has honoured us? In reality, CLEANTHES, consider what it is you assert, when you represent the Deity as

---

[1] [At this point in Hume's MS. a passage scored out reads as follows: 'Are you unacquainted with that principle of philosophy, that we have no idea of anything which has no likeness to ourselves, or to those objects that have been exposed to our senses and experience?' Omission of this sentence is obviously occasioned by the insertion of the new concluding paragraph of Part III. But first Hume has tried to retain it by changing the beginning of the sentence to: 'Reflect a moment on that principle of philosophy which you at present allege . . .']

similar to a human mind and understanding. What is the soul of man? A composition of various faculties, passions, sentiments, ideas; united, indeed, into one self or person, but still distinct from each other.* When it reasons, the ideas, which are the parts of its discourse, arrange themselves in a certain form or order; which is not preserved entire for a moment, but immediately gives place to another arrangement. New opinions, new passions, new affections, new feelings arise, which continually diversify the mental scene, and produce in it the greatest variety, and most rapid succession imaginable. How is this compatible with that perfect immutability and simplicity, which all true theists ascribe to the Deity? By the same act, say they, he sees past, present, and future: His love and his hatred, his mercy and his justice are one individual operation: He is entire in every point of space; and complete in every instant of duration. No succession, no change, no acquisition, no diminution. What he is implies not in it any shadow of distinction or diversity. And what he is, this moment, he ever has been, and ever will be, without any new judgment, sentiment, or operation. He stands fixed in one simple, perfect state; nor can you ever say, with any propriety, that this act of his is different from that other, or that this judgment or idea has been lately formed, and will give place, by succession, to any different judgment or idea.

I can readily allow, said CLEANTHES, that those who maintain the perfect simplicity of the supreme Being, to the extent in which you have explained it, are complete *mystics*, and chargeable with all the consequences which I have drawn from their opinion. They are, in a word, atheists, without knowing it. For though it be allowed, that the Deity possesses attributes, of which we have no comprehension; yet ought we never to ascribe to him any attributes, which are absolutely incompatible with that intelligent nature, essential to him. A mind, whose acts and sentiments and ideas are not distinct and successive; one, that is wholly simple, and totally immutable; is a mind which has no thought, no reason, no will, no sentiment, no love, no hatred; or in a word, is no mind at all. It is an abuse of terms to give it that appellation; and we may as well speak of limited extension without figure, or of number without composition.

Pray consider, said PHILO, whom you are at present inveighing against. You are honouring with the appellation of atheist all the sound, orthodox divines almost, who have treated of this subject; and you will, at last, be, yourself, found, according to your reckoning, the only sound theist in the world. But if idolaters be atheists, as, I think, may justly be asserted, and Christian theologians[1] the same; what becomes of the argument, so much celebrated, derived from the universal consent of mankind?*

But because I know you are not much swayed by names and authorities, I shall endeavour to show you, a little more distinctly, the inconveniences of that anthropomorphism, which you have embraced; and shall prove, that there is no ground to suppose a plan of the world to be formed in the divine mind, consisting of distinct ideas, differently arranged; in the same manner as an architect forms in his head the plan of a house which he intends to execute.

It is not easy, I own, to see, what is gained by this supposition, whether we judge of the matter by *reason* or by *experience*. We are still obliged to mount higher, in order to find the cause of this cause, which you had assigned as satisfactory and conclusive.

[If *reason* (I mean abstract reason, derived from enquiries *a priori*) be not alike mute with regard to all questions concerning cause and effect; this sentence at least it will venture to pronounce, That a mental[2] world or universe of ideas requires a cause as much as does a material world or[3] universe of objects; and if similar in its arrangement must require a similar cause. For what is there in this subject, which should occasion a different conclusion or inference? In an abstract view, they are entirely alike; and no difficulty attends the one supposition, which is not common to both of them.][4]

---

[1] [Christian theologians *for* Christians.]

[2] [mental *added*.]   [3] [material world or *added*.]

[4] [Paragraph in brackets substituted for: 'When we consult reason, all causes and effects seem equally explicable a *priori*; nor is it possible to assign either of them, by the mere abstract contemplation of their nature, without consulting *experience*, or considering what we have found to result from the operation of objects. And if this proposition be true in general, that *reason, judging* a priori, *finds all causes and effects alike explicable*; it must appear more so, when we compare the external world of objects with that world of thought, which is represented as its cause. If *reason* tells us, that the world of objects requires a cause, it must give us the same information concerning the world of thought: And if the one seems to reason to require a cause of any particular kind, the other must require a cause of a like kind. Any proposition, therefore, which we can form concerning the cause of the former, if it be consistent, or intelligible, or necessary, must also appear to reason consistent or intelligible or

Again, when we will needs force *experience* to pronounce some sentence, even to these subjects, which lie beyond her sphere; neither can she perceive any material difference in this particular, between these two kinds of worlds, but finds them to be governed by similar principles, and to depend upon an equal variety of causes in their operations. We have specimens in miniature of both of them. Our own mind resembles the one: A vegetable or animal body the other. Let experience, therefore, judge from these samples. Nothing seems more delicate with regard to its causes than thought; and as these causes never operate in two persons after the same manner, so we never find two persons, who think exactly alike. Nor indeed does the same person think exactly alike at any two different periods of time. A difference of age, of the disposition of his body, of weather, of food, of company, of books, of passions; any of these particulars or others more minute, are sufficient to alter the curious machinery of thought, and communicate to it very different movements and operations. As far as we can judge, vegetables and animal bodies are not more delicate in their motions, nor depend upon a greater variety or more curious adjustment of springs and principles.

How therefore shall we satisfy ourselves concerning the cause of that Being,[1] whom you suppose the Author of nature, or, according to your system of anthropomorphism, the ideal world, into which you trace the material? Have we not the same reason to trace that ideal world into another ideal world, or new intelligent principle? But if we stop, and go no farther; why go so far? Why not stop at the material world? How can we satisfy ourselves without going on *in infinitum*? And after all, what satisfaction is there in that infinite progression? Let us remember the story of the INDIAN philosopher and his elephant.* It was never more applicable than to the present subject. If the material world rests upon a similar ideal

necessary, when apply'd to the latter, such as you have described it; and *vice versa*. It is evident, then, that as far as abstract reason can judge, it is perfectly indifferent, whether we rest on the universe of matter or on that of thought; nor do we gain any thing by tracing the one into the other.' Hume has scored out this passage; then added twice on the margin: 'Print these lines, though eraz'd'; and then, in both cases, scored through the instruction. The paragraph substituted for it is written on the last page of Part IV.]

[1] [the cause of that Being *for* that Deity.]

world, this ideal world must rest upon some other; and so on, without end. It were better, therefore, never to look beyond the present material world. By supposing it to contain the principle of its order within itself, we really assert it to be God; and the sooner we arrive at that divine Being so much the better. When you go one step beyond the mundane system,[1] you only excite an inquisitive humour, which it is impossible ever to satisfy.

To say, that the different ideas, which compose the reason of the supreme Being, fall into order, of themselves, and by their own nature, is really to talk without any precise meaning.[2] If it has a meaning, I would fain know, why it is not as good sense to say, that the parts of the material world fall into order, of themselves, and by their own nature? Can the one opinion be intelligible, while the other is not so?

We have, indeed, experience of ideas, which fall into order, of themselves, and without any *known* cause: But, I am sure, we have a much larger experience of matter, which does the same; as in all instances of generation and vegetation, where the accurate analysis of the cause exceeds all human comprehension. We have also experience of particular systems of thought and of matter, which have no order; of the first, in madness, of the second, in corruption. Why then should we think, that order is more essential to one than the other? And if it requires a cause in both, what do we gain by your system, in tracing the universe of objects into a similar universe of ideas? The first step, which we make, leads us on for ever. It were, therefore, wise in us, to limit all our enquiries to the present world, without looking farther. No satisfaction can ever be attained by these speculations, which so far exceed the narrow bounds of human understanding.

It was usual with the PERIPATETICS, you know, CLEANTHES, when the cause of any phenomenon was demanded, to have recourse to their *faculties* or *occult qualities*, and to say, for instance, that bread nourished by its nutritive faculty, and senna purged by its purgative: But it has been discovered, that this subterfuge was nothing but the disguise of ignorance; and that these philosophers, though less ingenuous, really said the same thing with the sceptics or the vulgar, who fairly confessed, that they knew not the cause of

---

[1] [mundane system *for* universe.]
[2] [any precise meaning *for* a meaning.]

these phenomena. In like manner, when it is asked, what cause produces order in the ideas of the supreme Being, can any other reason be assigned by you, anthropomorphites, than that it is a *rational* faculty, and that such is the nature of the Deity? But why a similar answer will not be equally satisfactory in accounting for the order of the world, without having recourse to any such intelligent Creator as you insist on, may be difficult to determine. It is only to say, that *such* is the nature of material objects, and that they are all originally possessed of a *faculty* of order and proportion. These are only more learned and elaborate ways of confessing our ignorance; nor has the one hypothesis any real advantage above the other, except in its greater conformity to vulgar prejudices.

You have displayed this argument with great emphasis, replied CLEANTHES: You seem not sensible, how easy it is to answer it. Even in common life, if I assign a cause for any event; is it any objection, PHILO, that I cannot assign the cause of that cause, and answer every new question, which may incessantly be started? And what philosophers could possibly submit to so rigid a rule? Philosophers, who confess ultimate causes to be totally unknown, and are sensible, that the most refined principles, into which they trace the phenomena, are still to them as inexplicable as these phenomena themselves are to the vulgar. The order and arrangement of nature, the curious adjustment of final causes, the plain use and intention of every part and organ; all these bespeak in the clearest language an intelligent cause or Author. The heavens and the earth join in the same testimony: The whole chorus of nature raises one hymn to the praises of its Creator: You alone, or almost alone, disturb this general harmony. You start abstruse doubts, cavils, and objections: You ask me, what is the cause of this cause? I know not; I care not; that concerns not me. I have found a Deity; and here I stop my enquiry. Let those go farther, who are wiser or more enterprising.

[I pretend to be neither, replied PHILO: And for that very reason, I should never perhaps have attempted to go so far; especially when I am sensible, that I must at last be contented to sit down with the same answer, which, without farther trouble, might have satisfied me from the beginning. If I am still to remain in utter ignorance of causes, and can absolutely give an explication of nothing, I shall never esteem it any advantage to shove off for a moment a difficulty, which, you acknowledge, must immediately, in its full force, recur upon me. Naturalists indeed very justly explain particular effects by more general causes; though these general causes themselves should remain in the end totally inexplicable:* But they never surely thought it satisfactory to explain a particular effect by a particular cause, which was no more to be accounted for than the effect itself.][1] An ideal system, arranged of itself,[2] without a precedent design, is not a whit more explicable than a material one, which attains its order in a like manner; nor is there any more difficulty in the latter supposition than in the former.

---

[1] [Passage in brackets substituted for: 'Your answer may, perhaps, be good, said Philo, upon your principles, that the religious system can be proved by experience, and by experience alone; and that the Deity arose from some external cause. But these opinions, you know, will be adopted by very few. And as to all those, who reason upon other principles, and yet deny the mysterious simplicity of the divine nature, my objection still remains good. An ideal system, &c.' The new passage is written on the lower part of the last page of Part IV, with marks to indicate point of insertion.]

[2] [of itself *added*.]

PART V

But to show you still more inconveniences, continued Philo, in your anthropomorphism; please to take a new survey of your principles. *Like effects prove like causes.* This is the experimental argument; and this, you say too, is the sole theological[1] argument. Now it is certain, that the liker the effects are, which are seen, and the liker the causes, which are inferred, the stronger is the argument. Every departure on either side diminishes the probability, and renders the experiment less conclusive. You cannot doubt of[2] this principle: Neither ought you to reject its consequences.

All the new discoveries in astronomy, which prove the immense grandeur and magnificence of the works of nature, are so many additional arguments for a Deity, according to the true system of theism: But according to your hypothesis of experimental theism,[3] they become so many objections, by removing the effect still farther from all resemblance to the effects of human art and contrivance. For if Lucretius,[4]* even following the old system of the world, could exclaim,

> Quis regere immensi summam, quis habere profundi
> Indu manu validas potis est moderanter habenas?
> Quis pariter cœlos omnes convertere? et omnes
> Ignibus ætheriis terras suffire feraces?
> Omnibus inve locis esse omni tempore præsto?

If *Tully*[5]* esteemed this reasoning so natural, as to put it into the

---

[1] [theological *for* religious.]

[2] [doubt of *for* deny.]

[3] [of experimental theism *added.*]

[4] Lib. II, 1095. ['Who can rule the sum, who hold in his hand with controlling force the strong reins, of the immeasurable deep? who can at once make all the different heavens to roll and warm with ethereal fires all the fruitful earths, or be present in all places at all times' (Munro's translation).]

[5] *De Nat[ura] Deor[um]*, Lib. I [8. 'For with what eyes of the mind could your Plato have beheld that workshop of such stupendous toil, in which he represents the world as having been put together and built by God? How was so vast an undertaking set about? What tools, what levers, what machines, what servants, were employed in so great a work? How came air, fire, water, and earth to obey and submit to the architect's will?'].

mouth of his Epicurean. *Quibus enim oculis animi intueri potuit vester Plato fabricam illam tanti operis, qua construi a Deo atque ædificari mundum facit? quæ molitio? quæ ferramenta? qui vectes? quæ machinæ? qui ministri tanti muneris fuerunt? quemadmodum autem obedire et parere voluntati architecti aer, ignis, aqua, terra potuerunt?* If this argument, I say, had any force in former ages; how much greater must it have at present; when the bounds of nature are so infinitely enlarged, and such a magnificent scene is opened to us? It is still more unreasonable to form our idea of so unlimited a cause from our experience of the narrow productions of human design and invention.

The discoveries by microscopes, as they open a new universe in miniature, are still objections, according to you; arguments, according to me. The farther we push our researches of this kind, we are still led to infer the universal cause of All to be vastly different from mankind, or from any object of human experience and observation.

And what say you to the discoveries in anatomy, chemistry, botany? ... These surely are no objections, replied Cleanthes: They only discover new instances of art and contrivance. It is still the image of mind reflected on us from innumerable objects. Add, a mind *like the human*, said Philo. I know of no other, replied Cleanthes. And the liker the better, insisted Philo. To be sure, said Cleanthes.

Now, Cleanthes, said Philo, with an air of alacrity and triumph, mark the consequences. *First*, By this method of reasoning, you renounce all claim to infinity in any of the attributes of the Deity. For as the cause ought only to be proportioned to the effect, and the effect, so far as it falls under our cognisance, is not infinite; what pretensions have we, upon your suppositions,[1] to ascribe that attribute to the divine Being? You will still insist, that, by removing him so much from all similarity to human creatures, we give in to the most arbitrary hypothesis, and at the same time weaken all proofs of his existence.

Secondly, You have no reason, on your theory, for ascribing perfection to the Deity, even in his finite capacity; or for supposing him free from every error, mistake, or incoherence in his under-

---

[1] [upon your suppositions *added*.]

takings. There are many inexplicable difficulties in the works of nature, which, if we allow a perfect Author to be proved *a priori*, are easily solved, and become only seeming difficulties,* from the narrow capacity of man, who cannot trace infinite relations. But according to your method of reasoning, these difficulties become all real; and perhaps will be insisted on, as new instances of likeness to human art and contrivance. At least, you must acknowledge, that it is impossible for us to tell, from our limited views, whether this system contains any great faults, or deserves any considerable praise, if compared to other possible, and even real systems. Could a peasant, if the ÆNEID were read to him, pronounce that poem to be absolutely faultless, or even assign to it its proper rank among the productions of human wit; he, who had never seen any other production?

[¹But were this world ever so perfect a production, it must still remain uncertain, whether all the excellencies of the work can justly be ascribed to the workman. If we survey a ship, what an exalted idea must we form of the ingenuity of the carpenter, who framed so complicated, useful, and beautiful a machine? And what surprise must we entertain, when we find him a stupid mechanic, who imitated others, and copied an art, which, through a long succession of ages, after multiplied trials, mistakes, corrections, deliberations, and controversies, had been gradually improving? Many worlds might have been botched and bungled, throughout an eternity, ere this system was struck out: Much labour lost: Many fruitless trials made: And a slow, but continued improvement carried on during infinite ages in the art of world-making. In such subjects, who can determine, where the truth; nay, who can conjecture where the probability, lies; amidst a great number of hypotheses which may be proposed, and a still greater number which may be imagined?]

And what shadow of an argument, continued PHILO, can you produce, from your hypothesis, to prove the unity of the Deity? A great number of men join in building a house or ship, in rearing a city, in framing a commonwealth: Why may not several Deities combine in contriving and framing a world? This is only so much greater similarity to human affairs. By sharing the work among

¹ [This paragraph, and the paragraph on p. 70, in square brackets, are added on the last page of Part V, with marks to indicate points of insertion.]

several, we may so much farther limit the attributes of each, and get rid of that extensive power and knowledge, which must be supposed in one Deity, and which, according to you, can only serve to weaken the proof of his existence. And if such foolish, such vicious creatures as man can yet often unite in framing and executing one plan; how much more those Deities or Dæmons,* whom we may suppose several degrees more perfect?

[To multiply causes,* without necessity, is indeed contrary to true philosophy: But this principle applies not to the present case. Were one Deity antecedently proved by your theory, who were possessed of every attribute requisite to the production of the universe; it would be needless, I own (though not absurd) to suppose any other Deity existent. But while it is still a question, whether all these attributes are united in one subject, or dispersed among several independent Beings: By what phenomena in nature can we pretend to decide the controversy? Where we see a body raised in a scale, we are sure that there is in the opposite scale, however concealed from sight, some counterpoising weight equal to it: But it is still allowed to doubt, whether that weight be an aggregate of several distinct bodies, or one uniform united mass. And if the weight requisite very much exceeds any thing which we have ever seen conjoined in any single body, the former supposition becomes still more probable and natural. An intelligent Being of such vast power and capacity, as is necessary to produce the universe, or, to speak in the language of ancient philosophy, so prodigious an animal, exceeds all analogy, and even comprehension.]

But farther, CLEANTHES; men are mortal, and renew their species by generation; and this is common to all living creatures. The two great sexes of male and female, says MILTON, animate the world. Why must this circumstance, so universal, so essential, be excluded from those numerous and limited Deities? Behold then the theogony* of ancient times brought back upon us.

And why not become a perfect anthropomorphite? Why not assert the Deity or Deities to be corporeal, and to have eyes, a nose, mouth, ears, &c.? EPICURUS maintained, that no man had ever seen reason but in a human figure; therefore the gods must have a human figure. And this argument,* which is deservedly so much ridiculed by Cicero,[1] becomes, according to you, solid and philosophical.

In a word, CLEANTHES, a man, who follows your hypothesis, is able, perhaps, to assert, or conjecture, that the universe, sometime, arose from something like[2] design: But beyond that position he cannot ascertain one single circumstance, and is left afterwards to fix every point of his theology, by the utmost licence of fancy and hypothesis. This world, for aught he knows, is very faulty and imperfect, compared to a superior standard; and was only the first rude essay of some infant Deity, who afterwards abandoned it, ashamed of his lame performance; it is the work only of some dependent, inferior Deity; and is the object of derision to his superiors: it is the production of old age and dotage in some superannuated Deity; and ever since his death, has run on at adventures, from the first impulse and active force, which it received from him. . . . You justly give signs of horror, DEMEA, at these strange suppositions: But these, and a thousand more of the same kind, are CLEANTHES's suppositions, not mine. From the moment the attributes of the Deity are supposed finite, all these have place. And I cannot, for my part, think, that so wild and unsettled a system of theology is, in any respect, preferable to none at all.

These suppositions I absolutely disown, cried CLEANTHES: They strike me, however, with no horror; especially, when proposed in that rambling way in which they drop from you. On the contrary, they give me pleasure, when I see, that, by the utmost indulgence of your imagination, you never get rid of the hypothesis of design in the universe; but are obliged, at every turn, to have recourse to it. To this concession I adhere steadily; and this I regard as a sufficient foundation for religion.

---

[1] [Cicero *for* Divines.]

[2] [something like *for* some kind of.]

PART VI

It must be a slight fabric, indeed, said Demea, which can be erected on so tottering a foundation. While we are uncertain, whether there is one Deity or many; whether the Deity or Deities, to whom we owe our existence, be perfect or imperfect, subordinate or supreme, dead or alive; what trust or confidence can we repose in them? What devotion or worship address to them? What veneration or obedience pay them? To all the purposes of life, the theory of religion becomes altogether useless: And even with regard to speculative consequences, its uncertainty, according to you, must render it totally precarious and unsatisfactory.

To render it still more unsatisfactory, said Philo, there occurs to me another hypothesis, which must acquire an air of probability from the method of reasoning so much insisted on by Cleanthes. That like effects arise from like causes: This principle he supposes the foundation of all religion. But there is another principle of the same kind, no less certain, and derived from the same source of[1] experience; that where several known circumstances are *observed* to be similar, the unknown will[2] also be *found* similar. Thus, if we see the limbs of a human body, we conclude, that it is also attended with a human head, though hid from us. Thus, if we see, through a chink in a wall, a small part of the sun, we conclude, that, were the wall removed, we should see the whole body.[3] In short, this method of reasoning is so obvious and familiar, that no scruple can ever be made with regard to its solidity.

Now if we survey the universe, so far as it falls under our knowledge, it bears a great resemblance to an animal or organized body, and seems actuated with a like principle of life and motion. A continual circulation of matter in it produces no disorder: A

[1] [practice and *omitted*.]

[2] [will *for* must.]

[3] [*This sentence has been substituted for:* Thus, if we hear, in the dark, reason and sense delivered in an articulate voice, we infer, that there is also present a human figure, which we shall discover on the return of light. *There is also, on the margin, scored out the words:* If we see from a distance the buildings of a city, we infer that they contain inhabitants whom we shall discover on our approach to them.]

continual waste in every part is incessantly repaired: The closest sympathy is perceived throughout the entire system: And each part or member, in performing its proper offices, operates both to its own preservation and to that of the whole. The world, therefore, I infer, is an animal, and the Deity is the SOUL of the world, actuating it, and actuated by it.

You have too much learning, CLEANTHES, to be at all surprised at this opinion, which, you know, was maintained by almost all the theists of antiquity,* and chiefly prevails in their discourses and reasonings. For though sometimes the ancient philosophers reason from final causes,* as if they thought the world the workmanship of God; yet it appears rather their favourite notion to consider it as his body, whose organization renders it subservient to him. And it must be confessed, that as the universe resembles more a human body than it does the works of human art and contrivance; if our limited analogy could ever, with any propriety, be extended to the whole of nature, the inference seems juster in favour of the ancient than the modern theory.

There are many other advantages too, in the former theory, which recommended it to the ancient theologians. Nothing more repugnant to all their notions, because nothing more repugnant to common experience, than mind without body; a mere spiritual substance, which fell not under their senses nor comprehension, and of which they had not observed one single instance throughout all nature. Mind and body they knew, because they felt both: An order, arrangement, organization, or internal machinery in both they likewise knew, after the same manner: And it could not but seem reasonable to transfer this experience to the universe, and to suppose the divine mind and body to be also coeval, and to have, both of them, order and arrangement naturally inherent in them, and inseparable from them.

Here therefore is a new species of anthropomorphism, CLEANTHES, on which you may deliberate; and a theory which seems not liable to any considerable difficulties. You are too much superior surely to *systematical prejudices*, to find any more difficulty in supposing an animal body to be, originally, of itself, or from unknown causes, possessed of order and organization, than in supposing a similar order to belong[1] to mind. But the *vulgar*

---

[1] [order to belong *for* principle belonging.]

prejudice, that body and mind ought always to accompany each other, ought not, one should think, to be entirely neglected; since it is founded on *vulgar experience*, the only guide which you profess to follow in all these theological inquiries. And if you assert, that our limited experience is an unequal standard, by which to judge of the unlimited extent of nature; you entirely abandon your own hypothesis, and must thenceforward adopt our mysticism, as you call it, and admit of the absolute incomprehensibility of the divine nature.[1]

This theory, I own, replied CLEANTHES, has never before occurred to me, though a pretty natural one; and I cannot readily, upon so short an examination and reflection, deliver any opinion with regard to it. You are very scrupulous, indeed, said PHILO; were I to examine any system of yours, I should not have acted with half that caution and reserve, in starting objections and difficulties to it. However, if any thing occur to you, you will oblige us by proposing it.

Why then, replied CLEANTHES, it seems to me that, though the world does, in many circumstances, resemble an animal body; yet is the analogy also defective in many circumstances, the most material: No organs of sense; no seat of thought or reason; no one precise origin of motion and action. In short, it seems to bear a stronger resemblance to a vegetable than to an animal; and your inference would be so far inconclusive in favour of the soul of the world.

But in the next place, your theory seems to imply the eternity of the world; and that is a principle which, I think, can be refuted by the strongest reasons and probabilities. I shall suggest an argument to this purpose, which, I believe, has not been insisted on by any writer. Those, who reason from the late origin of arts and sciences, though their inference wants not force, may perhaps be refuted by considerations derived from the nature of human society, which is in continual revolution between ignorance and knowledge, liberty and slavery, riches and poverty; so that it is impossible for us, from our limited experience, to foretell with assurance what events may or may not be expected. Ancient learning and history seem to have been in great danger of entirely perishing after the inundation of

[1] [This last sentence scored out, with note on the margin: 'Print this sentence, though eraz'd.']

the barbarous nations; and had these convulsions continued a little longer, or been a little more violent, we should not probably have now known what passed in the world a few centuries before us. Nay, were it not for the superstition of the Popes, who preserved a little jargon of LATIN, in order to support the appearance of an ancient and universal church, that tongue must have been utterly lost: In which case, the Western world, being totally barbarous, would not have been in a fit disposition for receiving the GREEK language and learning, which was conveyed to them after the sacking of CONSTANTINOPLE.* When learning and books had been[1] extinguished, even the mechanical arts would have fallen considerably to decay; and it is easily imagined, that fable or tradition might ascribe to them a much later origin than the true one. This vulgar[2] argument, therefore, against the eternity of the world, seems a little precarious.

But here appears to be the foundation of a better argument. LUCULLUS* was the first that brought cherry-trees from ASIA to EUROPE; though that tree thrives so well in many EUROPEAN climates, that it grows in the woods without any culture. Is it possible, that, throughout a whole eternity, no EUROPEAN had ever passed into ASIA, and thought of transplanting so delicious a fruit into his own country? Or if the tree was once transplanted and propagated, how could it ever afterwards perish? Empires may rise and fall; liberty and slavery succeed alternately; ignorance and knowledge give place to each other; but the cherry-tree will still remain in the woods of GREECE, SPAIN and ITALY, and will never be affected by the revolutions of human society.

It is not two thousand years since vines were transplanted into FRANCE; though there is no climate in the world more favourable to them. It is not three centuries since horses, cows, sheep, swine, dogs, corn, were known in AMERICA. Is it possible, that, during the revolutions of a whole eternity, there never arose a COLUMBUS, who might open the communication between EUROPE and that continent? We may as well imagine, that all men would wear stockings for ten thousand years, and never have the sense to think of garters to tie them. All these seem convincing proofs of the youth, or rather infancy, of the world; as being founded on the operation of

---

[1] [totally *omitted.*]   [2] [vulgar *for* common.]

principles more constant and steady than those by which human society is governed and directed. Nothing less than a total convulsion of the elements will ever destroy all the EUROPEAN animals and vegetables, which are now to be found in the Western world.

And what argument have you against such convulsions? replied PHILO. Strong and almost incontestable proofs may be traced over the whole earth, that every part of this globe has continued for many ages entirely covered with water. And though order were supposed inseparable from matter, and inherent in it; yet may matter be susceptible of many and great revolutions, through the endless periods of eternal duration. The incessant changes, to which every part of it is subject, seem to intimate some such general transformations; though at the same time, it is observable, that all the changes and corruptions, of which we have ever had experience, are but passages from one state of order to another; nor can matter ever rest in total deformity and confusion. What we see in the parts, we may infer in the whole; at least, that is the method of reasoning on which you rest your whole theory. And were I obliged to defend any particular system of this nature (which I never willingly should do), I esteem none more plausible than that which ascribes an eternal, inherent principle of order to the world;[1] though attended with great and continual revolutions and alterations. This at once solves all difficulties;[2] and if the solution, by being so general, is not[3] entirely complete and satisfactory, it is, at least, a theory, that we must, sooner or later, have recourse to, whatever system we embrace. How could things have been as they are, were there not an original, inherent principle of order somewhere, in thought or in matter? And it is very[4] indifferent to which of these we give the preference. Chance has no place, on any hypothesis, sceptical or religious.[5] Every thing is surely governed by steady, inviolable laws. And were the inmost essence of things laid open to us, we should then discover a scene, of which, at present, we can have no idea. Instead of admiring the order of

[1] [to the world *for* in matter.]

[2] [solves all difficulties *for* answers all questions.]

[3] [by being so general, is not *for* be not.]

[4] [is very *for* seems.]

[5] [(1) *Originally:* Chance it is ridiculous to maintain on any hypothesis. (2) *Altered to:* Chance, or what is the same thing liberty, seems not to have place on any hypothesis, sceptical or religious. (3) *Finally revised as above.*]

natural beings, we should clearly see, that it was absolutely impossible for them, in the smallest article, ever to admit of any other disposition.

Were any one inclined to revive the ancient Pagan Theology, which maintained, as we learn from Hesiod,[1] that this globe was governed by 30,000 Deities, who arose from the unknown powers of nature: You would naturally object, CLEANTHES, that nothing is gained by this hypothesis, and that it is as easy to suppose all men and animals, beings more numerous, but less perfect, to have sprung immediately from a like origin. Push the same inference a step farther; and you will find a numerous society of Deities as explicable as one universal Deity, who possesses, within himself, the powers and perfections of the whole society. All these systems, then, of scepticism, polytheism, and theism, you must allow, on your principles, to be on a like footing,[2] and that no one of them has any advantages over the others. You may thence learn the fallacy of your principles.

[1] [which maintained . . . Hesiod *for* mentioned by Varro.]
[2] [on a like footing *for* alike explicable.]

PART VII

BUT here, continued PHILO, in examining the ancient system of the soul of the world, there strikes me, all on a sudden, a new idea, which, if just, must go near to subvert all your reasoning, and destroy even your first inferences, on which you repose such confidence. If the universe bears a greater likeness to animal bodies and to vegetables, than to the works of human art, it is more probable that its cause resembles the cause of the former than that of the latter, and its origin ought rather to be ascribed to generation or vegetation than to reason or design. Your conclusion, even according to your own principles, is therefore lame and defective.

Pray open up this argument a little farther, said DEMEA. For I do not rightly apprehend it, in that concise manner in which you have expressed it.

Our friend, CLEANTHES, replied PHILO, as you have heard, asserts, that since no question of fact can be proved otherwise than by experience, the existence of a Deity admits not of proof from any other medium. The world, says he, resembles the works of human contrivance: Therefore its cause must also resemble that of the other. Here we may remark, that the operation of one very small part of nature, to wit man, upon another very small part, to wit that inanimate matter lying within his reach, is the rule by which CLEANTHES judges of the origin of the whole; and he measures objects, so widely disproportioned, by the same individual standard. But to waive all objections drawn from this topic; I affirm, that there are other parts of the universe (besides the machines of human invention) which bear still a greater resemblance to the fabric of the world, and which therefore afford a better conjecture concerning the universal origin of this system.[1] These parts are animals and vegetables. The world plainly resembles more an animal or a vegetable, than it does a watch or a knitting-loom. Its cause, therefore, it is more probable, resembles the cause of the former. The cause of the former is generation or vegetation. The cause, therefore, of the world, we may infer to be some thing similar or analogous to generation or vegetation.

[1] [this system *for* the whole of nature.]

But how is it conceivable, said DEMEA, that the world can arise from any thing similar to vegetation or generation?

Very easily, replied PHILO. In like manner as a tree sheds its seed into the neighbouring fields, and produces other trees; so the great vegetable, the world, or this planetary system, produces within itself certain seeds, which, being scattered into the surrounding chaos, vegetate into new worlds. A comet, for instance, is the seed of a world; and after it has been fully ripened, by passing from sun to sun, and star to star, it is at last tossed into the unformed elements, which everywhere surround this universe, and immediately sprouts up into a new system.

Or if, for the sake of variety (for I see no other advantage), we should suppose this world to be an animal; a comet is the egg of this animal; and in like manner as an ostrich lays its egg in the sand, which, without any farther care, hatches the egg, and produces a new animal; so . . .

I understand you, says DEMEA: But what wild, arbitrary suppositions are these? What *data* have you for such extraordinary conclusions? And is the slight, imaginary resemblance of the world to a vegetable or an animal sufficient to establish the same inference with regard to both? Objects, which are in general so widely different; ought they to be a standard for each other?

Right, cries PHILO: This is the topic on which I have all along insisted. I have still asserted, that we have no *data* to establish any system of cosmogony. Our experience, so imperfect in itself, and so limited both in extent and duration, can afford us no probable conjecture concerning the whole of things. But if we must needs fix on some hypothesis; by what rule, pray, ought we to determine our choice? Is there any other rule than the greater similarity of the objects compared? And does not a plant or an animal, which springs from vegetation or generation, bear a stronger resemblance to the world, than does any artificial machine, which arises from reason and design?

But what is this vegetation and generation of which you talk? said DEMEA. Can you explain their operations, and anatomize that fine internal structure, on which they depend?

As much, at least, replied PHILO, as GLEANTHES can explain the operations of reason, or anatomize that internal structure, on which *it* depends. But without any such elaborate disquisitions, when I see an animal, I infer, that it sprang from generation; and that with as great certainty as you conclude a house to have been reared by[1] design. These words, *generation, reason*, mark only certain powers and energies in nature, whose effects are known, but whose essence is incomprehensible; and one of these principles, more than the other, has no privilege for being made a standard to the whole of nature.

In reality, DEMEA, it may reasonably be expected, that the larger the views are which we take of things, the better will they conduct us in our conclusions concerning such extraordinary and such magnificent subjects. In this little corner of the world alone, there are four principles,* *reason, instinct, generation, vegetation*, which are similar to each other, and are the causes of similar effects. What a number of other principles may we naturally suppose in the immense extent and variety of the universe, could we travel from planet to planet and from system to system, in order to examine each part of this mighty fabric?[2] Any one of these four principles above mentioned (and a hundred others which lie open to our conjecture) may afford us a theory,[3] by which to judge of the origin of the world; and it is a palpable and egregious partiality, to confine our view entirely to that principle, by which our own minds[4] operate. Were this principle more intelligible on that account, such a partiality might be somewhat excusable: But reason, in its internal fabric and structure, is really as little known to us as instinct or vegetation; and perhaps even that vague, undeterminate word, nature, to which the vulgar refer every thing, is not at the bottom more inexplicable. The effects of these principles are all known to us from experience: But the principles themselves, and their manner of operation, are totally unknown: Nor is it less intelligible, or less conformable to experience to say, that the world arose by vegetation from a seed shed by another world, than to say that it arose from a divine reason or contrivance, according to the sense in which CLEANTHES understands it.

But methinks, said DEMEA, if the world had a vegetative quality, and could sow the seeds of new worlds into the infinite chaos, this power would be still an additional argument for design in its Author. For whence could arise so wonderful a faculty but from

[1] [reason and *omitted*.] [2] [fabric *for* whole.]
[3] [theory *for* standard.] [4] [our own minds *for* we ourselves.]

design? Or how can order spring from any thing, which perceives not that order which it bestows?

You need only look around you, replied PHILO, to satisfy yourself with regard to this question. A tree bestows order and organization on that tree which springs from it, without knowing the order: an animal, in the same manner, on its offspring: a bird, on its nest: And instances of this kind are even more frequent in the world, than those of order, which arise from reason and contrivance.[1] To say that all this order in animals and vegetables proceeds ultimately from design is begging the question; nor can that great point be ascertained otherwise than by proving *a priori*, both that order is, from its nature,[2] inseparably attached to thought,[3] and that it can never, of itself, or from original unknown principles, belong to matter.

But farther, DEMEA; this objection, which you urge, can never be made use of by CLEANTHES, without renouncing a defence which he has already made against one of my objections. When I enquired concerning the cause of that supreme reason and intelligence, into which he resolves every thing; he told me, that the impossibility of satisfying such enquiries could never be admitted as an objection in any species of philosophy. *We must stop somewhere*, says he; *nor is it ever within the reach of human capacity to explain ultimate causes, or show the last connections of any objects. It is sufficient, if the steps, so far as we go, are supported by experience and observation.* Now that vegetation and generation, as well as reason, are experienced to be principles of order in nature, is undeniable. If I rest my system of cosmogony on the former, preferably to the latter, it is at my choice. The matter seems entirely arbitrary. And when CLEANTHES asks me what is the cause of my great vegetative or generative faculty, I am equally entitled to ask him the cause of his great reasoning principle.[4] These questions we have agreed to forbear on both sides; and it is chiefly his interest on the present occasion to stick to this agreement. Judging by our limited and imperfect experience, generation has some privileges above reason: For we see every day the latter arise from the former, never the former from the latter.

---

[1] [contrivance *for* perception.] [2] [from its nature *added*.]
[3] [thought *for* perception.] [4] [principle *for* faculty.]

Compare, I beseech you, the consequences on both sides. The world, say I, resembles an animal, therefore it is an animal, therefore it arose from generation. The steps, I confess, are wide; yet there is some small appearance of analogy in each step. The world, says CLEANTHES, resembles a machine, therefore it is a machine, therefore it arose from design. The steps are here equally wide, and the analogy less striking. And if he pretends to carry on *my* hypothesis a step farther, and to infer design or reason from the great principle of generation, on which I insist; I may, with better authority, use the same freedom to push farther *his* hypothesis, and infer a divine generation or theogony from his principle of reason. I have at least some faint shadow of experience, which is the utmost that can ever be attained in the present subject. Reason, in innumerable instances, is observed to arise from the principle of generation, and never to arise from any other principle.

[¹HESIOD, and all the ancient mythologists, were so struck with this analogy, that they universally explained the origin of nature from an animal birth, and copulation. PLATO too, so far as he is intelligible, seems to have adopted some such notion in his TIMÆUS.]*

[²The BRAHMINS assert, that the world arose from an infinite spider, who spun this whole complicated mass from his bowels, and annihilates afterwards the whole or any part of it, by absorbing it again, and resolving it into his own essence. Here is a species of cosmogony, which appears to us ridiculous; because a spider is a little contemptible animal, whose operations we are never likely to take for a model of the whole universe. But still here is a new species of analogy, even in our globe. And were there a planet wholly inhabited by spiders (which is very possible), this inference would there appear as natural and irrefragable as that which in our planet ascribes the origin of all things to design and intelligence, as explained by CLEANTHES. Why an orderly system may not be spun

---

¹ [This paragraph, written on the margin, with marks to show that it was intended to continue the preceding paragraph, originally began: 'And Hesiod, you know, as well as all the.' &c. It has later been altered as above, and instruction inserted 'New Paragraph'.]

² [This paragraph also is a later addition. It is written on the last page of Part VII, with marks to indicate point of insertion.]

from the belly as well as from the brain, it will be difficult for him to give a satisfactory reason.]

I must confess, PHILO, replied CLEANTHES, that of all men living, the task which you have undertaken, of raising doubts and objections, suits you best, and seems, in a manner, natural and unavoidable to you. So great is your fertility of invention, that I am not ashamed to acknowledge myself unable, on a sudden, to solve regularly such out-of-the-way difficulties as you incessantly start upon me: Though I clearly see, in general, their fallacy and error. And I question not, but you are yourself, at present, in the same case, and have not the solution so ready as the objection; while you must be sensible, that common sense and reason is entirely against you, and that such whimsies, as you have delivered, may puzzle, but never can convince us.

PART VIII

WHAT you ascribe to the fertility of my invention, replied PHILO, is entirely owing to the nature of the subject. In subjects, adapted to the narrow compass of human reason, there is commonly but one determination, which carries probability or conviction with it; and to a man of sound judgment, all other suppositions, but that one, appear entirely absurd and chimerical. But in such questions as the present, a hundred contradictory views may preserve a kind of imperfect analogy; and invention has here full scope to exert itself. Without any great effort of thought, I believe that I could, in an instant, propose other systems of cosmogony, which would have some faint appearance of truth; though it is a thousand, a million to one, if either yours or any one of mine be the true system.

For instance; what if I should revive the old EPICUREAN hypothesis? This is commonly, and I believe, justly, esteemed the most absurd system, that has yet been proposed; yet, I know not, whether, with a few alterations, it might not be brought to bear a faint appearance of probability. Instead of supposing matter infinite,* as EPICURUS did; let us suppose it finite. A finite number of particles is only susceptible of finite transpositions: And it must happen, in an eternal duration, that every possible order or position must be tried an infinite number of times. This world, therefore, with all its events, even the most minute, has before been produced and destroyed, and will again be produced and destroyed, without any bounds and limitations. No one, who has a conception of the powers of infinite, in comparison of finite, will ever scruple this determination.

But this supposes, said DEMEA, that matter can acquire motion, without any voluntary agent or first mover.

And where is the difficulty, replied PHILO, of that supposition? Every event, before experience, is equally difficult and incomprehensible; and every event, after experience, is equally easy and intelligible. Motion, in many instances, from gravity, from elasticity, from electricity, begins in matter, without any known voluntary agent; and to suppose always, in these cases, an unknown voluntary agent, is mere hypothesis; and hypothesis attended with no advantages. The beginning of motion* in matter itself is as conceivable *a priori* as its communication from mind and intelligence.

Besides, why may not motion have been propagated by impulse through all eternity, and the same stock of it, or nearly the same, be still upheld in the universe? As much as is lost by the composition of motion, as much is gained by its resolution. And whatever the causes are, the fact is certain, that matter is, and always has been in continual agitation, as far as human experience or tradition reaches. There is not probably, at present, in the whole universe, one particle of matter at absolute rest.

And this very consideration too, continued PHILO, which we have stumbled on in the course of the argument, suggests a new hypothesis[1] of cosmogony, that is not absolutely absurd and improbable. Is there a system, an order, an œconomy of things, by which matter can preserve that perpetual agitation, which seems essential to it, and yet maintain a constancy in the forms, which it produces? There certainly is such an œconomy: For this is actually the case with the present world. The continual motion of matter, therefore, in less than infinite transpositions, must produce this œconomy or order; and by its very nature, that order, when once established, supports itself, for many ages, if not to eternity. But wherever matter is so poised, arranged, and adjusted as to continue in perpetual motion, and yet preserve a constancy in the forms, its situation must, of necessity, have all the same appearance of art and contrivance which we observe at present. All the parts of each form must have a relation to each other, and to the whole: And the whole itself must have a relation to the other parts of the universe; to the element, in which the form subsists; to the materials, with which it repairs its waste and decay; and to every other form, which is hostile or friendly. A defect in any of these particulars destroys the form; and the matter, of which it is composed, is again set loose, and is thrown into irregular motions and fermentations, till it unite itself to some other regular form. If no such form be prepared to receive it, and if there be a great quantity of this corrupted matter in the universe, the universe itself is entirely disordered; whether it be the feeble embryo of a world in its first

---

[1] [hypothesis *for* system.]

beginnings, that is thus destroyed, or the rotten carcass of one, languishing in old age and infirmity. In either case, a chaos ensues; till finite, though innumerable revolutions produce at last some forms, whose parts and organs are so adjusted as to support the forms amidst a continued succession of matter.

[¹Suppose (for we shall endeavour to vary the expression), that matter were thrown into any position, by a blind, unguided force; it is evident that this first position must in all probability be the most confused and most disorderly imaginable, without any resemblance to those works of human contrivance, which, along with a symmetry of parts, discover an adjustment of means to ends and a tendency to self-preservation. If the actuating force cease after this operation, matter must remain for ever in disorder, and continue an immense chaos, without any proportion or activity. But suppose, that the actuating force, whatever it be, still continues in matter, this first position will immediately give place to a second, which will likewise in all probability be as disorderly as the first, and so on, through many successions of changes and revolutions. No particular order or position ever continues a moment unaltered. The original force, still remaining in activity, gives a perpetual restlessness to matter. Every possible situation is produced, and instantly destroyed. If a glimpse or dawn of order appears for a moment, it is instantly hurried away, and confounded, by that never-ceasing force, which actuates every part of matter.

Thus the universe goes on for many ages in a continued succession of chaos and disorder. But is it not possible that it may settle at last, so as not to lose its motion and active force (for that we have supposed inherent in it), yet so as to preserve an uniformity of appearance, amidst the continual motion and fluctuation of its parts? This we find to be the case with the universe at present. Every individual is perpetually changing, and every part of every individual, and yet the whole remains, in appearance, the same. May we not hope for such a position, or rather be assured of it, from the eternal revolutions of unguided matter, and may not this account for all the appearing wisdom and contrivance which is in the universe? Let us contemplate the subject a little, and we shall find, that this adjustment, if attained by matter, of a seeming

¹ [This and the next paragraph in brackets are written, with marks to indicate point of insertion, on the last page of Part VIII.]

stability in the forms, with a real and perpetual revolution or motion of parts, affords a plausible, if not a true solution of the difficulty.]

It is in vain, therefore, to insist upon the uses of the parts in animals or vegetables, and their curious adjustment to each other. I would fain know how an animal could subsist, unless its parts were so adjusted? Do we not find, that it immediately perishes whenever this adjustment ceases, and that its matter corrupting tries some new form? It happens, indeed, that the parts of the world are so well adjusted, that some regular form immediately lays claim to this corrupted matter: And if it were not so, could the world subsist? Must it not dissolve as well as the animal, and pass through new positions and situations; till in a great, but finite succession, it fall at last into the present or some such order?*

It is well, replied CLEANTHES, you told us, that this hypothesis was suggested on a sudden, in the course of the argument. Had you had leisure to examine it, you would soon have perceived the insuperable objections, to which it is exposed. No form, you say, can subsist, unless it possess those powers and organs,[1] requisite for its subsistence: Some new order or œconomy must be tried, and so on, without intermission; till at last some order, which can support and maintain itself, is fallen upon. But according to this hypothesis, whence arise the many conveniences and advantages which men and all animals possess? Two eyes, two ears, are not absolutely necessary for the subsistence of the species. Human race might have been propagated and preserved, without horses, dogs, cows, sheep, and those innumerable fruits and products which serve to our satisfaction and enjoyment. If no camels had been created for the use of man in the sandy deserts of AFRICA and ARABIA, would the world have been dissolved? If no loadstone had been framed to give that wonderful and useful direction to the needle, would human society and the human kind have been immediately extinguished? Though the maxims of nature be in general very frugal, yet instances of this kind are far from being rare; and any one of them is a sufficient proof of design, and of a benevolent design, which gave rise to the order and arrangement of the universe.

[1] [organs *for* members.]

At least, you may safely infer, said PHILO, that the foregoing hypothesis is so far incomplete and imperfect; which I shall not scruple to allow. But can we ever reasonably expect greater success in any attempts of this nature? Or can we ever hope to erect a system of cosmogony, that will be liable to no exceptions, and will contain no circumstance repugnant to our limited and imperfect experience of the[1] analogy of nature? Your theory itself cannot surely pretend to any such advantage; even though you have run into *anthropomorphism*, the better to preserve a conformity to common experience. Let us once more put it to trial. In all instances which we have ever seen, ideas are copied from real objects, and are ectypal, not archetypal,* to express myself in learned terms: You reverse this order, and give thought the precedence. In all instances which we have ever seen, thought has no influence upon matter, except where that matter is so conjoined with it, as to have an equal reciprocal influence upon it. No animal can move immediately any thing but the members of its own body; and indeed, the equality of action and re-action seems to be an universal law of nature: But your theory implies a contradiction to this experience. These instances, with many more, which it were easy to collect (particularly the supposition of a mind or system of thought that is eternal, or in other words, an animal ingenerable and immortal[2]), these instances, I say, may teach, all of us, sobriety in condemning each other, and let us see, that as no system of this kind ought ever to be received from a slight analogy, so neither ought any to be rejected on account of a small incongruity. For that is an inconvenience from which we can justly pronounce no one to be exempted.

All religious systems, it is confessed, are subject to great and insuperable difficulties. Each disputant triumphs in his turn; while he carries on an offensive war, and exposes the absurdities, barbarities, and pernicious tenets of his antagonist. But all of them, on the whole, prepare a complete triumph for the sceptic; who tells them, that no system ought ever to be embraced with regard to such subjects: For this plain reason, that no absurdity ought ever to be assented to with regard to any subject. A total suspense of judg-

---

[1] [our limited and imperfect experience of the *for* the usual.]

[2] [particularly the supposition . . . immortal *for* particularly the creation from nothing.]

ment is here our only reasonable resource. And if every attack, as is commonly observed, and no defence, among theologians, is successful; how complete must be *his* victory, who remains always, with all mankind, on the offensive, and has himself no fixed station or abiding city, which he is ever, on any occasion, obliged to defend?

PART IX

BUT if so many difficulties attend the argument *a posteriori*, said DEMEA; had we not better adhere to that simple and sublime argument *a priori*, which, by offering to us infallible demonstration, cuts off at once all doubt and difficulty? By this argument, too, we may prove the INFINITY of the divine attributes, which, I am afraid, can never be ascertained with certainty from any other topic. For how can an effect, which either is finite, or, for aught we know, may be so; how can such an effect, I say, prove an infinite cause? The unity too of the divine nature, it is very difficult, if not absolutely impossible, to deduce merely from contemplating the works of nature; nor will the uniformity alone of the plan, even were it allowed, give us any assurance of that attribute. Whereas the argument *a priori* . . .

You seem to reason, DEMEA, interposed CLEANTHES, as if those advantages and conveniences in the abstract argument were full proofs of its solidity. But it is first proper, in my opinion, to determine what argument of this nature you choose to insist on; and we shall afterwards, from itself, better than from its *useful* consequences, endeavour to determine what value we ought to put upon it.

The argument,* replied DEMEA, which I would insist on is the common one. Whatever exists must have a cause or reason of its existence; it being absolutely impossible for any thing to produce itself, or be the cause of its own existence. In mounting up, therefore, from effects to causes, we must either go on in tracing an infinite succession, without any ultimate cause at all, or must at last have recourse to some ultimate cause, that is *necessarily* existent: Now that the first supposition is absurd may be thus proved. In the infinite chain or succession of causes and effects, each single effect is determined to exist by the power and efficacy of that cause which immediately preceded; but the whole eternal chain or succession, taken together, is not determined or caused by any thing: And yet it is evident that it requires a cause or reason, as much as any particular object, which begins to exist in time. The question is still reasonable, why this particular succession of causes existed from eternity, and not any other succession, or no succession at all. If there be no necessarily existent Being, any supposition, which can be formed, is equally possible; nor is there any more absurdity in nothing's having existed from eternity, than there is in that succession of causes, which constitutes the universe. What was it, then, which determined something to exist rather than nothing, and bestowed being on a particular possibility, exclusive of the rest? *External causes*, there are supposed to be none. *Chance* is a word without a meaning. Was it *nothing*? But that can never produce any thing. We must, therefore, have recourse to a necessarily existent Being, who carries the REASON of his existence in himself; and who cannot be supposed not to exist without an express contradiction. There is consequently such a Being, that is, there is a Deity.

I shall not leave it to PHILO, said CLEANTHES (though I know that the starting objections is his chief delight), to point out the weakness of this metaphysical reasoning. It seems to me so obviously ill-grounded, and at the same time of so little consequence to the cause of true piety and religion, that I shall myself venture to show the fallacy of it.

I shall begin with observing, that there is an evident absurdity in pretending to demonstrate a matter of fact, or to prove it by any arguments *a priori*. Nothing is demonstrable, unless the contrary implies a contradiction.* Nothing, that is distinctly conceivable, implies a contradiction. Whatever we conceive as existent, we can also conceive as non-existent. There is no Being, therefore, whose non-existence implies a contradiction. Consequently there is no Being, whose existence is demonstrable. I propose this argument as entirely decisive, and am willing to rest the whole controversy upon it.

It is pretended that the Deity is a necessarily existent Being; and this necessity of his existence is attempted to be explained by asserting, that, if we knew his whole essence or nature, we should perceive it to be as impossible for him not to exist as for twice two not to be four. But it is evident, that this can never happen, while our faculties remain the same as at present. It will still be possible for us, at any time, to conceive the non-existence of what we formerly conceived to exist; nor can the mind ever lie under a necessity of supposing any object to remain always in being; in the same manner as we lie under a necessity of always conceiving twice two to be four. The words, therefore, *necessary exist-ence*, have no meaning; or, which is the same thing, none that is consistent.

But farther; why may not the material universe be the neces-sarily existent Being, according to this pretended explication of necessity? We dare not affirm that we know all the qualities of matter; and for aught we can determine, it may contain some qualities, which, were they known, would make its non-existence appear as great a contradiction as that twice two is five. I find only one argument employed to prove, that the material world is not the necessarily existent Being; and this argument is derived from the contingency both of the matter and the form of the world. 'Any particle of matter', it is said,[1] 'may be *conceived* to be annihilated; and any form may be *conceived* to be altered. Such an annihilation or alteration, therefore, is not impossible.' But it seems a great partiality not to perceive, that the same argument extends equally to the Deity, so far as we have any conception of him; and that the mind can at least imagine[2] him to be non-existent, or his attributes to be altered. It must be some unknown, inconceivable qualities, which can make his non-existence appear impossible, or his at-tributes unalterable: And no reason can be assigned, why these qualities may not belong to matter. As they are altogether unknown and inconceivable, they can never be proved incompatible with it.

Add to this, that in tracing an eternal succession of objects, it seems absurd to inquire for a general cause or first Author. How can any thing, that exists from eternity, have a cause, since that relation implies a priority in time and a beginning of existence?

In such a chain too, or succession of objects, each part is caused by that which preceded it, and causes that which succeeds it. Where then is the difficulty? But the WHOLE, you say, wants a cause. I answer, that the uniting of these parts into a whole, like the uniting of several distinct counties into one kingdom, or several distinct members into one body, is performed merely by an arbi-trary act of the mind, and has no influence on the nature of things. Did I show you the particular causes of each individual in a collection of twenty particles of matter, I should think it very unreasonable, should you afterwards ask me, what was the cause of

---

[1] Dr. Clarke.*   [2] [imagine *for* conceive.]

the whole twenty. This is sufficiently explained in explaining the cause of the parts.

['Though the reasonings, which you have urged, CLEANTHES, may well excuse me, said PHILO, from starting any farther difficulties; yet I cannot forbear insisting still upon another topic. It is observed by arithmeticians, that the products of 9 compose always either 9 or some lesser product of 9; if you add together all the characters, of which any of the former products is composed. Thus, of 18, 27, 36, which are products of 9, you make 9 by adding 1 to 8, 2 to 7, 3 to 6. Thus 369 is a product also of 9; and if you add 3, 6, and 9, you make 18, a lesser product of 9.² To a superficial observer, so wonderful a regularity may be admired as the effect either of chance or design; but a skilful algebraist immediately concludes it to be the work of necessity, and demonstrates, that it must for ever result from the nature of these numbers. Is it not probable, I ask, that the whole œconomy of the universe is conducted by a like necessity, though no human algebra can furnish a key which solves the difficulty? And instead of admiring the order of natural beings, may it not happen, that, could we penetrate into the intimate nature of bodies, we should clearly see why it was absolutely impossible, they could ever admit of any other disposition? So dangerous is it to introduce this idea of necessity into the present question! And so naturally does it afford an inference directly opposite to the religious hypothesis!

But dropping all these abstractions, continued PHILO; and confining ourselves to more familiar topics; I shall venture to add an observation,]³ that the argument *a priori* has seldom been found very convincing, except to people of a metaphysical head, who have accustomed themselves to abstract reasoning, and who finding from mathematics, that the understanding frequently leads to truth, through obscurity, and contrary to first appearances, have transferred the same habit of thinking to subjects where it ought not to have place. Other people, even of good sense and the best

¹ [Passage in brackets is written on the reverse side of the last sheet of Part IX with marks to indicate point of insertion. The whole passage is scored out by Hume and then the instruction added, also by Hume, on the margin: 'Print this passage.']

² *République de Lettres*, Août, 1685.

³ [*The original opening of this concluding paragraph runs:* I shall venture, said PHILO, to add to these reasonings of CLEANTHES an observation.]

inclined to religion, feel always some deficiency in such arguments, though they are not perhaps able to explain distinctly where it lies. A certain proof, that men ever did, and ever will, derive their religion from other sources than from this species of reasoning.

PART X

It is my opinion, I own, replied Demea, that each man feels, in a manner, the truth of religion within his own breast; and from a consciousness of his imbecility and misery, rather than from any reasoning, is led to seek protection from that Being, on whom he and all nature is dependent. So anxious or so tedious are even the best scenes of life, that futurity is still the object of all our hopes and fears. We incessantly look forward, and endeavour, by prayers, adoration, and sacrifice, to appease those unknown powers, whom we find, by experience, so able to afflict and oppress us. Wretched creatures that we are! What resource for us amidst the innumerable ills of life, did not religion suggest some methods of atonement, and appease those terrors, with which we are incessantly agitated and tormented?*

I am indeed persuaded, said Philo, that the best and indeed the only method of bringing every one to a due sense of religion is by just representations of the misery and wickedness of men. And for that purpose a talent of eloquence and strong imagery is more requisite than that of reasoning and argument. For is it necessary to prove, what every one feels within himself? It is only necessary to make us feel it, if possible, more intimately and sensibly.

The people, indeed, replied Demea, are sufficiently convinced of this great and melancholy truth. The miseries of life, the unhappiness of man, the general corruptions of our nature, the unsatisfactory enjoyment of pleasures, riches, honours; these phrases have become almost proverbial in all languages. And who can doubt of what all men declare from their own immediate feeling and experience?

In this point, said Philo, the learned are perfectly agreed with the vulgar; and in all letters, *sacred* and *profane*, the topic of human misery has been insisted on with the most pathetic eloquence that sorrow and melancholy could inspire. The poets, who speak from sentiment, without a system, and whose testimony has therefore the more authority, abound in images of this nature. From Homer down to Dr. Young,* the whole inspired tribe have ever been sensible, that no other representation of things would suit the feeling and observation of each individual.

As to authorities, replied DEMEA, you need not seek them. Look round this library of CLEANTHES. I shall venture to affirm, that, except authors of particular sciences, such as chemistry or botany, who have no occasion to treat of human life, there scarce is one of those innumerable writers, from whom the sense of human misery has not, in some passage or other, extorted a complaint and confession of it. At least, the chance is entirely on that side; and no one author has ever, so far as I can recollect, been so extravagant as to deny it.

There you must excuse me, said PHILO: LEIBNITZ has denied it;* and is perhaps the first,[1] who ventured upon so bold and paradoxical an opinion; at least, the first, who made it essential to his philosophical system.

And by being the first, replied DEMEA, might he not have been sensible of his error? For is this a subject in which philosophers can propose to make discoveries, especially in so late an age? And can any man hope by a simple denial (for the subject scarcely admits of reasoning) to bear down the united testimony of mankind, founded on sense and consciousness?

And why should man, added he, pretend to an exemption from the lot of all other animals? The whole earth, believe me, PHILO, is cursed and polluted. A perpetual war is kindled amongst all living creatures. Necessity, hunger, want, stimulate the strong and courageous: Fear, anxiety, terror, agitate the weak and infirm. The first entrance into life gives anguish to the new-born infant and to its wretched parent: Weakness, impotence, distress, attend each stage of that life: And it is at last finished in agony and horror.

Observe too, says PHILO, the curious artifices of nature, in order to embitter the life of every living being. The stronger prey upon the weaker, and keep them in perpetual terror and anxiety. The weaker too, in their turn, often prey upon the stronger, and vex and molest them without relaxation. Consider that innumerable race of insects, which either are bred on the body of each animal, or flying about infix their stings in him. These insects have others still less

---

[1] That sentiment had been maintained by Dr. King* [*De Origine Mali*, 1702] and some few others, before LEIBNITZ, though by none of so great fame as that German philosopher.

than themselves, which torment them. And thus on each hand, before and behind, above and below, every animal is surrounded with enemies, which incessantly seek his misery and destruction.

Man alone, said DEMEA, seems to be, in part, an exception to this rule. For by combination in society, he can easily master lions, tigers, and bears, whose greater strength and agility naturally enable them to prey upon him.

On the contrary, it is here chiefly, cried PHILO, that the uniform and equal maxims of nature are most apparent. Man, it is true, can, by combination, surmount all his *real* enemies, and become master of the whole animal creation: But does he not immediately raise up to himself *imaginary* enemies, the dæmons of his fancy, who haunt him with superstitious terrors, and blast every enjoyment of life? His pleasure, as he imagines, becomes, in their eyes, a crime: His food and repose give them umbrage and offence: His very sleep and dreams furnish new materials to anxious fear: And even death, his refuge from every other ill, presents only the dread of endless and innumerable woes. Nor does the wolf molest more the timid flock, than superstition does the anxious breast of wretched mortals.

Besides, consider, DEMEA; this very society, by which we surmount those wild beasts, our natural enemies; what new enemies does it not raise to us? What woe and misery does it not occasion? Man is the greatest enemy of man. Oppression, injustice, contempt, contumely, violence, sedition, war, calumny, treachery, fraud; by these they mutually torment each other: And they would soon dissolve that society which they had formed, were it not for the dread of still greater ills, which must attend their separation.

But though these external insults, said DEMEA, from animals, from men, from all the elements, which assault us, form a frightful catalogue of woes, they are nothing in comparison of those, which arise within ourselves, from the distempered condition of our mind and body. How many lie under the lingering torment of diseases? Hear the pathetic enumeration of the great poet.

> Intestine stone and ulcer, colic-pangs,
> Daemoniac frenzy, moping melancholy,
> And moon-struck madness, pining atrophy,
> Marasmus and wide-wasting pestilence.
> Dire was the tossing, deep the groans: DESPAIR

Tended the sick, busiest from couch to couch.
And over them triumphant DEATH his dart
Shook, but delay'd to strike, tho' oft invok'd
With vows, as their chief good and final hope.[1]

The disorders of the mind, continued DEMEA, though more secret, are not perhaps less dismal and vexatious. Remorse, shame,
anguish, rage, disappointment, anxiety, fear, dejection, despair;
who has ever passed through life without cruel inroads from these
tormentors? How many have scarcely ever felt any better sensa-
tions? Labour and poverty, so abhorred by every one, are the
certain lot of the far greater number: And those few privileged
persons, who enjoy ease and opulence, never reach contentment or
true felicity. All the goods of life united would not make a very
happy man: But all the ills united would make a wretch indeed; and
any one of them almost (and who can be free from every one), nay
often the absence of one good (and who can possess all) is sufficient to render life ineligible.

Were a stranger to drop, on a sudden, into this world, I would
show him, as a specimen of its ills, an hospital full of diseases, a
prison crowded with malefactors and debtors, a field of battle
strowed with carcases, a fleet floundering in the ocean, a nation
languishing under tyranny, famine, or pestilence. To turn the gay
side of life to him, and give him a notion of its pleasures; whither
should I conduct him? to a ball, to an opera, to court? He might
justly think, that I was only showing him a diversity of distress and
sorrow.

There is no evading such striking instances, said PHILO, but by
apologies, which still farther aggravate the charge. Why have all
men, I ask, in all ages, complained incessantly of the miseries
of life? ... They have no just reason, says one: These complaints proceed only from their discontented, repining, anxious
disposition. ... And can there possibly, I reply, be a more certain
foundation of misery, than such a wretched temper?

But if they were really as unhappy as they pretend, says my
antagonist, why do they remain in life? ...

Not satisfied with life, afraid of death.*

---

[1] [Milton: *Paradise Lost*, XI.]

This is the secret chain, say I, that holds us. We are terrified, not bribed to the continuance of our existence.

It is only a false delicacy, he may insist, which a few refined spirits indulge, and which has spread these complaints among the whole race of mankind. . . . And what is this delicacy, I ask, which you blame? Is it any thing but a greater sensibility to all the pleasures and pains of life? and if the man of a delicate, refined temper, by being so much more alive than the rest of the world, is only so much more unhappy; what judgment must we form in general of human life?

Let men remain at rest, says our adversary; and they will be easy. They are willing artificers of their own misery. . . . No! reply I; an anxious languor follows their repose: Disappointment, vexation, trouble, their activity and ambition.

I can observe something like what you mention in some others, replied CLEANTHES: But I confess, I feel little or nothing of it in myself; and hope that it is not so common as you represent it.

If you feel not human misery yourself, cried DEMEA, I congratulate you on so happy a singularity. Others, seemingly the most prosperous, have not been ashamed to vent their complaints in the most melancholy strains. Let us attend to the great, the fortunate Emperor, CHARLES V, when, tired with human grandeur, he resigned all his extensive dominions into the hands of his son. In the last harangue, which he made on that memorable occasion, he publicly avowed, *that the greatest prosperities which he had ever enjoyed, had been mixed with so many adversities, that he might truly say he had never enjoyed any satisfaction or contentment.** But did the retired life, in which he sought for shelter, afford him any greater happiness? If we may credit his son's account, his repentance commenced the very day of his resignation.

CICERO's fortune, from small beginnings, rose to the greatest lustre and renown; yet what pathetic complaints of the ills of life do his familiar letters, as well as philosophical discourses, contain? And suitably to his own experience, he introduces CATO, the great, the fortunate CATO, protesting in his old age, that, had he a new life in his offer, he would reject the present.*

Ask yourself, ask any of your acquaintance, whether they would live over again the last ten or twenty years of their life. No! but the next twenty, they say, will be better:

> And from the dregs of life, hope to receive
> What the first sprightly running could not give.[1]

Thus at last they find (such is the greatness of human misery; it reconciles even contradictions) that they complain, at once, of the shortness of life, and of its vanity and sorrow.

And is it possible, CLEANTHES, said PHILO, that after all these reflections, and infinitely more, which might be suggested, you can still persevere in your anthropomorphism, and assert the moral attributes of the Deity, his justice, benevolence, mercy, and rectitude, to be of the same nature with these virtues in human creatures? His power we allow infinite: Whatever he wills is executed: But neither man nor any other animal are happy: Therefore he does not will their happiness. His wisdom is infinite: He is never mistaken in choosing the means to any end: But the course of nature tends not to human or animal felicity: Therefore it is not established for that purpose. Through the whole compass of human knowledge, there are no inferences more certain and infallible than these. In what respect, then, do his benevolence and mercy resemble the benevolence and mercy of men?

EPICURUS's old questions are yet unanswered. Is he willing to prevent evil, but not able? then is he impotent. Is he able, but not willing? then is he malevolent. Is he both able and willing? whence then is evil?*

You ascribe, CLEANTHES (and I believe justly) a purpose and intention to nature. But what, I beseech you, is the object of that curious artifice and machinery, which she has displayed in all animals? The preservation alone of individuals and propagation of the species. It seems enough for her purpose, if such a rank be barely upheld in the universe, without any care or concern for the happiness of the members that compose it. No resource for this purpose: No machinery, in order merely to give pleasure or ease: No fund of pure joy and contentment: No indulgence without some want or necessity accompanying it. At least, the few phenomena of this nature are overbalanced by opposite phenomena of still greater importance.

Our sense of music, harmony, and indeed beauty of all kinds, gives satisfaction, without being absolutely necessary to the pre-

---

[1] [Dryden, *Aurengzebe*, Act iv, sc. i. Hume has written 'hope' *for* 'think'.]

servation and propagation of the species. But what racking pains, on the other hand, arise from gouts, gravels, megrims, tooth-aches, rheumatisms; where the injury to the animal-machinery is either small or incurable? Mirth, laughter, play, frolic, seem gratuitous satisfactions, which have no farther tendency: Spleen, melancholy, discontent, superstition, are pains of the same nature. How then does the divine benevolence display itself, in the sense of you anthropomorphites? None but we mystics, as you were pleased to call us, can account for this strange mixture of phenomena, by deriving it from attributes, infinitely perfect, but incomprehensible.

And have you at last, said CLEANTHES smiling, betrayed your intentions, PHILO? Your long agreement with DEMEA did indeed a little surprise me; but I find you were all the while erecting a concealed battery against me. And I must confess, that you have now fallen upon a subject worthy of your noble spirit of opposition and controversy. If you can make out the present point, and prove mankind to be unhappy or corrupted, there is an end at once of all religion. For to what purpose establish the natural attributes of the Deity, while the moral are still doubtful and uncertain?*

You take umbrage very easily, replied DEMEA, at opinions the most innocent, and the most generally received even amongst the religious and devout themselves: And nothing can be more surprising than to find a topic like this, concerning the wickedness and misery of man, charged with no less than atheism and profaneness. Have not all pious divines and preachers, who have indulged their rhetoric on so fertile a subject; have they not easily, I say, given a solution of any difficulties which may attend it? This world is but a point in comparison of the universe: This life but a moment in comparison of eternity. The present evil phenomena, therefore, are rectified in other regions, and in some future period of existence. And the eyes of men, being then opened to larger views of things, see the whole connection of general laws, and trace, with adoration, the benevolence and rectitude of the Deity, through all the mazes and intricacies of his providence.

No! replied CLEANTHES, No! These arbitrary suppositions can never be admitted, contrary to matter of fact, visible and uncontroverted. Whence can any cause be known but from its known effects? Whence can any hypothesis be proved but from the apparent phenomena? To establish one hypothesis upon another is building entirely in the air; and the utmost we ever attain, by these conjectures and fictions, is to ascertain the bare possibility of our opinion; but never can we, upon such terms, establish its reality.

The only method of supporting divine benevolence (and it is what I willingly embrace) is to deny absolutely the misery and wickedness of man. Your representations are exaggerated: Your melancholy views mostly fictitious: Your inferences contrary to fact and experience. Health is more common than sickness: Pleasure than pain: Happiness than misery. And for one vexation which we meet with, we attain, upon computation, a hundred enjoyments.

Admitting your position, replied PHILO, which yet is extremely doubtful, you must, at the same time, allow, that, if pain be less frequent than pleasure, it is infinitely more violent and durable. One hour of it is often able to outweigh a day, a week, a month of our common insipid enjoyments: And how many days, weeks, and months are passed by several in the most acute torments? Pleasure, scarcely in one instance, is ever able to reach ecstasy and rapture: And in no one instance can it continue for any time at its highest pitch and altitude. The spirits evaporate; the nerves relax; the fabric is disordered; and the enjoyment quickly degenerates into fatigue and uneasiness. But pain often, Good God, how often! rises to torture and agony; and the longer it continues, it becomes still more genuine agony and torture. Patience is exhausted; courage languishes; melancholy seizes us; and nothing terminates our misery but the removal of its cause, or another event, which is the sole cure of all evil, but which, from our natural folly, we regard with still greater horror and consternation.

But not to insist upon these topics, continued PHILO, though most obvious, certain, and important; I must use the freedom to admonish you, CLEANTHES, that you have put this controversy upon a most dangerous issue, and are unawares introducing a total scepticism into the most essential articles of natural and revealed theology. What! no method of fixing a just foundation for religion, unless we allow the happiness of human life, and maintain a continued existence even in this world, with all our present pains, infirmities, vexations, and follies, to be eligible and desirable! But this is contrary to every one's feeling and experience: It is contrary to an authority so established as nothing can subvert: No decisive proofs can ever be produced against this authority; nor is it possible for you to compute, estimate, and compare all the pains and all the pleasures in the lives of all men and of all animals: And thus by your resting the whole system of religion on a point, which, from its very nature, most for ever be uncertain, you tacitly confess, that that system is equally uncertain.

But allowing you, what never will be believed; at least, what you never possibly[1] can prove, that animal, or at least,[2] human happiness, in this life, exceeds its misery; you have yet done nothing: For this is not, by any means, what we expect from infinite power, infinite wisdom, and infinite goodness. Why is there any misery at all in the world? Not by chance surely. From some cause then. Is it from the intention of the Deity? But he is perfectly benevolent. Is it contrary to his intention? But he is almighty. Nothing can shake the solidity of this reasoning, so short, so clear, so decisive; except we assert, that these subjects exceed all human capacity, and that our common measures of truth and falsehood are not applicable to them; a topic, which I have all along insisted on, but which you have, from the beginning, rejected with scorn and indignation.

But I will be contented to retire still from this intrenchment:[3] For I deny that you can ever force me in it: I will allow, that pain or misery in man is *compatible* with infinite power and goodness in the Deity, even in your sense of these attributes: What are you advanced by all these concessions? A mere possible compatibility is not sufficient. You must *prove* these pure, unmixed, and un-controllable attributes from the present mixed and confused phenomena, and from these alone. A hopeful[4] undertaking! Were the phenomena ever so pure and unmixed, yet being finite, they would be insufficient for that purpose. How much more, where they are also so jarring and discordant?

Here, CLEANTHES, I find myself at ease in my argument. Here I triumph. Formerly, when we argued concerning the natural attributes of intelligence and design, I needed all my sceptical and metaphysical subtilty to elude your grasp. In many views of the

---

[1] [possibly *omitted and then restored.*]
[2] [animal, or at least *added.*]
[3] [retrenchment *for* defence: *altered to* intrenchment *by Hume's nephew.*]
[4] [hopeful *for* strange.]

universe, and of its parts, particularly the latter, the beauty and fitness of final causes strike us with such irresistible force, that all objections appear (what I believe[1] they really are) mere cavils and sophisms; nor can we then imagine how it was ever possible for us to repose any weight on them. But there is no view of human life, or of the condition of mankind, from which, without the greatest violence, we can infer the moral attributes, or learn that infinite benevolence, conjoined with infinite power and infinite wisdom, which we must discover by the eyes of faith alone. It is your turn now to tug the labouring oar, and to support your philosophical subtilties against the dictates of plain reason and experience.

---

[1] [I believe *for* perhaps. This alteration may have been made in 1776.]

PART XI

I SCRUPLE not to allow, said CLEANTHES, that I have been apt to suspect the frequent repetition of the word, *infinite*, which we meet with in all theological writers, to savour more of panegyric than of philosophy, and that any purposes of reasoning, and even of religion, would be better served, were we to rest contented with more accurate and more moderate expressions. The terms, *admirable, excellent, superlatively great, wise*, and *holy*; these sufficiently fill the imaginations of men; and any thing beyond, besides that it leads into absurdities, has no influence on the affections or sentiments. Thus, in the present subject, if we abandon all human analogy, as seems your intention, DEMEA, I am afraid we abandon all religion, and retain no conception of the great object of our adoration. If we preserve human analogy, we must for ever find it impossible to reconcile any mixture of evil in the universe with infinite attributes; much less, can we ever prove the latter from the former. But supposing the Author of nature to be finitely perfect, though far exceeding mankind; a satisfactory account may then be given of natural and moral evil, and every untoward phenomenon be explained and adjusted. A less evil may then be chosen, in order to avoid a greater: Inconveniences be submitted to, in order to reach a desirable end: And in a word, benevolence, regulated by wisdom, and limited by necessity, may produce just such a world as the present. You, PHILO, who are so prompt at starting views, and reflections, and analogies; I would gladly hear, at length, without interruption, your opinion of this new theory; and if it deserve our attention, we may afterwards, at more leisure, reduce it into form.

My sentiments, replied PHILO, are not worth being made a mystery of; and therefore, without any ceremony, I shall deliver what occurs to me with regard to the present subject. It must, I think, be allowed, that, if a very limited intelligence, whom we shall suppose utterly unacquainted with the universe, were assured, that it were the production of a very good, wise, and powerful Being, however finite, he would, from his conjectures, form *beforehand* a different notion of it from what we find it to be by experience; nor would he ever imagine, merely from these attributes of the cause, of which he is informed, that the effect could be so full of vice and misery and disorder, as it appears in this life. Supposing now, that this person were brought into the world, still assured, that it was the workmanship of such a sublime and benevolent Being; he might, perhaps, be surprised at the disappointment; but would never retract his former belief, if founded on any very solid argument; since such a limited intelligence must be sensible of his own blindness and ignorance, and must allow, that there may be many solutions of those phenomena, which will for ever escape his comprehension. But supposing, which is the real case with regard to man, that this creature is not antecedently convinced of a supreme intelligence, benevolent, and powerful, but is left to gather such a belief from the appearances of things; this entirely alters the case, nor will he ever find any reason for such a conclusion. He may be fully convinced of the narrow limits of his understanding; but this will not help him in forming an inference concerning the goodness of superior powers, since he must form that inference from what he knows, not from what he is ignorant of. The more you exaggerate his weakness and ignorance, the more diffident you render him, and give him the greater suspicion, that such subjects are beyond the reach of his faculties. You are obliged, therefore, to reason with him merely from the known phenomena, and to drop every arbitrary supposition or conjecture.

Did I show you a house or palace, where there was not one apartment convenient or agreeable; where the windows, doors, fires, passages, stairs, and the whole œconomy of the building were the source of noise, confusion, fatigue, darkness, and the extremes of heat and cold; you would certainly blame the contrivance, without any farther examination. The architect would in vain display his subtilty, and prove to you, that if this door or that window were altered, greater ills would ensue. What he says, may be strictly true: The alteration of one particular, while the other parts of the building remain, may only augment the inconveniences. But still you would assert in general, that, if the architect had had skill and good intentions, he might have formed such a plan of the whole, and might have adjusted the parts in such a manner, as would have remedied all or most of these inconveniences. His ignorance, or even your own ignorance of such a plan, will never convince you of the impossibility of it. If you find many inconveniences and deformities in the building, you will always, without entering into any detail, condemn the architect.

In short, I repeat the question: Is the world considered in general, and as it appears to us in this life,[1] different from what a man or such a limited being would, *beforehand*, expect from a very powerful, wise, and benevolent Deity? It must be strange prejudice to assert the contrary. And from thence I conclude, that, however consistent the world may be, allowing certain suppositions and conjectures, with the idea of such a Deity, it can never afford us an inference concerning his existence. The consistence is not absolutely denied, only the inference.* Conjectures, especially where infinity is excluded from the divine attributes, may, perhaps, be sufficient to prove a consistence; but can never be foundations for any inference.

There seem to be *four* circumstances, on which depend all, or the greatest part of the ills, that molest sensible creatures; and it is not impossible but all these circumstances may be necessary and unavoidable. We know so little beyond common life, or even of common life, that, with regard to the œconomy of a universe, there is no conjecture, however wild, which may not be just; nor any one, however plausible, which may not be erroneous. All that belongs to human understanding, in this deep ignorance and obscurity, is to be sceptical, or at least cautious; and not to admit of any hypothesis, whatever; much less, of any which is supported by no appearance of probability. Now this I assert to be the case with regard to all the causes of evil, and the circumstances on which it depends. None of them appear to human reason, in the least degree, necessary or unavoidable; nor can we suppose them such, without the utmost licence of imagination.

The *first* circumstance which introduces evil, is that contrivance or œconomy of the animal creation, by which pains, as well as pleasures, are employed to excite all creatures to action, and make them vigilant in the great work of self-preservation. Now pleasure alone, in its various degrees, seems to human understanding sufficient for this purpose. All animals might be constantly in a state of enjoyment; but when urged by any of the necessities of nature, such as thirst, hunger, weariness; instead of pain, they

---

[1] [in this life *added*.]

might feel a diminution of pleasure, by which they might be prompted to seek that object, which is necessary to their subsistence. Men pursue pleasure as eagerly as they avoid pain; at least, might have been so constituted. It seems, therefore, plainly possible to carry on the business of life without any pain. Why then is any animal ever rendered susceptible of such a sensation? If animals can be free from it an hour, they might enjoy a perpetual exemption from it; and it required as particular a contrivance of their organs to produce that feeling, as to endow them with sight, hearing, or any of the senses. Shall we conjecture, that such a contrivance was necessary, without any appearance of reason? And shall we build on that conjecture as on the most certain truth?

But a capacity of pain would not alone produce pain, were it not for the *second* circumstance, viz. the conducting of the world by general laws; and this seems nowise necessary to a very perfect Being. It is true; if every thing were conducted by particular volitions,* the course of nature would be perpetually broken, and no man could employ his reason in the conduct of life. But might not other particular volitions remedy this inconvenience? In short, might not the Deity exterminate all ill, wherever it were to be found; and produce all good, without any preparation or long progress of causes and effects?

Besides, we must consider, that, according to the present œconomy of the world, the course of nature, though supposed exactly regular, yet to us appears not so, and many events are uncertain, and many disappoint our expectations. Health and sickness, calm and tempest, with an infinite number of other accidents, whose causes are unknown and variable, have a great influence both on the fortunes of particular persons and on the prosperity of public societies: And indeed all human life, in a manner, depends on such accidents. A Being, therefore, who knows the secret springs of the universe, might easily, by particular volitions, turn all these accidents to the good of mankind, and render the whole world happy, without discovering himself in any operation. A fleet, whose purposes were salutary to society, might always meet with a fair wind: Good princes enjoy sound health and long life: Persons born to power and authority, be framed with good tempers and virtuous dispositions. A few such events as these, regularly and wisely conducted, would change the face of the world; and yet would no more seem to disturb the course of nature or confound human conduct, than the present œconomy of things, where the causes are secret, and variable, and compounded. Some small touches, given to CALIGULA's brain in his infancy, might have converted him into a TRAJAN: One wave, a little higher than the rest, by burying CÆSAR and his fortune in the bottom of the ocean, might have restored liberty to a considerable part of mankind. There may, for aught we know, be good reasons, why providence interposes not in this manner; but they are unknown to us: And though the mere supposition, that such reasons exist, may be sufficient to *save* the conclusion concerning the divine attributes, yet surely it can never be sufficient to *establish* that conclusion.

If every thing in the universe be conducted by general laws, and if animals be rendered susceptible of pain, it scarcely seems possible but some ill must arise in the various shocks of matter, and the various concurrence and opposition of general laws: But this ill would be very rare, were it not for the *third* circumstance, which I proposed to mention, viz. the great frugality with which all powers and faculties are distributed to every particular being. So well adjusted are the organs and capacities of all animals, and so well fitted to their preservation, that, as far as history or tradition reaches, there appears not to be any single species which has yet been extinguished in the universe.[1] Every animal has the requisite endowments; but these endowments are bestowed with so scrupulous an œconomy, that any considerable diminution must entirely destroy the creature. Wherever one power is increased, there is a proportional abatement in the others. Animals, which excel in swiftness, are commonly defective in force. Those, which possess both, are either imperfect in some of their senses, or are oppressed with the most craving wants. The human species, whose chief excellency is reason and sagacity, is of all others the most necessitous, and the most deficient in bodily advantages; without clothes, without arms, without food, without lodging, without any

[1] [*In Hume's manuscript there is here the following note, scored out*: CÆSAR, speaking of the woods in Germany, mentions some animals as subsisting there, which are now utterly extinct. *De Bello Gall*: lib. 6. These, and some few more instances, may be exceptions to the proposition here delivered. STRABO (lib. 4) quotes from POLYBIUS an account of an animal about the Tyrol, which is not now to be found. If POLYBIUS was not deceived, which is possible, the animal must have been then very rare, since STRABO cites but one authority, and speaks doubtfully.]

convenience of life, except what they owe to their own skill and industry. In short, nature seems to have formed an exact calculation of the necessities of her creatures; and like a *rigid master*, has afforded them little[1] more powers or endowments, than what are strictly sufficient to supply those necessities. An *indulgent parent* would have bestowed a large stock, in order to guard against accidents, and secure the happiness and welfare of the creature, in the most unfortunate concurrence of circumstances. Every course of life would not have been so surrounded[2] with precipices, that the least departure from the true path, by mistake or necessity, must involve us in misery and ruin. Some reserve, some fund would have been provided to ensure happiness; nor would the powers and the necessities have been adjusted with so rigid an œconomy. The Author of nature is inconceivably powerful: His force is supposed great, if not altogether inexhaustible: Nor is there any reason, as far as we can judge, to make him observe this strict frugality in his dealings with his creatures. [[3]It would have been better, were his power extremely limited, to have created fewer animals, and to have endowed these with more faculties for their happiness and preservation. A builder is never esteemed prudent, who undertakes a plan, beyond what his stock will enable him to finish.]

[In order to cure most of the ills of human life, I require not that man should have the wings of the eagle, the swiftness of the stag, the force of the ox, the arms of the lion, the scales of the crocodile or rhinoceros; much less do I demand the sagacity of an angel or cherubim. I am contented to take an increase in one single power or faculty of his soul. Let him be endowed with a greater propensity to industry and labour; a more vigorous spring and activity of mind; a more constant bent to business and application. Let the whole species possess naturally an equal diligence with that which many individuals are able to attain by habit and reflection; and the most beneficial consequences, without any allay of ill, is the immediate and necessary result of this endowment. Almost all the moral, as well as natural evils of human life arise from idleness; and were

---

[1] [little *for* no.]   [2] [surrounded *for* bordered.]

[3] [This passage in brackets is first written on the margin, then scored out and rewritten on the last page of Part XI, with marks to indicate point of insertion. The next paragraph, also here given in brackets, is added, in immediate sequence, on the same page.]

our species, by the original constitution of their frame, exempt from this vice or infirmity, the perfect cultivation of land, the improvement of arts and manufactures, the exact execution of every office and duty, immediately follow; and men at once may fully reach that state of society, which is so imperfectly attained by the best-regulated government. But as industry is a power, and the most valuable of any, nature seems determined, suitably to her usual maxims, to bestow it on men with a very sparing hand; and rather to punish him severely for his deficiency in it, than to reward him for his attainments. She has so contrived his frame, that nothing but the most violent necessity can oblige him to labour; and she employs all his other wants to overcome, at least in part, the want of diligence, and to endow him with some share of a faculty, of which she has thought fit naturally to bereave him. Here our demands may be allowed very humble, and therefore the more reasonable.[1] If we required the endowments of superior penetration and judgment, of a more delicate taste of beauty, of a nicer sensibility to benevolence and friendship; we might be told, that we impiously pretend to break the order of nature, that we want to exalt ourselves into a higher rank of being, that the presents which we require, not being suitable to our state and condition, would only be pernicious to us. But it is hard; I dare to repeat it, it is hard, that being placed in a world so full of wants and necessities; where almost every being and element is either our foe or refuses us their assistance; we should also have our own temper to struggle with, and should be deprived of that faculty which can alone fence against these multiplied evils.]

The *fourth* circumstance, whence arises the misery and ill of the universe, is the inaccurate workmanship of all the springs and principles of the great machine of nature. It must be acknowledged, that there are few parts of the universe, which seem not to serve some purpose, and whose removal would not produce a visible defect and disorder in the whole. The parts hang all together; nor can one be touched without affecting the rest, in a greater or less degree. But at the same time, it must be observed, that none of these parts or principles, however useful, are so accurately adjusted, as to keep precisely within those bounds in which their

[1] [reasonable *for* legitimate.]

utility consists; but they are, all of them, apt, on every occasion, to run into the one extreme or the other. One would imagine, that this grand production had not received the last hand of the maker; so little finished is every part, and so coarse are the strokes, with which it is executed. Thus, the winds are requisite to convey the vapours along the surface of the globe, and to assist men in navigation: But how oft, rising up to tempests and hurricanes, do they become pernicious? Rains are necessary to nourish all the plants and animals of the earth: But how often are they defective? how often excessive? Heat is requisite to all life and vegetation; but is not always found in the due proportion. On the mixture and secretion of the humours and juices of the body depend the health and prosperity of the animal: But the parts perform not regularly their proper function. What more useful than all the passions of the mind, ambition, vanity, love, anger? But how oft do they break their bounds, and cause the greatest convulsions in society? There is nothing so advantageous in the universe, but what frequently becomes pernicious, by its excess or defect; nor has nature guarded, with the requisite accuracy, against all disorder or confusion. The irregularity is never, perhaps,[1] so great as to destroy any species; but is often sufficient to involve the individuals in ruin and misery.

On the concurrence, then, of these *four* circumstances does all or the greatest part of natural evil* depend. Were all living creatures incapable of pain, or were the world administered by particular volitions, evil never could have found access into the universe: And were animals endowed with a large stock of powers and faculties, beyond what strict necessity requires; or were the several springs and principles of the universe so accurately framed as to preserve always the just temperament and medium; there must have been very little ill in comparison of what we feel at present. What then shall we pronounce on this occasion? Shall we say, that these circumstances are not necessary, and that they might easily have been altered in the contrivance of the universe? This decision seems too presumptuous for creatures so blind and ignorant. Let us be more modest in our conclusions. Let us allow, that, if the goodness of the Deity (I mean a goodness like the human) could be

---

[1] [perhaps *added.*]

established on any tolerable reasons[1] *a priori*, these phenomena, however untoward, would not be sufficient to subvert that principle; but might easily, in some unknown manner, be reconcilable to it. But let us still assert, that as this goodness is not antecedently established, but must be inferred from the phenomena, there can be no grounds for such an inference, while there are so many ills in the universe, and while these ills might so easily have been remedied, as far as human understanding can be allowed to judge on such a subject. I am sceptic enough to allow, that the bad appearances, notwithstanding all my reasonings, may be compatible with such attributes as you suppose: But surely they can never prove these attributes. Such a conclusion cannot result from scepticism; but must arise from the phenomena, and from our confidence in the reasonings which we deduce from these phenomena.

[Look round this universe. What an immense profusion of beings, animated and organized, sensible and active! You admire this prodigious variety and fecundity. But inspect a little more narrowly these living existences, the only beings worth regarding. How hostile and destructive to each other! How insufficient all of them for their own happiness! How contemptible or odious to the spectator! The whole presents nothing but the idea of a blind nature, impregnated by a great[2] vivifying principle, and pouring forth from her lap, without discernment or parental care, her maimed and abortive children.[3]]

Here the MANICHÆAN system* occurs as a proper hypothesis to solve the difficulty: And no doubt, in some respects, it is very specious, and has more probability than the common hypothesis, by giving a plausible account of the strange mixture of good and ill which appears in life. But if we consider, on the other hand, the perfect uniformity and agreement of the parts of the universe, we shall not discover in it any marks of the combat of a malevolent with a benevolent Being. There is indeed an opposition of pains and pleasures in the feelings of sensible creatures: But are not all the operations of nature carried on by an opposition of principles, of hot and cold, moist and dry, light and heavy? The true conclu-

---

[1] [on any tolerable reasons *added*.]   [2] [a great *for* an infinitely.]
[3] [This passage in brackets is written, with marks to indicate point of insertion, on the last sheet of Part XI, immediately prior to the other additions given above, pp. 110–11.]

sion is, that the original source[1] of all things is entirely indifferent to all these principles, and has no more regard to good above ill than to heat above cold, or to drought above moisture, or to light above heavy.

There may *four* hypotheses be framed concerning the first[2] causes of the universe: *that* they are endowed with perfect good- ness, *that* they have perfect malice, *that* they are opposite and have both goodness and malice, *that* they have neither goodness nor malice. Mixed phenomena can never prove the two former un- mixed principles. And the uniformity and steadiness of general laws seem to oppose the third. The fourth, therefore, seems by far the most probable.

What I have said concerning natural evil will apply to moral, with little or no variation; and we have no more[3] reason to infer, that the rectitude of the supreme Being resembles human rectitude than that his benevolence resembles the human. Nay, it will be thought, that we have still greater cause to exclude from him moral sentiments, such as we feel them; since moral evil, in the opinion of many, is much more predominant above moral good than natural evil above natural good.

But even though this should not be allowed, and though the virtue, which is in mankind, should be acknowledged much su- perior to the vice; yet so long as there is any vice at all in the universe, it will very much puzzle you anthropomorphites, how to account for it. You must assign a cause for it, without having recourse to the first cause. But as every effect must have a cause, and that cause another; you must either carry on the progression *in infinitum*, or rest on[4] that original principle, who is the ultimate cause of all things. . . .*

Hold! Hold! cried DEMEA: Whither does your imagination hurry you? I joined in alliance with you, in order to prove the incompre- hensible nature of the divine Being, and refute the principles of CLEANTHES, who would measure every thing by a human rule and standard. But I now find you running into all the topics of the greatest libertines and infidels;[5] and betraying that holy cause,

---

[1] [source *for* cause.]   [2] [first *for* original.]
[3] [no more *for* the same.]   [4] [rest on *for* stop at.]
[5] [infidels *for* sceptics.]

which you seemingly espoused. Are you secretly, then, a more dangerous enemy than CLEANTHES himself?

And are you so late in perceiving it? replied CLEANTHES. Believe me, DEMEA; your friend PHILO, from the beginning, has been amusing himself at both our expence; and it must be confessed, that the injudicious reasoning of our vulgar theology has given him but too just a handle of ridicule. (The total infirmity of human reason, the absolute incomprehensibility of the divine nature, the great and universal misery and still greater wickedness of men; these are strange topics surely to be so fondly cherished by orthodox divines and doctors. In ages of stupidity and ignorance, indeed, these principles may safely be espoused; and perhaps, no views of things are more proper to promote superstition, than such as encourage the blind amazement, the diffidence, and melancholy of mankind. But at present . . .)

Blame not so much, interposed PHILO, the ignorance of these reverend gentlemen. They know how to change their style with the times. Formerly it was a most popular theological topic to maintain, that human life was vanity and misery, and to exaggerate all the ills and pains which are incident to men. But of late years, divines, we find, begin to retract this position, and maintain, though still with some hesitation, that there are more goods that evils, more pleasures than pains, even in this life. When religion stood entirely upon temper and education, it was thought proper to encourage melancholy; as indeed, mankind never have recourse to superior powers so readily as in that disposition. But as men have now learned to form principles, and to draw consequences, it is necessary to change the batteries, and to make use of such arguments as will endure, at least some scrutiny and examination. This variation is the same (and from the same causes) with that which I formerly remarked with regard to scepticism.

Thus PHILO continued to the last his spirit of opposition, and his censure of established opinions. But I could observe, that DEMEA did not at all relish the latter part of the discourse; and he took occasion soon after, on some pretence or other, to leave the company.

PART XII

AFTER DEMEA'S departure CLEANTHES and PHILO continued the conversation in the following manner. Our friend, I am afraid, said CLEANTHES, will have little inclination to revive this topic of discourse, while you are in company; and to tell truth, PHILO, I should rather wish to reason with either of you apart on a subject so sublime and interesting. Your spirit of controversy, joined to your abhorrence of vulgar superstition, carries you strange lengths, when engaged in an argument; and there is nothing so sacred and venerable, even in your own eyes, which you spare on that occasion.

I must confess, replied PHILO, that I am less cautious on the subject of natural religion than on any other; both because I know that I can never, on that head, corrupt the principles of any man of common sense, and because no one, I am confident, in whose eyes I appear a man of common sense, will ever mistake my intentions. You, in particular, CLEANTHES, with whom I live in unreserved intimacy; you are sensible, that, notwithstanding the freedom of my conversation, and my love of singular arguments, no one has a deeper sense of religion impressed on his mind, or pays more profound adoration to the divine Being, as he discovers himself to reason, in the inexplicable contrivance and artifice of nature. A purpose, an intention, a design strikes everywhere the most careless, the most stupid thinker; and no man can be so hardened in absurd systems, as at all times to reject it. *That nature does nothing in vain*, is a maxim established in all the schools, merely from the contemplation of the works of nature, without any religious purpose; and, from a firm conviction of its truth, an anatomist, who had observed a new organ or canal, would never be satisfied till he had also discovered its use and intention. One great foundation of the COPERNICAN system is the maxim, *that nature acts by the simplest methods, and chooses the most proper means to any end*; and astronomers often, without thinking of it, lay this strong foundation of piety and religion. [¹The same thing is observable in other parts

---

¹ [Added on the margin.]

of philosophy: And] thus all the sciences almost lead us insensibly to acknowledge a first intelligent Author; and their authority is often so much the greater, as they do not directly profess that intention.*

It is with pleasure I hear GALEN reason concerning the structure of the human body. The anatomy of a man, says he,[1] discovers above 600 different muscles; and whoever duly considers these, will find, that in each of them nature must have adjusted at least ten different circumstances, in order to attain the end which she proposed; proper figure, just magnitude, right disposition of the several ends, upper and lower position of the whole, the due insertion of the several nerves, veins, and arteries: So that, in the muscles alone, above 6000 several views and intentions must have been formed and executed. The bones he calculates to be 284: The distinct purposes, aimed at in the structure of each, above forty. What a prodigious display of artifice, even in these simple and homogeneous parts? But if we consider the skin, ligaments, vessels, glandules, humours, the several limbs and members of the body; how must our astonishment rise upon us, in proportion to the number and intricacy of the parts so artificially adjusted? The farther we advance in these researches, we discover new scenes of art and wisdom: But descry still, at a distance, farther scenes beyond our reach; in the fine internal structure of the parts, in the œconomy of the brain, in the fabric of the seminal vessels. All these artifices are repeated in every different species of animal, with wonderful variety, and with exact propriety, suited to the different intentions of nature, in framing each species. And if the infidelity of GALEN, even when these natural sciences were still imperfect, could not withstand such striking appearances; to what pitch of pertinacious obstinacy must a philosopher in this age have attained, who can now doubt of a supreme intelligence?

Could I meet with one of this species (who, I thank God, are very rare) I would ask him: Supposing there were a God, who did not discover himself immediately to our senses; were it possible for him to give stronger proofs of his existence, than what appear on the whole face of nature? What indeed could such a divine

[1] De formatione foetus. [*De Foetuum Formatione Libellus*, cap. vi; Galeni *Opera* (1822), lib. iv, pp. 691 sqq.]

Being do, but copy the present œconomy of things; render many of his artifices so plain, that no stupidity could mistake them; afford glimpses of still greater artifices, which demonstrate his prodigious superiority above our narrow apprehensions; and conceal altogether a great many from such imperfect creatures? Now according to all rules of just reasoning, every fact must pass for undisputed, when it is supported by all the arguments which its nature admits of, even though these arguments be not, in themselves, very numerous or forcible: How much more, in the present case, where no human imagination can compute their number, and no understanding estimate their cogency?

I shall farther add, said CLEANTHES, to what you have so well urged, that one great advantage of the principle of theism, is, that it is the only system of cosmogony which can be rendered intelligible and complete, and yet can throughout preserve a strong analogy to what we every day see and experience in the world. The comparison of the universe to a machine of human contrivance is so obvious and natural, and is justified by so many instances of order and design in nature,[1] that it must immediately strike all unprejudiced apprehensions, and procure universal approbation. Whoever attempts to weaken this theory, cannot pretend to succeed by establishing in its place any other that is precise and determinate: It is sufficient for him, if he start doubts and difficulties; and by remote and abstract views of things, reach that suspence of judgment, which is here the utmost boundary of his wishes. But besides that this state of mind is in itself unsatisfactory, it can never be steadily maintained against such striking appearances as continually engage us into the religious hypothesis.[2] A false, absurd system, human nature, from the force of prejudice, is capable of adhering to with obstinacy and perseverance: But no system at all, in opposition to a theory, supported by strong and obvious[3] reason, by natural propensity, and by early education, I think it absolutely impossible to maintain or defend.

So little, replied PHILO, do I esteem this suspense of judgment in the present case to be possible, that I am apt to suspect there enters

---

[1] [design in nature *for* contrivance.]   [2] [hypothesis *for* theory.]
[3] [and obvious *added*.]

somewhat of a dispute of words into this controversy, more than is usually imagined. That the works of nature bear a great analogy to the productions of art is evident; and according to all the rules of good reasoning, we ought to infer, if we argue at all concerning them, that their causes have a proportional analogy. But as there arc also considerable differences, we have reason to suppose a proportional difference in the causes; and in particular ought to attribute a much higher degree of power and energy to the supreme cause than any we have ever observed in mankind. Here then the existence of a DEITY is plainly ascertained by reason; and if we make it a question, whether, on account of these analogies, we can properly call him a *mind* or *intelligence*, notwithstanding the vast difference, which may reasonably be supposed between him and human minds; what is this but a mere verbal controversy? No man can deny the analogies between the effects: To restrain ourselves from enquiring concerning the causes is scarcely possible: From this enquiry, the legitimate conclusion is, that the causes have also an analogy: And if we are not contented with calling the first and supreme cause a GOD or DEITY, but desire to vary the expression; what can we call him but MIND or THOUGHT, to which he is justly supposed to bear a considerable resemblance?

[[[1]All men of sound reason are disgusted with verbal disputes, which abound so much in philosophical and theological enquiries; and it is found, that the only remedy for this abuse must arise from clear definitions, from the precision of those ideas which enter into any argument, and from the strict and uniform use of those terms which are employed. But there is a species of controversy, which, from the very nature of language and of human ideas, is involved in perpetual ambiguity, and can never, by any precaution or any definitions, be able to reach a reasonable certainty or precision. These are the controversies concerning the degrees of any quality or circumstance. Men may argue to all eternity, whether Hannibal be a great, or a very great, or a superlatively great man, what degree of beauty Cleopatra possessed, what epithet of praise Livy or Thucydides is entitled to, without bringing the controversy to any determination. The disputants may here agree in their sense

[1] [This paragraph in double brackets is written on the concluding sheet of the manuscript, with marks to indicate point of insertion. The double bracket is here used to mark this addition as having been made in the final revision, in 1776.]

and differ in the terms, or *vice versa*; yet never be able to define their terms, so as to enter into each other's meaning: Because the degrees of these qualities are not, like quantity or number, susceptible of any exact mensuration, which may be the standard in the controversy. That the dispute concerning theism is of this nature, and consequently is merely verbal, or perhaps, if possible, still more incurably ambiguous, will appear upon the slightest enquiry. I ask the theist, if he does not allow, that there is a great and immeasurable, because incomprehensible, difference between the *human* and the *divine* mind: The more pious he is, the more readily will he assent to the affirmative, and the more will he be disposed to magnify the difference: He will even assert, that the difference is of a nature which cannot be too much magnified. I next turn to the atheist, who, I assert, is only nominally so, and can never possibly be in earnest; and I ask him, whether, from the coherence and apparent sympathy in all the parts of this world, there be not a certain degree of analogy among all the operations of nature, in every situation and in every age; whether the rotting of a turnip, the generation of an animal, and the structure of human thought be not energies that probably bear some remote analogy to each other: It is impossible he can deny it: He will readily acknowledge it. Having obtained this concession, I push him still farther in his retreat; and I ask him, if it be not probable, that the principle which first arranged, and still maintains, order in this universe, bears not also some remote inconceivable analogy to the other operations of nature, and among the rest to the œconomy of human mind and thought. However reluctant, he must give his assent. Where then, cry I to both these antagonists, is the subject of your dispute? The theist allows, that the original intelligence is very different from human reason: The atheist allows, that the original principle of order bears some remote analogy to it. Will you quarrel, Gentlemen, about the degrees, and enter into a controversy, which admits not of any precise meaning, nor consequently of any determination? If you should be so obstinate, I should not be surprised to find you insensibly change sides; while the theist on the one hand exaggerates the dissimilarity between the supreme Being, and frail, imperfect, variable, fleeting, and mortal creatures; and the atheist on the other magnifies the analogy among all the operations of nature, in every period, every situation, and every position. Consider then, where the real point of controversy lies, and if you cannot lay aside your disputes, endeavour, at least, to cure yourselves of your animosity.]]

And here I must also acknowledge, CLEANTHES, that, as the works of nature have a much greater analogy to the effects of *our* art and contrivance, than to those of *our* benevolence and justice; we have reason to infer that the natural attributes of the Deity have a greater resemblance to those of man, than his moral have to human virtues. But what is the consequence? Nothing but this, that the moral qualities of man are more defective in their kind than his natural abilities. For, as the supreme Being is allowed to be absolutely and entirely perfect, whatever differs most from him departs the farthest from the supreme standard of rectitude and perfection.[1]

These, CLEANTHES, are my unfeigned sentiments on this subject; and these sentiments, you know, I have ever cherished and maintained. But in proportion to my veneration for true religion, is my abhorrence of vulgar superstitions; and I indulge a peculiar pleasure, I confess, in pushing such principles, sometimes into absurdity, sometimes into impiety. And you are sensible, that all bigots, notwithstanding their great aversion to the latter above the former, are commonly equally guilty of both.

My inclination, replied CLEANTHES, lies, I own, a contrary way. Religion, however corrupted, is still better than no religion at all. The doctrine of[2] a future state is so strong and necessary a security to morals, that we never ought to abandon or neglect it. For if finite and temporary rewards and punishments have so great an effect, as

---

[1] [It seems evident, that the dispute between the sceptics and dogmatists is entirely verbal, or at least regards only the degrees of doubt and assurance, which we ought to indulge with regard to all reasoning: And such disputes are commonly, at the bottom, verbal, and admit not of any precise determination. No philosophical dogmatist denies, that there are difficulties both with regard to the senses and to all science; and that these difficulties are in a regular, logical method, absolutely insolveable. No sceptic denies, that we lie under an absolute necessity, notwithstanding these difficulties, of thinking, and believing, and reasoning with regard to all kind of subjects, and even of frequently assenting with confidence and security. The only difference, then, between these sects, if they merit that name, is, that the sceptic, from habit, caprice, or inclination, insists most on the difficulties; the dogmatist, for like reasons, on the necessity.][a]

[a] [The above note, written on the concluding page of the original Part XII, below the word 'Finis', with marks to indicate point of insertion, has been scored out, and rewritten on the concluding sheet of the manuscript.*]

[2] [The doctrine of *added*.]

we daily find: How much greater must be expected from such as are infinite and eternal?*

How happens it then, said PHILO, if vulgar superstition[1]* be so salutary to society, that all history abounds so much with accounts of its pernicious consequences on public affairs? Factions, civil wars, persecutions, subversions of government, oppression, slavery; these are the dismal consequences which always attend its prevalency over the minds of men. If the religious spirit be ever mentioned in any historical narration, we are sure to meet afterwards with a detail of the miseries which attend it. And no period of time can be happier or more prosperous, than those in which it is never regarded, or heard of.

〔The reason of this observation, replied CLEANTHES, is obvious. The proper office of religion* is to regulate the heart of men, humanize their conduct, infuse the spirit of temperance, order, and obedience; and as its operation is silent, and only enforces the motives of morality and justice, it is in danger of being overlooked, and confounded with these other motives. When it distinguishes itself, and acts as a separate principle over men, it has departed from its proper sphere, and has become only a cover to faction and ambition.〕

And so will all religion, said PHILO, except the philosophical and rational kind. Your reasonings are more easily eluded than my facts. The inference is not just, because finite and temporary rewards and punishments have so great influence, that therefore such as are infinite and eternal must have so much greater.[2] Consider, I beseech you, the attachment, which we have to present things, and the little concern which we discover for objects so remote and uncertain. When divines are declaiming against the common behaviour and conduct of the world, they always represent this prin-

---

[1] [superstition *for* religion.]

[2] [*In the manuscript the following passage is scored out:* If indeed we consider the matter merely in an abstract light: If we compare only the importance of the motives, and then reflect on the natural self-love of mankind; we shall not only look for a great effect from religious considerations; but we must really esteem them absolutely irresistible and infallible in their operation. For what other motive can reasonably counterbalance them even for a moment? But this is not found to hold in reality; and therefore, we may be certain that there is some other principle of human nature, which we have here overlooked, and which diminishes, at least, the force of these motives. This principle is the attachment, which we have, &c.]

ciple as the strongest imaginable (which indeed it is) and describe almost all human kind as lying under the influence of it, and sunk into the deepest lethargy and unconcern about their religious interests. Yet these same divines, when they refute their speculative antagonists, suppose the motives of religion to be so powerful, that, without them, it were impossible for civil society to subsist; nor are they ashamed of so palpable a contradiction. It is certain, from experience, that the smallest grain of natural honesty and benevolence has more effect on men's conduct, than the most pompous views suggested by theological theories and systems. A man's natural inclination works incessantly upon him; it is for ever present to the mind; and mingles itself with every view and consideration: Whereas religious motives, where they act at all, operate only by starts and bounds; and it is scarcely possible for them to become altogether habitual to the mind. The force of the greatest gravity, say the philosophers, is infinitely small, in comparison of that of the least impulse; yet it is certain that the smallest gravity will, in the end, prevail above a great impulse; because no strokes or blows can be repeated with such constancy as attraction and gravitation.

Another advantage of inclination: It engages on its side all the wit and ingenuity of the mind; and when set in opposition to religious principles, seeks every method and art of eluding them: In which it is almost always successful. Who can explain the heart of man, or account for those strange salvos and excuses, with which people satisfy themselves, when they follow their inclinations, in opposition to their religious duty? This is well understood in the world; and none but fools ever repose less trust in a man, because they hear, that, from study and philosophy, he has entertained some speculative doubts with regard to theological subjects. And when we have to do with a man, who makes a great profession of religion and devotion; has this any other effect upon several, who[1] pass for prudent, than to put them on their guard, lest they be cheated and deceived by him?

We must farther consider, that philosophers, who cultivate reason and reflection, stand less in need of such motives to keep them under the restraint of morals: And that the vulgar, who alone

---

[1] [greatly *added, and then scored out.*]

may need them, are utterly incapable of so pure a religion as represents the Deity to be pleased with nothing but virtue in human behaviour. The recommendations to the Divinity are generally supposed to be either frivolous observances, or rapturous ecstasies, or a bigoted credulity. [1]We need not run back into antiquity, or wander into remote regions, to find instances of this degeneracy. Amongst ourselves, some have been guilty of that atrociousness, unknown to the EGYPTIAN and GRECIAN superstitions, of declaiming, in express terms, against morality, and representing it as a sure forfeiture of the divine favour, if the least trust or reliance be laid upon it.

But even though superstition or enthusiasm* should not put itself in direct opposition to morality; the very diverting of the attention, the raising up a new and frivolous species of merit,* the preposterous distribution which it makes of praise and blame, must have the most pernicious consequences, and weaken extremely men's attachment to the natural motives of justice and humanity.

Such a principle of action likewise, not being any of the[2] familiar motives of human conduct, acts only by intervals on the temper, and must be roused by continual efforts, in order to render the pious zealot satisfied with his own conduct, and make him fulfil his devotional task. Many religious exercises are entered into with seeming fervour, where the heart, at the time, feels cold and languid: A habit of dissimulation is by degrees contracted: And fraud and falsehood become the predominant principle. Hence the reason of that vulgar observation,[3] that the highest zeal in religion and the deepest hypocrisy, so far from being inconsistent, are often or commonly united in the same individual character.

The bad effects of such habits, even in common life, are easily imagined: But where the interests of religion are concerned, no morality can be forcible enough to bind the enthusiastic zealot. The sacredness of the cause sanctifies every measure which can be made use of to promote it.

The steady attention alone to so important an interest as that of eternal salvation is apt to extinguish the benevolent affections, and

---

[1] ['We need . . .' *to end of paragraph scored out, and instruction added on the margin,* 'Print this passage'.]

[2] [natural or *omitted.*]

[3] [vulgar observation *for* common phenomenon.]

beget a narrow, contracted selfishness. And when such a temper is encouraged, it easily eludes all the general precepts of charity and benevolence.

Thus the motives of vulgar superstition have no great[1] influence on general conduct; nor is their operation very favourable to morality, in the instances where they predominate.

Is there any maxim in politics more certain and infallible, than that both the number and authority of priests should be confined within very narrow limits, and that the civil magistrate ought, for ever, to keep his *fasces* and *axes** from such dangerous hands? But if the spirit of popular religion were so salutary to society, a contrary maxim ought to prevail. The greater number of priests, and their greater authority and riches, will always augment the religious spirit. And though the priests have the guidance of this spirit, why may we not expect a superior sanctity of life, and greater benevolence and moderation, from persons who are set apart for religion, who are continually inculcating it upon others, and who must themselves imbibe a greater share of it? Whence comes it then, that, in fact, the utmost a wise magistrate can propose with regard to popular religions, is, as far as possible, to make a saving game of it, and to prevent their pernicious consequences with regard to society? Every expedient which he tries for so humble a purpose is surrounded with inconveniences. If he admits only one religion among his subjects, he must sacrifice, to an uncertain prospect of tranquillity, every consideration of public liberty, science, reason, industry, and even his own independency. If he gives indulgence to several sects, which is the wiser maxim, he must preserve a very philosophical indifference to all of them, and carefully restrain the pretensions of the prevailing sect; otherwise he can expect nothing but endless disputes, quarrels, factions, persecutions, and civil commotions.

True religion, I allow, has no such pernicious consequences: But we must treat of religion, as it has commonly[2] been found in the world;* nor have I any thing to do with that speculative tenet of[3] theism, which, as it is a species of philosophy, must partake of the beneficial influence of that principle,[4] and at the same time must lie

---

[1] [no great *for* little.] [2] [commonly *for* always.]
[3] [refined *omitted*.] [4] [of that principle *added*.]

under a like inconvenience, of being always confined to very few persons.[1]

Oaths are requisite in all courts of judicature; but it is a question whether their authority arises from any popular religion. It is the solemnity and importance of the occasion, the regard to reputation, and the reflecting on the general interests of society, which are the chief restraints upon mankind. Custom-house oaths and political oaths are but little regarded even by some who pretend to principles of honesty and religion: And a Quaker's asseveration is with us justly put upon the same footing with the oath of any other person. I know, that POLYBIUS[2] ascribes the infamy of GREEK faith to the prevalency of the EPICUREAN philosophy; but I know also, that PUNIC faith had as bad a reputation in ancient times, as IRISH evidence has in modern; though we cannot account for these vulgar observations by the same reason. Not to mention, that GREEK faith was infamous before the rise of the EPICUREAN philosophy; and EURIPIDES,[3] in a passage which I shall point out to you, has glanced a remarkable stroke of satire against his nation, with regard to this circumstance.

Take care, PHILO, replied CLEANTHES, take care: Push not matters too far: Allow not your zeal against false religion to undermine your veneration for the true. Forfeit not this principle, the chief, the only great comfort in life; and our principal support amidst all the attacks of adverse fortune. The most agreeable reflection, which it is possible for human imagination to suggest, is that of genuine theism, which represents us as the workmanship of a Being perfectly good, wise, and powerful; who created us for happiness, and who, having implanted in us immeasurable desires of good, will prolong our existence to all eternity, and will transfer us into an infinite variety of scenes, in order to satisfy those desires, and render our felicity complete and durable. Next to such a Being himself (if the comparison be allowed) the happiest lot which

---

[1] [*Hume has added on margin, and then scored out:* Since government, reason, learning, friendship, love, and every human advantage are attended with inconveniences, as we daily find, what may be expected in all the various models of superstition; a quality, composed of whatever is the most absurd, corrupted, and barbarous of our nature? Were there any one exception to that universal mixture of good and ill, which is found in life, this might be pronounced thoroughly and entirely ill.]

[2] Lib. 6, cap. 54.   [3] *Iphigenia in Tauride.**

we can imagine, is that of being under his guardianship and protection.

These appearances, said PHILO, are most engaging and alluring; and with regard to the true philosopher, they are more than appearances. But it happens here, as in the former case, that, with regard to the greater part of mankind, the appearances are deceitful, and that the terrors of religion commonly prevail above its comforts.

It is allowed, that men never have recourse to devotion so readily as when dejected with grief or depressed with sickness. Is not this a proof, that the religious spirit is not so nearly allied to joy as to sorrow?

But men, when afflicted, find consolation in religion, replied CLEANTHES. Sometimes, said PHILO: But it is natural to imagine, that they will form a notion of those unknown Beings, suitably to the present gloom and melancholy of their temper, when they betake themselves to the contemplation of them. Accordingly, we find the tremendous images to predominate in all[1] religions; and we ourselves, after having employed the most exalted expression in our decriptions of the Deity, fall into the flattest contradiction, in affirming, that the damned are infinitely superior in number to the elect.

I shall venture to affirm, that there never was a popular religion, which represented the state of departed souls in such a light, as would render it eligible for human kind, that there should be such a state. These fine models of religion are the mere product of philosophy. For as death lies between the eye and the prospect of futurity, that event is so shocking to nature, that it must throw a gloom on all the regions which lie beyond it; and suggest to the generality of mankind the idea of CERBERUS and FURIES; devils, and torrents of fire and brimstone.

It is true; both fear and hope enter into religion; because both these passions, at different times, agitate the human mind, and each of them forms a species of divinity, suitable to itself. But when a man is in a cheerful disposition, he is fit for business or company or entertainment of any kind; and he naturally applies himself to these, and thinks not of religion When melancholy, and dejected,

---

[1] [all *for* most.]

he has nothing to do but brood upon the terrors of the invisible world, and to plunge himself still deeper in affliction. It may, indeed, happen, that after he has, in this manner, engraved the religious opinions deep into his thought and imagination, there may arrive a change of health or circumstances, which may restore his good humour, and raising cheerful prospects of futurity, make him run into the other extreme of joy and triumph. But still it must be acknowledged, that, as terror is the primary principle of religion, it is the passion which always predominates in it, and admits but of short intervals of pleasure.

Not to mention, that these fits of excessive, enthusiastic joy, by exhausting the spirits, always prepare the way for equal fits of superstitious terror and dejection; nor is there any state of mind so happy as the calm and equable. But this state it is impossible to support, where a man thinks, that he lies, in such profound darkness and uncertainty, between an eternity of happiness and an eternity of misery. No wonder, that such an opinion disjoints the ordinary frame of the mind, and throws it into the utmost confusion. And though that opinion is seldom so steady in its operation as to influence all the actions; yet it is apt to make a considerable breach in the temper, and to produce that gloom and melancholy, so remarkable in all devout people.*

It is contrary to common sense to entertain apprehensions or terrors, upon account of any opinion whatsoever, or to imagine that we run any risk hereafter, by the freest use of our reason. Such a sentiment implies both an *absurdity* and an *inconsistency*. It is an absurdity to believe that the Deity has human passions, and one of the lowest of human passions, a restless appetite for applause. It is an inconsistency to believe, that, since the Deity has this human passion, he has not others also; and, in particular, a disregard to the opinions of creatures so much inferior.

[¹*To know God*, says Seneca, *is to worship him.** All other worship is indeed absurd, superstitious, and even impious. It degrades him to the low condition of mankind, who are delighted with entreaty, solicitation, presents, and flattery. Yet is this impiety the smallest of which superstition is guilty. Commonly, it de-

---

¹ [This passage in brackets, an addition made in an early revision, is written on the margin, then scored out, and rewritten, together with the next paragraph, on the second last sheet of the manuscript.]

presses the Deity far below the condition of mankind; and represents him as a capricious Dæmon, who exercises his power without reason and without humanity! And were that divine Being disposed to be offended at the vices and follies of silly mortals, who are his own workmanship; ill would it surely fare with the votaries of most popular superstitions. Nor would any of human race merit his *favour*, but a very few, the philosophical theists, who entertain, or rather indeed endeavour to entertain, suitable notions of his divine perfections: As the only persons entitled to his *compassion* and *indulgence* would be the philosophical sceptics, a sect almost equally rare, who, from a natural diffidence of their own capacity, suspend, or endeavour to suspend all judgment with regard to such sublime and such extraordinary subjects.]

[[[1]If the whole of natural theology, as some people seem to maintain, resolves itself into one simple, though somewhat ambiguous, at least undefined proposition, *that the cause or causes of order in the universe probably bear some remote analogy to human intelligence:* If this proposition be not capable of extension, variation, or more particular explication: If it afford no inference that affects human life, or can be the source of any action[2] or forbearance: And if the analogy, imperfect as it is, can be carried no farther than to the human intelligence; and cannot be transferred,[3] with any appearance of probability, to the other qualities of the mind: If this really be the case, what can the most inquisitive, contemplative, and religious man do more than give a plain, philosophical assent to the proposition, as often as it occurs; and believe that the arguments, on which it is established, exceed the objections which lie against it? Some astonishment indeed will naturally arise from the greatness of the object: Some melancholy from its obscurity: Some contempt of human reason, that it can give no solution more satisfactory with regard to so extraordinary and magnificent a question. But believe me, CLEANTHES, the most natural sentiment, which a well-disposed mind will feel on this occasion, is a longing desire and expectation, that Heaven would .

---

[1] [This paragraph, in double brackets, written on the second last sheet of the manuscript, after the above paragraph, is an addition made in the final revision, in 1776.]

[2] [steady sentiment *omitted*.]

[3] [transferred *for* extended.]

be pleased to dissipate, at least alleviate, this profound ignorance, by affording some more particular revelation to mankind, and making discoveries of the nature, attributes, and operations of the divine object of our Faith. A person, seasoned with a just sense of the imperfections of natural reason, will fly to revealed truth with the greatest avidity: While the haughty dogmatist, persuaded that he can erect a complete system of theology by the mere help of philosoply, disdains any farther aid, and rejects this adventitious instructor. To be a philosophical sceptic is, in a man of letters, the first and most essential step towards being a sound, believing Christian; a proposition which I would willingly recommend to the attention of PAMPHILUS: And I hope CLEANTHES will forgive me for interposing so far in the education and instruction of his pupil.]]

CLEANTHES and PHILO pursued not this conversation much farther; and as nothing ever made greater impression on me, than all the reasonings of that day; so I confess, that, upon a serious review of the whole, I cannot but think, that PHILO's principles are more probable than DEMEA's; but that those of CLEANTHES approach still nearer to the truth.*

FINIS

AN ABSTRACT OF THE DIALOGUES

Pamphilus to Hermippus: reasons for the dialogue form—the question at issue is the nature of the divine being—the three speakers briefly introduced: the 'accurate philosophical turn' of Cleanthes, the 'careless scepticism' of Philo, the 'rigorous othodoxy' of Demea.

Part I.   Religion based upon the 'science of natural theology' distinguished from religion as piety—excessive or Pyrrhonian scepticism about common life (which Cleanthes tries to attribute to Philo) contrasted with mitigated scepticism about abstruse philosophical conclusions (which Philo attributes to himself). Ordinary philosophy is and ought to be close to common life; abstruse philosophy is close to religion—the methods of natural science and natural theology compared. Religion looks for support wherever it can be found.

Part II.   Demea and Philo confirm that the question concerns the nature, not the being, of a deity—'proof *a priori*' establishes the being, 'argument *a posteriori*' (the design argument) establishes the nature and being of God but, by comparison with proof *a priori*, only as probable. First statement of the design argument by Cleanthes followed by restatement and criticisms by Philo: it is a weak analogical argument; it fails to satisfy the requirement of causal inferences that 'species of objects' be conjoined.

Part III.   The 'articulate voice heard in the clouds' and the 'vegetable library' suppositions lead Cleanthes to a statement of the 'informal' design argument which would be immune to mitigated scepticism. Demea contributes some observations about the difference between the materials and the manner of divine and human thinking. Plotinus and mystics give an alternative view of religion to that of Cleanthes.

Part IV.   The relation between mysticism, anthropomorphism, the ineffability of God, and atheism. If a mental world is required as a cause for the material world, why does that mental world not itself require a cause, and thus lead to an infinite regress of causes? The alternative is to rest content with the self-ordering of the physical world and never start the infinite regress of explanatory causes.

Part V.   The problem of anthropomorphism continued—ambiguities and limitations inherent in the design argument (e.g. a polytheistic outcome).

Part VI.   Whether the world is like the body of an animal directed by a mind—whether mind and matter are distinct—whether the world is young, ancient, or eternal—the nature of order.

Part VII.   Discussion (mainly by Philo) whether some principle (e.g. animal or vegetable generation) other than reason or intelligent purposes could account for the world as it is and the order which it has.

Part VIII.   Investigation of a new hypothesis of cosmogony, namely that the universe could be as it is through a process of natural selection operating within a large but finite physical universe: the natural selection being the persistence of forms (things) and processes (repeating chains of events) which once hit on by chance are well adapted to endure. But nature is more generous, more orderly and more well adapted than this would lead us to expect. So: 'A total suspense of judgment is here our only reasonable resource.'

Part IX.   Examination of 'the argument *a priori*' for the necessary existence of a deity. The argument is stated by Demea in a version drawn from Dr Samuel Clarke. It is decisively rejected by Cleanthes who mainly appeals to arguments and distinctions of the sort already set out in Hume's general philosophical works.

Part X.   Discussion of the problem of evil. The speakers agree about the prevalence of misery. Philo sharpens this into the particular question—if God is both able and willing to prevent evil, why is there so much, or indeed why is there *any* evil in the world?—a solution is offered and dismissed. Even if pain and misery can be shown to be compatible with the goodness and power of God, their real existence in the world destroys the design argument's inference from the world to a God having moral qualities and infinite, or even very great, power.

Part XI.   Continuation of the discussion of evil as a problem for inferring God from the world. Four sources of evil examined; but at best these may establish the compatibility of evil with God, not the inference *from* a world containing evil *to* a God of unmixed goodness. The true inference (suggests Philo) is to a disinterested, amoral, origin of the universe. Demea departs.

Part XII. Philo confesses that the existence of a deity is 'plainly ascertained by reason' in the design everywhere apparent in nature. He then begins to show how little this apparent concession amounts to—discussion of the relation between religion and morality, and of the difference between true and corrupt religion—Philo concludes with further statements of the very limited conclusion 'ascertained by reason'.

THE NATURAL HISTORY
OF RELIGION

INTRODUCTION

As every enquiry, which regards religion, is of the utmost importance, there are two questions in particular, which challenge our
attention, to wit, that concerning its foundation in reason, and that
concerning its origin in human nature. Happily, the first question,
which is the most important, admits of the most obvious, at least,
the clearest solution. The whole frame of nature bespeaks an intelligent author; and no rational enquirer can, after serious reflection,
suspend his belief a moment with regard to the primary principles
of genuine Theism and Religion. But the other question, concerning the origin of religion in human nature, is exposed to some more
difficulty. The belief of invisible, intelligent power has been very
generally diffused over the human race, in all places and in all
ages;* but it has neither perhaps been so universal as to admit of no
exception, nor has it been, in any degree, uniform in the ideas,
which it has suggested. Some nations have been discovered, who
entertained no sentiments of Religion, if travellers and historians
may be credited; and no two nations, and scarce any two men, have
ever agreed precisely in the same sentiments. It would appear,
therefore, that this preconception springs not from an original
instinct or primary impression of nature, such as gives rise to self-
love, affection between the sexes, love of progeny, gratitude, resentment; since every instinct of this kind has been found absolutely universal in all nations and ages, and has always a precise
determinate object, which it inflexibly pursues. The first religious
principles must be secondary; such as may easily be perverted by
various accidents and causes, and whose operation too, in some
cases, may, by an extraordinary concurrence of circumstances,
be altogether prevented. What those principles are, which give
rise to the original belief, and what those accidents and causes
are, which direct its operation, is the subject of our present
enquiry.

I THAT POLYTHEISM WAS THE PRIMARY RELIGION OF MEN

It appears to me, that, if we consider the improvement of human society, from rude beginnings to a state of greater perfection, polytheism or idolatry was, and necessarily must have been, the first and most ancient religion of mankind. This opinion I shall endeavour to confirm by the following arguments.

It is a matter of fact incontestable, that about 1700 years ago all mankind were polytheists. The doubtful and sceptical principles of a few philosophers, or the theism, and that too not entirely pure, of one or two nations, form no objection worth regarding. Behold then the clear testimony of history. The farther we mount up into antiquity, the more do we find mankind plunged into polytheism. No marks, no symptoms of any more perfect religion. The most ancient records of human race still present us with that system as the popular and established creed. The north, the south, the east, the west, give their unanimous testimony to the same fact. What can be oppposed to so full an evidence?

As far as writing or history reaches, mankind, in ancient times, appear universally to have been polytheists. Shall we assert, that, in more ancient times, before the knowledge of letters, or the discovery of any art or science, men entertained the principles of pure theism? That is, while they were ignorant and barbarous, they discovered truth: But fell into error, as soon as they acquired learning and politeness.

But in this assertion you not only contradict all appearance of probability, but also our present experience concerning the principles and opinions of barbarous nations. The savage tribes of AMERICA, AFRICA, and ASIA are all idolaters. Not a single exception to this rule. Insomuch, that, were a traveller to transport himself into any unknown region; if he found inhabitants cultivated with arts and science, though even upon that supposition there are odds against their being theists, yet could he not safely, till farther inquiry, pronounce any thing on that head: But if he found them ignorant and barbarous, he might beforehand declare them idolaters; and there scarcely is a possibility of his being mistaken.

It seems certain, that, according to the natural progress of human thought, the ignorant multitude must first entertain some groveling and familiar notion of superior powers, before they stretch their

conception to that perfect Being, who bestowed order on the whole
frame of nature.* We may as reasonably imagine, that men inhabited palaces before huts and cottages, or studied geometry before
agriculture; as assert that the Deity appeared to them a pure spirit,
omniscient, omnipotent, and omnipresent, before he was apprehended to be a powerful, though limited being, with human passions and appetites, limbs and organs. The mind rises gradually,
from inferior to superior: By abstracting from what is imperfect, it
forms an idea of perfection: And slowly distinguishing the nobler
parts of its own frame from the grosser, it learns to transfer only the
former, much elevated and refined, to its divinity. Nothing could
disturb this natural progress of thought, but some obvious and
invincible argument, which might immediately lead the mind into
the pure principles of theism, and make it overleap, at one bound,
the vast interval which is interposed between the human and the
divine nature. But though I allow, that the order and frame of the
universe, when accurately examined, affords such an argument;
yet I can never think, that this consideration could have an influence on mankind, when they formed their first rude notions of
religion.

The causes of such objects, as are quite familiar to us, never
strike our attention or curiosity; and however extraordinary or
surprising these objects in themselves, they are passed over, by the
raw and ignorant multitude, without much examination or enquiry.
ADAM, rising at once, in paradise, and in the full perfection of his
faculties, would naturally, as represented by MILTON,* be astonished at the glorious appearances of nature, the heavens, the air, the
earth, his own organs and members; and would be led to ask,
whence this wonderful scene arose. But a barbarous, necessitous
animal (such as a man is on the first origin of society), pressed by
such numerous wants and passions, has no leisure to admire the
regular face of nature, or make enquiries concerning the cause of
those objects, to which from his infancy he has been gradually
accustomed. On the contrary, the more regular and uniform, that is,
the more perfect nature appears, the more is he familiarized to it,
and the less inclined to scrutinize and examine it. A monstrous
birth excites his curiosity, and is deemed a prodigy. It alarms him
from its novelty; and immediately sets him a trembling, and
sacrificing, and praying. But an animal, compleat in all its limbs

and organs, is to him an ordinary spectacle, and produces no religious opinion or affection. Ask him, whence that animal arose; he will tell you, from the copulation of its parents. And these, whence? From the copulation of theirs. A few removes satisfy his curiosity, and set the objects at such a distance, that he entirely loses sight of them. Imagine not, that he will so much as start the question, whence the first animal; much less, whence the whole system, or united fabric of the universe arose. Or, if you start such a question to him, expect not, that he will employ his mind with any anxiety about a subject, so remote, so uninteresting, and which so much exceeds the bounds of his capacity.

But farther, if men were at first led into the belief of one Supreme Being, by reasoning from the frame of nature, they could never possibly leave that belief, in order to embrace polytheism; but the same principles of reason, which at first produced and diffused over mankind, so magnificent an opinion, must be able, with greater facility, to preserve it. The first invention and proof of any doctrine is much more difficult than the supporting and retaining of it.

There is a great difference between historical facts and speculative opinions; nor is the knowledge of the one propagated in the same manner with that of the other. An historical fact, while it passes by oral tradition from eyewitnesses and contemporaries, is disguised in every successive narration, and may at last retain but very small, if any, resemblance of the original truth, on which it was founded. The frail memories of men, their love of exaggeration, their supine carelessness; these principles, if not corrected by books and writing, soon pervert the account of historical events; where argument or reasoning has little or no place, nor can ever recal the truth, which has once escaped those narrations. It is thus the fables of HERCULES, THESEUS, BACCHUS are supposed to have been originally founded in true history, corrupted by tradition. But with regard to speculative opinions, the case is far otherwise. If these opinions be founded on arguments so clear and obvious as to carry conviction with the generality of mankind, the same arguments, which at first diffused the opinions, will still preserve them in their original purity. If the arguments be more abstruse, and more remote from vulgar apprehension, the opinions will always be confined to a few persons; and as soon as men leave the contemplation of the arguments, the opinions will immediately be lost and be buried in oblivion. Whichever side of this dilemma we take, it must appear impossible, that theism could, from reasoning, have been the primary religion of human race, and have afterwards, by its corruption, given birth to polytheism and to all the various superstitions of the heathen world. Reason, when obvious, prevents these corruptions: When abstruse, it keeps the principles entirely from the knowledge of the vulgar, who are alone liable to corrupt any principle or opinion.

II   ORIGIN OF POLYTHEISM

If we would, therefore, indulge our curiosity, in enquiring concerning the origin of religion, we must turn our thoughts towards polytheism, the primitive religion of uninstructed mankind.

Were men led into the apprehension of invisible, intelligent power by a contemplation of the works of nature, they could never possibly entertain any conception but of one single being, who bestowed existence and order on this vast machine, and adjusted all its parts, according to one regular plan or connected system. For though, to persons of a certain turn of mind, it may not appear altogether absurd, that several independent beings, endowed with superior wisdom, might conspire in the contrivance and execution of one regular plan; yet is this a merely arbitrary supposition, which, even if allowed possible, must be confessed neither to be supported by probability nor necessity. All things in the universe are evidently of a piece. Every thing is adjusted to every thing. One design prevails throughout the whole.* And this uniformity leads the mind to acknowledge one author; because the conception of different authors, without any distinction of attributes or operations, serves only to give perplexity to the imagination, without bestowing any satisfaction on the understanding. The statue of LAOCOON, as we learn from PLINY, was the work of three artists: But it is certain, that, were we not told so, we should never have imagined, that a groupe of figures, cut from one stone, and united in one plan, was not the work and contrivance of one statuary. To ascribe any single effect to the combination of several causes, is not surely a natural and obvious supposition.

On the other hand, if, leaving the works of nature, we trace the footsteps of invisible power in the various and contrary events of human life, we are necessarily led into polytheism and to the acknowledgment of several limited and imperfect deities. Storms and tempests ruin what is nourished by the sun. The sun destroys what is fostered by the moisture of dews and rains. War may be favourable to a nation, whom the inclemency of the seasons afflicts with famine. Sickness and pestilence may depopulate a kingdom, amidst the most profuse plenty. The same nation is not, at the same time, equally successful by sea and by land. And a nation, which now triumphs over its enemies, may anon submit to their more prosperous arms. In short, the conduct of events, or what we call the plan of a particular providence, is so full of variety and uncertainty, that, if we suppose it immediately ordered by any intelligent beings, we must acknowledge a contrariety in their designs and intentions, a constant combat of opposite powers, and a repentance or change of intention in the same power, from impotence or levity. Each nation has its tutelar deity. Each element is subjected to its invisible power or agent. The province of each god is separate from that of another. Nor are the operations of the same god always certain and invariable. To-day he protects: To-morrow he abandons us. Prayers and sacrifices, rites and ceremonies, well or ill performed, are the sources of his favour or enmity, and produce all the good or ill fortune, which are to be found amongst mankind.

We may conclude, therefore, that, in all nations, which have embraced polytheism, the first ideas of religion arose not from a contemplation of the works of nature, but from a concern with regard to the events of life, and from the incessant hopes and fears, which actuate the human mind. Accordingly, we find, that all idolaters, having separated the provinces of their deities, have recourse to that invisible agent, to whose authority they are immediately subjected, and whose province it is to superintend that course of actions, in which they are, at any time, engaged. JUNO is invoked at marriages; LUCINA at births. NEPTUNE receives the prayers of seamen; and MARS of warriors. The husbandman cultivates his field under the protection of CERES; and the merchant acknowledges the authority of MERCURY. Each natural event is supposed to be governed by some intelligent agent; and nothing prosperous or adverse can happen in life, which may not be the subject of peculiar prayers or thanksgivings.[1]

It must necessarily, indeed, be allowed, that, in order to carry men's intention beyond the present course of things, or lead them into any inference concerning invisible intelligent power, they must be actuated by some passion, which prompts their thought and reflection; some motive, which urges their first enquiry. But what passion shall we here have recourse to, for explaining an effect of such mighty consequences? Not speculative curiosity, surely, or the pure love of truth. That motive is too refined for such gross apprehensions; and would lead men into enquiries concerning the frame of nature, a subject too large and comprehensive for their narrow capacities. No passions, therefore, can be supposed to work upon such barbarians, but the ordinary affections of human life; the anxious concern for happiness, the dread of future misery, the terror of death, the thirst of revenge, the appetite for food and other necessaries. Agitated by hopes and fears of this nature, especially the latter, men scrutinize, with a trembling curiosity, the course of future causes, and examine the various and contrary events of human life. And in this disordered scene, with eyes still more disordered and astonished, they see the first obscure traces of divinity.

III   THE SAME SUBJECT CONTINUED

We are placed in this world, as in a great theatre, where the true springs and causes of every event are entirely concealed from us; nor have we either sufficient wisdom to foresee, or power to prevent those ills, with which we are continually threatened. We hang in perpetual suspence between life and death, health and sickness, plenty and want; which are distributed amongst the human species by secret and unknown causes, whose operation is oft unexpected, and always unaccountable. These *unknown causes*, then, become the constant object of our hope and fear; and while the passions are kept in perpetual alarm by an anxious expectation of the events, the imagination is equally employed in forming ideas of those powers, on which we have so entire a dependance. Could

[1] [See Hume's Note A, p. 186.]

men anatomize nature, according to the most probable, at least the most intelligible philosophy, they would find, that these causes are nothing but the particular fabric and structure of the minute parts of their own bodies and of external objects; and that, by a regular and constant machinery, all the events are produced, about which they are so much concerned. But this philosophy exceeds the comprehension of the ignorant multitude, who can only conceive the *unknown causes* in a general and confused manner; though their imagination, perpetually employed on the same subject, must labour to form some particular and distinct idea of them. The more they consider these causes themselves, and the uncertainty of their operation, the less satisfaction do they meet with in their researches; and, however unwilling, they must at last have abandoned so arduous an attempt, were it not for a propensity in human nature, which leads into a system, that gives them some satisfaction.

There is an universal tendency among mankind to conceive all beings like themselves, and to transfer to every object, those qualities, with which they are familiarly acquainted, and of which they are intimately conscious. We find human faces in the moon, armies in the clouds;* and by a natural propensity, if not corrected by experience and reflection, ascribe malice or good-will to every thing, that hurts or pleases us. Hence the frequency and beauty of the *prosopopœia* in poetry; where trees, mountains and streams are personified, and the inanimate parts of nature acquire sentiment and passion. And though these poetical figures and expressions gain not on the belief, they may serve, at least, to prove a certain tendency in the imagination, without which they could neither be beautiful nor natural. Nor is a river-god or hamadryad always taken for a mere poetical or imaginary personage; but may sometimes enter into the real creed of the ignorant vulgar; while each grove or field is represented as possessed of a particular *genius* or invisible power, which inhabits and protects it. Nay, philosophers cannot entirely exempt themselves from this natural frailty; but have oft ascribed it to inanimate matter the horror of a *vacuum*, sympathies, antipathies, and other affections of human nature. The absurdity is not less, while we cast our eyes upwards; and transferring, as is too usual, human passions and infirmities to the deity, represent him as jealous and revengeful, capricious and partial, and, in short, a wicked and foolish man, in every respect but his superior power and authority. No wonder, then, that mankind, being placed in such an absolute ignorance of causes, and being at the same time so anxious concerning their future fortune, should immediately acknowledge a dependence on invisible powers, possessed of sentiment and intelligence. The *unknown causes* which continually employ their thought, appearing always in the same aspect, are all apprehended to be of the same kind or species. Nor is it long before we ascribe to them thought and reason and passion, and sometimes even the limbs and figures of men, in order to bring them nearer to a resemblance with ourselves.

In proportion as any man's course of life is governed by accident, we always find, that he encreases in superstition; as may particularly be observed of gamesters and sailors, who, though, of all mankind, the least capable of serious reflection, abound most in frivolous and superstitious apprehensions. The gods, says CORIOLANUS in DIONYSIUS,[1] have an influence in every affair; but above all, in war; where the event is so uncertain. All human life, especially before the institution of order and good government, being subject to fortuitous accidents; it is natural, that superstition should prevail every where in barbarous ages, and put men on the most earnest enquiry concerning those invisible powers, who dispose of their happiness or misery. Ignorant of astronomy and the anatomy of plants and animals, and too little curious to observe the admirable adjustment of final causes; they remain still unacquainted with a first and supreme creator, and with that infinitely perfect spirit, who alone, by his almighty will, bestowed order on the whole frame of nature. Such a magnificent idea is too big for their narrow conceptions, which can neither observe the beauty of the work, nor comprehend the grandeur of its author. They suppose their deities, however potent and invisible, to be nothing but a species of human creatures, perhaps raised from among mankind, and retaining all human passions and appetites, together with corporeal limbs and organs. Such limited beings, though masters of human fate, being, each of them, incapable of extending his influence every where, must be vastly multiplied, in order to answer

all we know

---

[1] Dionysius of Halicarnassus, *Roman Antiquities*, bk. VIII, ch. 2, para. 2 [Loeb, v. 7].

that variety of events, which happen over the whole face of nature. Thus every place is stored with a crowd of local deities; and thus polytheism has prevailed, and still prevails, among the greatest part of uninstructed mankind.[1]

Any of the human affections may lead us into the notion of invisible, intelligent power; hope as well as fear, gratitude as well as affliction: But if we examine our own hearts, or observe what passes around us, we shall find, that men are much oftener thrown on their knees by the melancholy than by the agreeable passions. Prosperity is easily received as our due, and few questions are asked concerning its cause or author. It begets cheerfulness and activity and alacrity and a lively enjoyment of every social and sensual pleasure: And during this state of mind, men have little leisure or inclination to think of the unknown invisible regions. On the other hand, every disastrous accident alarms us, and sets us on enquiries concerning the principles whence it arose: Apprehensions spring up with regard to futurity: And the mind, sunk into diffidence, terror, and melancholy, has recourse to every method of appeasing those secret intelligent powers, on whom our fortune is supposed entirely to depend.

No topic is more usual with all popular divines than to display the advantages of affliction, in bringing men to a due sense of religion; by subduing their confidence and sensuality, which, in times of prosperity, make them forgetful of a divine providence. Nor is this topic confined merely to modern religions. The ancients have also employed it. *Fortune has never liberally, without envy,* says a GREEK historian,[2] *bestowed an unmixed happiness on mankind; but with all her gifts has ever conjoined some disastrous*

---

[1] The following lines of EURIPIDES are so much to the present purpose, that I cannot forbear quoting them:

Οὐκ ἔστιν οὐδὲν πιστόν, οὔτ᾽ εὐδοξία,
Οὔτ᾽ αὖ καλῶς πράσσοντα μὴ πράξειν κακῶς.
φύρουσι δ᾽ αὖθ οἱ θεοὶ πάλιν τε καὶ πρόσω,
Ταραγμὸν ἐντιθέντες, ὡς ἀγνωσίᾳ
Σέβωμεν αὐτοώς.

Hecuba, 11. 956–960

'There is nothing secure in the world; no glory, no prosperity. The gods toss all life into confusion; mix every thing with its reverse; that all of us, from our ignorance and uncertainty, may pay them the more worship and reverence.'

[2] Diodorus Siculus, bk. III, ch. 47 [Loeb, ii. 321].

circumstance, <u>*in order to chastize men into a reverence for the*</u> ~~<u>*gods, whom, in a continued course of prosperity, they are apt to*</u>~~ <u>*neglect and forget.*</u>

What age or period of life is the most addicted to superstition? The weakest and most timid. What sex? The same answer must be given. *The leaders and examples of every kind of superstition,* says STRABO,[1] *are the women.* These excite the men to devotion and supplications, and the observance of religious days. It is rare to meet with one that lives apart from the females, and yet is addicted to such practices. And nothing can, for this reason, be more improbable, than the account given of an order of men among the* GETES, *who practised celibacy, and were notwithstanding the most religious fanatics.* A method of reasoning, which would lead us to entertain a bad idea of the devotion of monks; did we not know by an experience, not so common, perhaps, in STRABO's days, that one may practise celibacy, and profess chastity; and yet maintain the closest connexions and most entire sympathy with that timorous and pious sex.

IV   DEITIES NOT CONSIDERED· AS CREATORS OR FORMERS OF
THE WORLD

The only point of theology, in which we shall find a consent of mankind almost universal, is, <u>that there is invisible, intelligent power in the world</u>: But whether this power be supreme or sub~~ordinate, whether~~ confined to one being, or distributed among several, what attributes, qualities, connexions, or principles of action ought to be ascribed to those beings; concerning all these points, there is the widest difference in the popular systems of theology. Our ancestors in EUROPE, before the revival of letters, believed, as we do at present, that there was one supreme God, the author of nature, whose power, though in itself uncontroulable, was yet often exerted by the interposition of his angels and subordinate ministers, who executed his sacred purposes. But they also believed, that all nature was full of other invisible powers; fairies, goblins, elves, sprights; beings, stronger and mightier than men, but much inferior to the celestial natures, who surround the

---

[1] *Geography,* bk. VII, ch. 3 [Loeb, iii. 183].

throne of God. Now, suppose, that any one, in those ages, had denied the existence of God and of his angels; would not his impiety justly have deserved the appellation of atheism, even though he had still allowed, by some odd capricious reasoning, that the popular stories of elves and fairies were just and well-grounded? The difference, on the one hand, between such a person and a genuine theist is infinitely greater than that, on the other, between him and one that absolutely excludes all invisible intelligent power. And it is a fallacy, merely from the casual resemblance of names, without any conformity of meaning, to rank such opposite opinions under the same denomination.*

To any one, who considers justly of the matter, it will appear, that the gods of all polytheists are not better than the elves or fairies of our ancestors, and merit as little any pious worship or veneration. These pretended religionists are really a kind of superstitious atheists, and acknowledge no being, that corresponds to our idea of a deity. No first principle of mind or thought: No supreme government and administration: No divine contrivance or intention in the fabric of the world.

The Chinese,[1] when their prayers are not answered, beat their idols. The deities of the Laplanders are any large stone which they meet with of an extraordinary shape.[2] The Egyptian mythologists, in order to account for animal worship, said, that the gods, pursued by the violence of earthborn men, who were their enemies, had formerly been obliged to disguise themselves under the semblance of beasts.[3] The Caunii, a nation in the Lesser Asia, resolving to admit no strange gods among them, regularly, at certain seasons, assembled themselves compleatly armed, beat the air with their lances, and proceeded in that manner to their frontiers; in order, as they said, to expel the foreign deities.[4] *Not even the immortal gods*, said some German nations to Cæsar, *are a match for the* Suevi.[5]

Many ills, says Dione in Homer to Venus wounded by Diomede, many ills, my daughter, have the gods inflicted on men: And many

[1] Père le Comte, *Nouveaux Memoires sur l'état Present de la Chine.*

[2] Jean-François Regnard, *Voiage de Laponie.*

[3] Diodorus Siculus, bk. I, ch. 86 [Loeb, i. 293]. Lucian, *On Sacrifices*, para. 14 [Loeb iii. 169]. Ovid alludes to the same tradition, *Metamorphoses*, bk. V, ll. 321–31 [Loeb, i. 261]. So also Manilius, *Astronomica*, bk. IV, l. 800 [Loeb, 284–5].

[4] Herodotus, bk. I, ch. 172 [Loeb, i. 215].

[5] Caesar, *Gallic War*, bk. IV, para. 7 [Loeb, 189].

ills, in return, have men inflicted on the gods.[1] We need but open any classic author to meet with these gross representations of the deities; and LONGINUS[2] with reason observes, that such ideas of the divine nature, if literally taken, contain a true atheism.

Some writers[3] have been surprized, that the impieties of ARISTOPHANES should have been tolerated, nay publicly acted and applauded by the Athenians; a people so superstitious and so jealous of the public religion, that, at that very time, they put SOCRATES to death for his imagined incredulity. But these writers do not consider, that the ludicrous, familiar images, under which the gods are represented by that comic poet, instead of appearing impious, were the genuine lights in which the ancients conceived their divinities. What conduct can be more criminal or mean, than that of JUPITER in the AMPHITRION?* Yet that play, which represented his gallante exploits, was supposed so agreeable to him, that it was always acted in ROME by public authority, when the state was threatened with pestilence, famine, or any general calamity.[4] The ROMANS supposed, that, like all old letchers, he would be highly pleased with the recital of his former feats of prowess and vigour, and that no topic was so proper, upon which to flatter his vanity.

The LACEDEMONIANS, says XENOPHON,[5] always, during war, put up their petitions very early in the morning, in order to be beforehand with their enemies, and, by being the first solicitors, preengage the gods in their favour. We may gather from SENECA,[6] that it was usual, for the votaries in the temples, to make interest with the beadle or sexton, that they might have a seat near the image of the deity, in order to be the best heard in their prayers and applications to him. The TYRIANS, when beseiged by ALEXANDER, threw chains on the statue of HERCULES, to prevent that deity from deserting to the enemy.[7] AUGUSTUS, having twice lost his fleet by

[1] Homer, *Iliad*, bk. V, ll. 381–84.

[2] Longinus, *On the Sublime*, ch. 9, para. 7 [Loeb, 147].

[3] Pierre Brumoy, *Théâtre des Grecs*; and Fontenelle, *Histoire des Oracles*.

[4] Arnobius, *Seven Books against the Heathen*, bk. VII, ch. 33.

[5] Xenophon, Constitution of the Lacedaemonians, para. 13 [Loeb, *Scripta Minora*, 181].

[6] Seneca, *Moral Epistles*, XLI [Loeb, i. 273].

[7] Quintus Curtius, *History of Alexander*, bk. IV, ch. 3, paras. 21–22. [Loeb, i. 195]. Diodorus Siculus, bk. XVII, ch. 4, para. 8 [Loeb, viii. 235 f].

storms, forbad NEPTUNE to be carried in procession along with the other gods; and fancied, that he had sufficiently revenged himself by that expedient.[1] After GERMANICUS's death, the people were so enraged at their gods, that they stoned them in their temples; and openly renounced all allegiance to them.[2]

To ascribe the origin and fabric of the universe to these imperfect beings never enters into the imagination of any polytheist or idolater. HESIOD, whose writings, with those of HOMER, contained the canonical system of the heavens;[3] HESIOD, I say, supposes gods and men to have sprung equally from the unknown powers of nature.[4] And throughout the whole theogony of that author, PANDORA is the only instance of creation or a voluntary production; and she too was formed by the gods merely from despight to PROMETHEUS, who had furnished men with stolen fire from the celestial regions.[5] The ancient mythologists, indeed, seem throughout to have rather embraced the idea of generation than that of creation or formation; and to have thence accounted for the origin of this universe.

OVID, who lived in a learned age, and had been instructed by philosophers in the principles of a divine creation or formation of the world; finding, that such an idea would not agree with the popular mythology, which he delivers, leaves it, in a manner, loose and detached from his system. *Quisquis fuit ille Deorum?*[6] Whichever of the gods it was, says he, that dissipated the chaos, and introduced order into the universe. It could neither be SATURN, he knew, nor JUPITER, nor NEPTUNE, nor any of the received deities of paganism. His theological system had taught him nothing upon that head; and he leaves the matter equally undetermined.

DIODORUS SICULUS,[7] beginning his work with an enumeration of

[1] Suetonius, *The Twelve Caesars*, 'The Deified Augustus', ch. 16 [Loeb, i. 143].

[2] Suetonius, *The Twelve Caesars*, 'Gaius Caligula', ch. 5 [Loeb, i. 409].

[3] Herodotus, bk. II, ch. 53 [Loeb, i. 409]. Lucian, 'Zeus Catechized', 'On Funerals', etc.

[4] Ὡς ὁμόθεν γεγάσι Θεοι Θνητοι τ'άνθρωποι. Hesiod, *Works and Days*, l. 108 [how the gods and mortal men spring from one source. Loeb, 11].

[5] Hesiod, *Theogony*, l. 570 [Loeb, 121].

[6] Ovid, *Metamorphoses*, bk. I, l. 32 [Loeb, i. 5].

[7] Diodorus Siculus, bk. I, chs. 6–7 [Loeb, i. 23–9].

the most reasonable opinions concerning the origin of the world, makes no mention of a deity or intelligent mind; though it is evident from his history, that he was much more prone to superstition than to irreligion. And in another passage,[1] talking of the ICHTHYOPHAGI, a nation in INDIA, he says, that, there being so great difficulty in accounting for their descent, we must conclude them to be *aborigines*, without any beginning of their generation, propagating their race from all eternity; as some of the physiologers,* in treating of the origin of nature, have justly observed. 'But in such subjects as these,' adds the historian, 'which exceed all human capacity, it may well happen, that those, who discourse the most, know the least; reaching a specious appearance of truth in their reasonings, while extremely wide of the real truth and matter of fact.'

A strange sentiment in our eyes, to be embraced by a professed and zealous religionist![2] But it was merely by accident, that the question concerning the origin of the world did ever in ancient times enter into religious systems, or was treated of by theologers. The philosophers alone made profession of delivering systems of this kind; and it was pretty late too before these bethought themselves of having recourse to a mind of supreme intelligence, as the first cause of all. So far was it from being esteemed profane in those days to account for the origin of things without a deity, that THALES, ANAXIMENES, HERACLITUS, and others, who embraced that system of cosmogony, past unquestioned; while ANAXAGORAS,* the first undoubted theist, among the philosophers, was perhaps the first that ever was accused of atheism.[3]

We are told by SEXTUS EMPIRICUS,[4] that EPICURUS, when a boy, reading with his preceptor these verses of HESIOD,

> Eldest of beings, *chaos* first arose;
> Next *earth*, wide-stretch'd, the *seat* of all:

---

[1] Diodorus Siculus, bk. III, ch. 20 [Loeb, ii. 141].

[2] The same author, who can thus account for the origin of the world without a Deity, esteems it impious to explain from physical causes, the common accidents of life, earthquakes, inundations, and tempests; and devoutly ascribes these to the anger of Jupiter or Neptune. A plain proof, whence he derived his ideas of religion. See Diodorus Siculus, bk. XV, ch. 48 [Loeb, vii. 83].

[3] [See Hume's Note B, p. 186.]

[4] *Against the Physicists*, bk. II, paras. 18–19 [Loeb, iii. 221].

the young scholar first betrayed his inquisitive genius, by asking, *And chaos whence?* But was told by his preceptor, that he must have recourse to the philosophers for a solution of such questions. And from this hint EPICURUS left philology and all other studies, in order to betake himself to that science, whence alone he expected satisfaction with regard to these sublime subjects.

The common people were never likely to push their researches so far, or derive from reasoning their systems of religion; when philologers and mythologists, we see, scarcely ever discovered so much penetration. And even the philosophers, who discourse of such topics, readily assented to the grossest theory, and admitted the joint origin of gods and men from night and chaos: from fire, water, air, or whatever they established to be the ruling element.

Nor was it only on their first origin, that the gods were supposed dependent on the powers of nature. Throughout the whole period of their existence they were subjected to the dominion of fate or destiny. *Think of the force of necessity,* says AGRIPPA to the ROMAN people, that force, *to which even the gods must submit.*[1] And the Younger PLINY,[2] agreeably to this way of thinking, tells us, that amidst the darkness, horror, and confusion, which ensued upon the first eruption of VESUVIUS, several concluded, that all nature was going to wrack, and that gods and men were perishing in one common ruin.

It is great complaisance, indeed, if we dignify with the name of religion such an imperfect system of theology, and put it on a level with later systems, which are founded on principles more just and more sublime. For my part, I can scarcely allow the principles even of MARCUS AURELIUS, PLUTARCH, and some other *Stoics* and *Academics,** though much more refined than the pagan superstition, to be worthy of the honourable appellation of theism. For if the mythology of the heathens resemble the ancient EUROPEAN system of spiritual beings, excluding God and angels, and leaving only fairies and sprights; the creed of these philosophers may justly be said to exclude a deity, and to leave only angels and fairies.

---

[1] Dionysius of Halicarnassus, *Roman Antiquities*, bk. VI, ch. 54 [Loeb, iv. 19].
[2] Pliny, *Letters*, bk. VI, Letter 20 [Loeb, 495. This is Pliny's personal and terrifying account of the eruption.]

V   VARIOUS FORMS OF POLYTHEISM: ALLEGORY, HERO-WORSHIP

But it is chiefly our present business to consider the gross polytheism of the vulgar, and to trace all its various appearances, in the
principles of human nature, whence they are derived.

Whoever learns by argument, the existence of invisible intelligent power, must reason from the admirable contrivance of natural
objects, and must suppose the world to be the workmanship of that
divine being, the original cause of all things. But the vulgar polytheist, so far from admitting that idea, deifies every part of the
universe, and conceives all the conspicuous productions of nature,
to be themselves so many real divinities. The sun, moon, and stars,
are all gods according to his system: Fountains are inhabited by
nymphs, and trees by hama-dryads: Even monkeys, dogs, cats, and
other animals often become sacred in his eyes, and strike him with
a religious veneration. And thus, however strong men's propensity
to believe invisible, intelligent power in nature, their propensity is
equally strong to rest their attention on sensible, visible objects;
and in order to reconcile these opposite inclinations, they are led to
unite the invisible power with some visible object.

The distribution also of distinct provinces to the several deities
is apt to cause some allegory, both physical and moral, to enter into
the vulgar systems of polytheism. The god of war will naturally be
represented as furious, cruel, and impetuous: The god of poetry as
elegant, polite, and amiable: The god of merchandise, especially in
early times, as thievish and deceitful. The allegories, supposed in
HOMER and other mythologists, I allow, have often been so
strained, that men of sense are apt entirely to reject them, and to
consider them as the production merely of the fancy and conceit of
critics and commentators. But that allegory really has place in the
heathen mythology is undeniable even on the least reflection.
CUPID the son of VENUS; the Muses the daughters of Memory;
PROMETHEUS, the wise brother, and EPIMETHEUS the foolish; HYGIEIA
or the goddess of health descended from ÆSCULAPIUS or the god of
Physic: Who sees not, in these, and in many other instances, the
plain traces of allegory? When a god is supposed to preside over
any passion, event, or system of actions, it is almost unavoidable to
give him a genealogy, attributes, and adventures, suitable to his
supposed powers and influence; and to carry on that similitude and
comparison, which is naturally so agreeable to the mind of man.

Allegories, indeed, entirely perfect, we ought not to expect as the productions of ignorance and superstition; there being no work of genius that requires a nicer hand, or has been more rarely executed with success. That *Fear* and *Terror* are the sons of MARS is just; but why by VENUS?[1] That *Harmony* is the daughter of VENUS is regular; but why by MARS?[2] That *Sleep* is the brother of *Death* is suitable; but why describe him as enamoured of one of the Graces?[3] And since the ancient mythologists fall into mistakes so gross and palpable, we have no reason surely to expect such refined and long-spun allegories, as some have endeavoured to deduce from their fictions.

LUCRETIUS was plainly seduced by the strong appearance of allegory, which is observable in the pagan fictions. He first addresses himself to VENUS as to that generating power, which animates, renews, and beautifies the universe: But is soon betrayed by the mythology into incoherencies, while he prays to that allegorical personage to appease the furies of her lover MARS: An idea not drawn from allegory, but from the popular religion, and which LUCRETIUS, as an EPICUREAN, could not consistently admit of.

The deities of the vulgar are so little superior to human creatures, that, where men are affected with strong sentiments of veneration or gratitude for any hero or public benefactor, nothing can be more natural than to convent him into a god, and fill the heavens, after this manner, with continual recruits from among mankind. Most of the divinities of the ancient world are supposed to have once been men, and to have been beholden for their *apotheosis* to the admiration and affection of the people. The real history of their adventures, corrupted by tradition, and elevated by the marvellous, became a plentiful source of fable; especially in passing through the hands of poets, allegorists, and priests, who successively improved upon the wonder and astonishment of the ignorant multitude.

Painters too and sculptors came in for their share of profit in the sacred mysteries; and furnishing men with sensible representations of their divinities, whom they cloathed in human figures, gave great encrease to the public devotion, and determined its object. It

[1] Hesiod, *Theogony*, l. 935.
[2] *Ibid*, [ll. 936–7] and Plutarch, 'Life of Pelopidas', ch. 19 [Loeb, v. 387].
[3] Homer, *Iliad*, bk. XIV, ll. 263–7.

was probably for want of these arts in rude and barbarous ages, that men deified plants, animals, and even brute, unorganized matter; and rather than be without a sensible object of worship, affixed divinity to such ungainly forms. Could any statuary of SYRIA, in early times, have formed a just figure of APOLLO, the conic stone, HELIOGABALUS,* had never become the object of such profound adoration, and been received as a representation of the solar deity.[1]

STILPO was banished by the council of AREOPAGUS, for affirming that the MINERVA in the citadel was no divinity; but the workmanship of PHIDIAS, the sculptor.[2] What degree of reason must we expect in the religious belief of the vulgar in other nations; when ATHENIANS and AREOPAGITES* could entertain such gross misconceptions?

These then are the general principles of polytheism, founded in human nature, and little or nothing dependent on caprice and accident. As the *causes*, which bestow happiness or misery, are, in general, very little known and very uncertain, our anxious concern endeavours to attain a determinate idea of them; and finds no better expedient than to represent them as intelligent voluntary agents, like ourselves; only somewhat superior in power and wisdom. The limited influence of these agents, and their great proximity to human weakness, introduce the various distribution and division of their authority; and thereby give rise to allegory. The same principles naturally deify mortals, superior in power, courage, or understanding, and produce hero-worship, together with fabulous history and mythological tradition, in all its wild and unaccountable forms. And as an invisible spiritual intelligence is an object too refined for vulgar apprehension, men naturally affix it to some sensible representation; such as either the more conspicuous parts of nature, or the statues, images, and pictures, which a more refined age forms of its divinities.

Almost all idolaters, of whatever age or country, concur in these

[1] Herodian, *History of the Empire*, bk. V, ch. 3, paras. 3–5 [Loeb, ii. 19]. Jupiter Ammon is represented by Quintus Curtius as a deity of the same kind, *History of Alexander*, bk. IV, ch. 7, para. 23 [Loeb, i. 233]. The Arabians and Pessinuntians adored also shapeless unformed stones as their deity: Arnobius, *Seven Books against the Heathen*, bk. VI, ch. 11.

[2] Diogenes Laertius, *Lives of Eminent Philosophers*, bk. II, ch. 11, 'Stilpo', para. 116 [Loeb, i. 245].

general principles and conceptions; and even the particular characters and provinces, which they assign to their deities, are not extremely different.[1] The GREEK and ROMAN travellers and conquerors, without much difficulty, found their own deities every where; and said, This is MERCURY, that VENUS; this MARS, that NEPTUNE; by whatever title the strange gods might be denominated. The goddess HERTHA of our SAXON ancestors seems to be no other, according to TACITUS,[2] than the *Mater Tellus*, of the ROMANS; and his conjecture was evidently just.

VI   ORIGIN OF THEISM FROM POLYTHEISM

The doctrine of one supreme deity, the author of nature, is very ancient, has spread itself over great and populous nations, and among them has been embraced by all ranks and conditions of men: But whoever thinks that it has owed its success to the prevalent force of those invincible reasons, on which it is undoubtedly founded, would show himself little acquainted with the ignorance and stupidity of the people, and their incurable prejudices in favour of their particular superstitions. Even at this day, and in EUROPE, ask any of the vulgar, why he believes in an omnipotent creator of the world; he will never mention the beauty of final causes, of which he is wholly ignorant: He will not hold out his hand, and bid you contemplate the suppleness and variety of joints in his fingers, their bending all one way, the counterpoise which they receive from the thumb, the softness and fleshy parts of the inside of his hand, with all the other circumstances, which render that member fit for the use, to which it was destined. To these he has been long accustomed; and he beholds them with listlessness and unconcern. He will tell you of the sudden and unexpected death of such a one: The fall and bruise of such another: The excessive drought of this season: The cold and rains of another. These he ascribes to the immediate operation of providence: And such events, as, with good reasoners, are the chief difficulties in admitting a supreme intelligence, are with him the sole arguments for it.

---

[1] See Caesar on the religion of the Gauls, *The Gallic War*, bk. VI, paras. 16–17 [Loeb, 197].

[2] Tacitus, *Germania*, para. 40 [Loeb, 197].

Many theists, even the most zealous and refined, have denied a *particular* providence,* and have asserted, that the Sovereign mind or first principle of all things, having fixed general laws, by which nature is governed, gives free and uninterrupted course to these laws, and disturbs not, at every turn, the settled order of events by particular volitions. From the beautiful connexion, say they, and rigid observance of established rules, we draw the chief argument for theism; and from the same principles are enabled to answer the principal objections against it. But so little is this understood by the generality of mankind, that, wherever they observe any one to ascribe all events to natural causes, and to remove the particular interposition of a deity, they are apt to suspect him of the grossest infidelity. *A little philosophy*, says lord BACON, *makes men atheists: A great deal reconciles them to religion.* For men, being taught, by superstitious prejudices, to lay the stress on a wrong place; when that fails them, and they discover, by a little reflection, that the course of nature is regular and uniform, their whole faith totters, and falls to ruin. But being taught, by more reflection, that this very regularity and uniformity is the strongest proof of design and of a supreme intelligence, they return to that belief, which they had deserted; and they are now able to establish it on a firmer and more durable foundation.

Convulsions in nature, disorders, prodigies, miracles, though the most opposite to the plan of a wise superintendent, impress mankind with the strongest sentiments of religion; the causes of events seeming then the most unknown and unaccountable. Madness, fury, rage, and an inflamed imagination, though they sink men nearest to the level of beasts, are, for a like reason, often supposed to be the only dispositions, in which we can have any immediate communication with the Deity.

We may conclude, therefore, upon the whole, that, since the vulgar, in nations, which have embraced the doctrine of theism, still build it upon irrational and superstitious principles, they are never led into that opinion by any process of argument, but by a certain train of thinking, more suitable to their genius and capacity.

It may readily happen, in an idolatrous* nation, that though men admit the existence of several limited deities, yet is there some one God, whom, in a particular manner, they make the object of their worship and adoration. They may either suppose, that, in the distribution of power and territory among the gods, their nation was subjected to the jurisdiction of that particular deity; or reducing heavenly objects to the model of things below, they may represent one god as the prince or supreme magistrate of the rest, who, though of the same nature, rules them with an authority, like that which an earthly sovereign exercises over his subjects and vassals. Whether this god, therefore, be considered as their peculiar patron, or as the general sovereign of heaven, his votaries will endeavour, by every art, to insinuate themselves into his favour; and supposing him to be pleased, like themselves, with praise and flattery, there is no eulogy or exaggeration, which will be spared in their addresses to him. In proportion as men's fears or distresses become more urgent, they still invent new strains of adulation; and even he who outdoes his predecessor in swelling up the titles of his divinity, is sure to be outdone by his surccessor in newer and more pompous epithets of praise. Thus they proceed; till at last they arrive at infinity itself, beyond which there is no farther progress: And it is well, if, in striving to get farther, and to represent a magnificent simplicity, they run not into inexplicable mystery, and destroy the intelligent nature of their deity, on which alone any rational worship or adoration can be founded. While they confine themselves to the notion of a perfect being, the creator of the world, they coincide, by chance, with the principles of reason and true philosophy; though they are guided to that notion, not by reason, of which they are in a great measure incapable, but by the adulation and fears of the most vulgar superstition.

We often find, amongst barbarous nations, and even sometimes amongst civilized, that, when every strain of flattery has been exhausted towards arbitrary princes, when every human quality has been applauded to the utmost; their servile courtiers represent them, at last, as real divinities, and point them out to the people as objects of adoration. How much more natural, therefore, is it, that a limited deity, who at first supposed only the immediate author of the particular goods and ills in life, should in the end be represented as sovereign maker and modifier of the universe?

Even where this notion of a supreme deity is already established; though it ought naturally to lessen every other worship, and abase every object of reverence, yet if a nation has entertained the opinion of a subordinate tutelar divinity, saint, or angel; their addresses to that being gradually rise upon them, and encroach on the adoration due to their supreme deity. The Virgin Mary, ere checked by the reformation, had proceeded, from being merely a good woman, to usurp many attributes of the Almighty: God and St NICHOLAS go hand in hand, in all the prayers and petitions of the MUSCOVITES.

Thus the deity, who, from love, converted himself into a bull, in order to carry off EUROPA; and who, from ambition, dethroned his father, SATURN, became the OPTIMUS MAXIMUS of the heathens. [Thus, the God of ABRAHAM, ISAAC, and JACOB, became the supreme deity or JEHOVAH of the JEWS.]*

The JACOBINS,* who denied the immaculate conception, have ever been very unhappy in their doctrine, even though political reasons have kept the ROMISH church from condemning it. The CORDELIERS* have run away with all the popularity. But in the fifteenth century, as we learn from BOULAINVILLIERS,[1] an ITALIAN *Cordelier* maintained, that, during the three days, when CHRIST was interred, the hypostatic union was dissolved, and that his human nature was not a proper object of adoration, during that period. Without the art of divination, one might fortel, that so gross and impious a blasphemy would not fail to be anathematized by the people. It was the occasion of great insults on the part of the JACOBINS; who now got some recompense for their misfortunes in the war about the immaculate conception.

Rather than relinquish this propensity to adulation, religionists, in all ages, have involved themselves in the greatest absurdities and contradictions.

HOMER, in one passage, calls OCEANUS and TETHYS the original parents of all things, conformably to the established mythology and tradition of the GREEKS: Yet, in other passages, he could not forbear complimenting JUPITER, the reigning deity, with that magnificent appellation; and accordingly denominates him the father of gods and men. He forgets, that every temple, every street was full of the ancestors, uncles, brothers, and sisters of this JUPITER; who was in reality nothing but an upstart parricide and usurper. A like contradiction is observable in HESIOD; and is so much the less

---

[1] *Histoire Abrégée*, p. 499. [It is not clear to what edition of Boulainvilliers's *Abridged Chronology of the History of France* Hume is referring.]

excusable, as his professed intention was to deliver a true genealogy of the gods.

Were there a religion (and we may suspect Mahometanism of this inconsistence) which [sometimes painted the Deity in the most sublime colours, as the creator of heaven and earth; sometimes degraded him nearly to the level with human creatures in his powers and faculties;]* while at the same time it ascribed to him suitable infirmities, passions, and partialities, of the moral kind: That religion, after it was extinct, would also be cited as an instance of those contradictions, which arise from the gross, vulgar, natural conceptions of mankind, opposed to their continual propensity towards flattery and exaggeration. Nothing indeed would prove more strongly the divine origin of any religion, than to find (and happily this is the case with Christianity) that it is free from a contradiction, so incident to human nature.

VII   CONFIRMATION OF THIS DOCTRINE

It appears certain, that, though the original notions of the vulgar represent the Divinity as a limited being, and consider him only as the particular cause of health or sickness; plenty or want; prosperity or adversity; yet when more magnificent ideas are urged upon them, they esteem it dangerous to refuse their assent. Will you say, that your deity is finite and bounded in his perfections; may be overcome by a greater force; is subject to human passions, pains, and infirmities; has a beginning, and may have an end? This they dare not affirm; but thinking it safest to comply with the higher encomiums, they endeavour, by an affected ravishment and devotion, to ingratiate themselves with him. As a confirmation of this, we may observe, that the assent of the vulgar is, in this case, merely verbal, and that they are incapable of conceiving those sublime qualities, which they seemingly attribute to the Deity. Their real idea of him, notwithstanding their pompous language, is still as poor and frivolous as ever.

That original intelligence, say the MAGIANS,* who is the first principle of all things, discovers himself *immediately* to the mind and understanding alone; but has placed the sun as his image in the visible universe; and when that bright luminary diffuses its beams over the earth and the firmament, it is a faint copy of the glory, which resides in the higher heavens. If you would escape the displeasure of this divine being, you must be careful never to set your bare foot upon the ground, nor spit into a fire, nor throw any water upon it, even though it were consuming a whole city.[1] Who can express the perfections of the Almighty? say the Mahometans. Even the noblest of his works, if compared to him, are but dust and rubbish. How much more must human conception fall short of his infinite perfections? His smile and favour renders men for ever happy; and to obtain it for your children, the best method is to cut off from them, while infants, a little bit of skin, about half the breadth of a farthing. Take two bits of cloth,[2] say the *Roman catholics*, about an inch or an inch and a half square, join them by the corners with two strings or pieces of tape about sixteen inches long, throw this over your head, and make one of the bits of cloth lie upon your breast, and the other upon your back, keeping them next your skin: There is not a better secret for recommending yourself to that infinite Being, who exists from eternity to eternity.

The GETES, commonly called immortal, from their steady belief of the soul's immortality, were genuine theists and unitarians. They affirmed ZAMOLXIS, their deity, to be the only true god; and asserted the worship of all other nations to be addressed to mere fictions and chimeras. But were their religious principles any more refined, on account of these magnificent pretensions? Every fifth year they sacrificed a human victim, whom they sent as a messenger to their deity, in order to inform him of their wants and necessities. And when it thundered, they were so provoked, that, in order to return the defiance, they let fly arrows at him, and declined not the combat as unequal. Such at least is the account, which HERODOTUS gives of the theism of the immortal GETES.[3]

VIII   FLUX AND REFLUX OF POLYTHEISM AND THEISM

It is remarkable, that the principles of religion have a kind of flux and reflux in the human mind, and that men have a natural tendency to rise from idolatry to theism, and to sink again from theism

[1] Thomas Hyde, *Historia Religionis Veterum Persarum* [*History of the Ancient Persian Religion, etc.*, Oxford 1700].

[2] Called the Scapulaire.

[3] Herodotus, bk. IV, ch. 94 [Loeb, ii. 295].

into idolatry. The vulgar, that is, indeed, all mankind, a few excepted, being ignorant and uninstructed, never elevate their contemplation to the heavens, or penetrate by their disquisitions into the secret structure of vegetable or animal bodies; so far as to discover a supreme mind or original providence, which bestowed order on every part of nature. They consider these admirable works in a more confined and selfish view; and finding their own happiness and misery to depend on the secret influence and unforeseen concurrence of external objects, they regard, with perpetual attention, the *unknown causes*, which govern all these natural events, and distribute pleasure and pain, good and ill, by their powerful, but silent, operation. The unknown causes are still appealed to on every emergence; and in this general appearance or confused image, are the perpetual objects of human hopes and fears, wishes and apprehensions. By degrees, the active imagination of men, uneasy in this abstract conception of objects, about which it is incessantly employed, begins to render them more particular, and to clothe them in shapes more suitable to its natural comprehension. It represents them to be sensible, intelligent beings, like mankind; actuated by love and hatred, and flexible by gifts and entreaties, by prayers and sacrifices. Hence the origin of religion: And hence the origin of idolatry or polytheism.

But the same anxious concern for happiness, which begets the idea of these invisible, intelligent powers, allows not mankind to remain long in the first simple conception of them; as powerful, but limited beings; masters of human fate, but slaves to destiny and the course of nature. Men's exaggerated praises and compliments still swell their idea upon them; and elevating their deities to the utmost bounds of perfection, at last beget the attributes of unity and infinity, simplicity and spirituality. Such refined ideas, being somewhat disproportioned to vulgar comprehension, remain not long in their original purity; but require to be supported by the notion of inferior mediators or subordinate agents, which interpose between mankind and their supreme deity. These demi-gods or middle beings, partaking more of human nature, and being more familiar to us, become the chief objects of devotion, and gradually recal that idolatry, which had been formerly banished by the ardent prayers and panegyrics of timorous and indigent mortals. But as these idolatrous religions fall every day into grosser and more vulgar conceptions, they at last destroy themselves, and by the vile representations, which they form of their deities, make the tide turn again towards theism. But so great is the propensity, in this alternate revolution of human sentiments, to return back to idolatry, that the utmost precaution is not able effectually to prevent it. And of this, some theists, particularly the JEWS and MAHOMETANS, have been sensible; as appears by their banishing all the arts of statuary and painting, and not allowing the representations, even of human figures, to be taken by marble or colours; lest the common informity of mankind should thence produce idolatry. The feeble apprehensions of men cannot be satisfied with conceiving their deity as a pure spirit and perfect intelligence; and yet their natural terrors keep them from imputing to him the least shadow of limitation and imperfection. They fluctuate between these opposite sentiments. The same infirmity still drags them downwards, from an omnipotent and spiritual deity, to a limited and corporeal one, and from a corporeal and limited deity to a statue or visible representation. The same endeavour at elevation still pushes them upwards, from the statue or material image to the invisible power; and from the invisible power to an infinitely perfect deity, the creator and sovereign of the universe.

IX COMPARISON OF THESE RELIGIONS, WITH REGARD TO PERSECUTION AND TOLERATION

Polytheism or idolatrous worship, being founded entirely in vulgar traditions, is liable to this great inconvenience, that any practice or opinion, however barbarous or corrupted, may be authorized by it; and full scope is given, for knavery to impose on credulity, till morals and humanity be expelled the religious systems of mankind. At the same time, idolatry is attended with this evident advantage, that, by limiting the powers and functions of its deities, it naturally admits the gods of other sects and nations to a share of divinity, and renders all the various deities, as well as rites, ceremonies, or traditions, compatible* with each other.[1] Theism is opposite both in its advantages and disadvantages. As that system supposes one sole deity, the perfection of reason and goodness, it

---

[1] [See Hume's Note C, p. 186.]

should, if justly prosecuted, banish every thing frivolous, un-reasonable, or inhuman from religious worship, and set before men the most illustrious example, as well as the most commanding motives, of justice and benevolence. These mighty advantages are not indeed over-balanced (for that is not possible), but somewhat diminished, by inconveniences, which arise from the vices and prejudices of mankind. While one sole object of devotion is acknowledged, the worship of other deities is regarded as absurd and impious. Nay, this unity of object seems naturally to require the unity of faith and ceremonies, and furnishes designing men with a pretence for representing their adversaries as profane, and the objects of divine as well as human vengeance. For as each sect is positive that its own faith and worship are entirely acceptable to the deity, and as no one can conceive, that the same being should be pleased with different and opposite rites and principles; the several sects fall naturally into animosity, and mutually discharge on each other that sacred zeal and rancour, the most furious and implacable of all human passions.

The tolerating spirit of idolaters, both in ancient and modern times, is very obvious to any one, who is the least conversant in the writings of historians or travellers. When the oracle of DELPHI was asked, what rites or worship was most acceptable to the gods? Those which are legally established in each city, replied the oracle.[1] Even priests, in those ages, could, it seems, allow salvation to those of the different communion. The ROMANS commonly adopted the gods of the conquered people; and never disputed the attributes of those local and national deities, in whose territories they resided. The religious wars and persecutions of the EGYPTIAN idolators are indeed an exception to this rule; but are accounted for by ancient authors from reasons singular and remarkable. Different species of animals were the deities of the different sects among the EGYPTIANS; and the deities being in continual war, engaged their votaries in the same contention. The worshippers of dogs could not long remain in peace with the adorers of cats or wolves.[2] But where that reason took not place, the EGYPTIAN superstition was not so incompatible as is commonly imagined; since we learn from

[1] Xenophon, *Memorabilia of Socrates*, bk. I, ch. 3, para. 1 [Loeb, iv. 45].
[2] Plutarch, *Moralia*, 'Isis and Osiris', ch. 72 [Loeb, v. 167 f.].

HERODOTUS,[1] that very large contributions were given by AMASIS towards rebuilding the temple of DELPHI.

The intolerance of almost all religions, which have maintained the unity of God, is as remarkable as the contrary principle of polytheists. The implacable narrow spirit of the JEWS is well known. MAHOMETANISM set out with still more bloody principles; and even to this day, deals out damnation, though not fire and faggot, to all other sects. And if, among CHRISTIANS, the ENGLISH and DUTCH have embraced the principles of toleration, this singularity has proceeded from the steady resolution of the civil magistrate, in opposition to the continued efforts of priests and bigots.

The disciples of ZOROASTER shut the doors of heaven against all but the MAGIANS.[2] Nothing could more obstruct the progress of the PERSIAN conquests, than the furious zeal of that nation against the temples and images of the GREEKS. And after the overthrow of that empire we find ALEXANDER, as a polytheist, immediately reestablishing the worship of the BABYLONIANS which their former princes, as monotheists, had carefully abolished.[3] Even the blind and devoted attachment of that conqueror to the GREEK superstition hindered not but he himself sacrificed according to the BABYLONISH rites and ceremonies.[4]

So social is polytheism, that the utmost fierceness and antipathy, which it meets with in an opposite religion, is scarcely able to disgust it, and keep it at a distance. AUGUSTUS praised extremely the reserve of his grandson, CAIUS CÆSAR, when this latter prince, passing by JERUSALEM, deigned not to sacrifice according to the JEWISH law. But for what reason did AUGUSTUS so much approve of this conduct? Only, because that religion was by the PAGANS esteemed ignoble and barbarous.[5]

I may venture to affirm, that few corruptions of idolatry and polytheism are more pernicious to society than this corruption of

[1] Herodotus, bk. II, ch. 180 [Loeb, i. 495].

[2] Thomas Hyde, *Historia Religionis Veterum Persarum, etc.*

[3] Arrian, *Anabasis of Alexander*, bk. III, ch. 16 [Loeb, i. 275], bk. VII, ch. 17 [Loeb ii. 263].

[4] *Ibid.*, bk. III, ch. 16.

[5] Suetonius, *The Twelve Caesars*, 'The Deified Augustus', ch. 93 [Loeb, i. 263].

theism,[1] when carried to the utmost height. The human sacrifices of the CARTHAGINIANS, MEXICANS, and many barbarous nations,[2] scarcely exceed the inquisition and persecutions of ROME and MADRID. For besides, that the effusion of blood may not be so great in the former case as in the latter; besides this, I say, the human victims, being chosen by lot, or by some exterior signs, affect not, in so considerable a degree, the rest of the society. Whereas virtue, knowledge, love of liberty, are the qualities, that call down the fatal vengeance of inquisitors;* and when expelled, leave the society in the most shameful ignorance, corruption, and bondage. The illegal murder of one man by a tyrant is more pernicious than the death of a thousand by pestilence, famine, or any undistinguishing calamity.

In the temple of DIANA at ARICIA near ROME, whoever murdered the present priest, was legally entitled to be installed his successor.[3] A very singular institution! For, however barbarous and bloody the common superstitions often are to the laity, they usually turn to the advantage of the holy order.

X WITH REGARD TO COURAGE OR ABASEMENT

From the comparison of theism and idolatry, we may form some other observations, which will also confirm the vulgar observation, that the corruption of the best things gives rise to the worst.

Where the deity is represented as infinitely superior to mankind, this belief, though altogether just, is apt, when joined with superstitious terrors, to sink the human mind into the lowest submission and abasement, and to represent the monkish virtues* of mortification, penance, humility, and passive suffering, as the only qualities which are acceptable to him. But where the gods are conceived to be only a little superior to mankind, and to have been, many of them, advanced from that inferior rank, we are more at our ease, in our addresses to them, and may even, without profaneness, aspire sometimes to a rivalship and emulation of them. Hence

---

[1] Corruptio optimi pessima [corruption of the best is worst: *cf.* Hume's essay 'Of Superstition and Enthusiasm'].

[2] [See Hume's Note D, p. 187.]

[3] Strabo, *Geography*, bk. V, ch. 3 [Loeb ii. 423]. Suetonius, 'Gaius Caligula', ch. 35 [Loeb i. 459—it is not clear here to what Hume is referring his reader].

activity, spirit, courage, magnanimity, love of liberty, and all the virtues which aggrandize a people.

The heroes in paganism correspond exactly to the saints in popery, and holy dervises in MAHOMETANISM. The place of HERCULES, THESEUS, HECTOR, ROMULUS, is now supplied by DOMINIC, FRANCIS, ANTHONY, and BENEDICT. Instead of the destruction of monsters, the subduing of tyrants, the defence of our native country; whippings and fastings, cowardice and humility, abject submission and slavish obedience, are become the means of obtaining celestial honours among mankind.

One great incitement to the pious ALEXANDER in his warlike expeditions was his rivalship of HERCULES and BACCHUS, whom he justly pretended to have excelled.[1] BRASIDAS, that generous and noble SPARTAN, after falling in battle, had heroic honours paid him by the inhabitants of AMPHIPOLIS, whose defence he had embraced.[2] And in general, all founders of states and colonies among the GREEKS were raised to this inferior rank of divinity, by those who reaped the benefit of their labours.

This gave rise to the observation of MACHIAVEL,[3] that the doctrines of the CHRISTIAN religion (meaning the catholic; for he knew no other) which recommend only passive courage and suffering, had subdued the spirit of mankind, and had fitted them for slavery and subjection. An observation, which would certainly be just, were there not many other circumstances in human society which controul the genius and character of a religion.

BRASIDAS seized a mouse, and being bit by it, let it go. *There is nothing so contemptible*, said he, *but what may be safe, if it has but courage to defend itself.*[4] BELLARMINE patiently and humbly allowed the fleas and other odious vermin to prey upon him. *We shall have heaven*, said he, *to reward us for our sufferings: But these poor creatures have nothing but the enjoyment of the present life.*[5] Such difference is there between the maxims of a GREEK hero and a CATHOLIC saint.

[1] Arrian, *passim* [*The Anabasis of Alexander*, e.g. bk. IV, ch. 10].

[2] Thucydides, *The Peloponnesian War*, bk. V, ch. 11 [Loeb, iii. 23].

[3] Machiavelli, *Discourses*, bk. II, ch. 2.

[4] Plutarch, *Moralia*, 'Sayings of Kings and Commanders', Brasidas [Loeb, iii. 123].

[5] Pierre Bayle, *Dictionnaire Historique et Critique*, article 'Bellarmine'.

XI WITH REGARD TO REASON OR ABSURDITY

Here is another observation to the same purpose, and a new proof that the corruption of the best things begets the worst. If we examine, without prejudice, the ancient heathen mythology, as contained in the poets, we shall not discover in it any such monstrous absurdity, as we may at first be apt to apprehend. Where is the difficulty in conceiving, that the same powers or principles, whatever they were, which formed this visible world, men and animals, produced also a species of intelligent creatures, of more refined substance and greater authority than the rest? That these creatures may be capricious, revengeful, passionate, voluptuous, is easily conceived; nor is any circumstance more apt, among ourselves, to engender such vices, than the licence of absolute authority. And in short, the whole mythological system is so natural, that, in the vast variety of planets and world, contained in this universe, it seems more than probable, that, somewhere or other, it is really carried into execution.

The chief objection to it with regard to this planet, is, that it is not ascertained by any just reason or authority. The ancient tradition, insisted on by heathen priests and theologers, is but a weak foundation; and transmitted also such a number of contradictory reports, supported, all of them, by equal authority, that it became absolutely impossible to fix a preference amongst them. A few volumes, therefore, must contain all the polemical writings of pagan priests: And their whole theology must consist more of traditional stories and superstitious practices than of philosophical argument and controversy.

But where theism forms the fundamental principle of any popular religion, that tenet is so conformable to sound reason, that philosophy is apt to incorporate itself with such a system of theology. And if the other dogmas of that system be contained in a sacred book, such as the Alcoran, or be determined by any visible authority, like that of the ROMAN pontiff, speculative reasoners naturally carry on their assent, and embrace a theory, which has been instilled into them by their earliest education, and which also possesses some degree of consistence and uniformity. But as these appearances are sure, all of them, to prove deceitful, philosophy will soon find herself very unequally yoked with her new associate;

and instead of regulating each principle, as they advance together, she is at every turn perverted to serve the purposes of superstition. For besides the unavoidable incoherences, which must be reconciled and adjusted; one may safely affirm, that all popular theology, especially the scholastic, has a kind of appetite for absurdity and contradiction. If that theology went not beyond reason and common sense, her doctrines would appear too easy and familiar. Amazement must of necessity be raised: Mystery affected: Darkness and obscurity sought after: And a foundation of merit afforded to the devout votaries, who desire an opportunity of subduing their rebellious reason, by the belief of the most unintelligible sophisms.

Ecclesiastical history sufficiently confirms these reflections. When a controversy is started, some people always pretend with certainty to foretell the issue. Whichever opinion, say they, is most contrary to plain sense is sure to prevail; even where the general interest of the system requires not that decision. Though the reproach of heresy may, for some time, be bandied about among the disputants, it always rests at last on the side of reason. Any one, it is pretended, that has but learning enough of this kind to know the definition of ARIAN, PELAGIAN, ERASTIAN, SOCINIAN, SABELLIAN, EUTYCHIAN, NESTORIAN, MONOTHELITE, &c. not to mention PROTESTANT,* whose fate is yet uncertain, will be convinced of the truth of this observation. It is thus a system becomes more absurd in the end, merely from its being reasonable and philosophical in the beginning.

To oppose the torrent of scholastic religion by such feeble maxims as these, that *it is impossible for the same thing to be and not to be*, that *the whole is greater than a part*, that *two and three make five*; is pretending to stop the ocean with a bullrush. Will you set up profane reason against sacred mystery? No punishment is great enough for your impiety. And the same fires, which were kindled for heretics, will serve also for the destruction of philosophers.*

XII WITH REGARD TO DOUBT OR CONVICTION

We meet every day with people so sceptical with regard to history, that they assert it impossible for any nation ever to believe such absurd principles as those of GREEK and EGYPTIAN paganism; and at the same time so dogmatical with regard to religion, that they think the same absurdities are to be found in no other communion. CAMBYSES entertained like prejudices; and very impiously ridiculed, and even wounded, APIS, the great god of the EGYPTIANS, who appeared to his profane senses nothing but a large spotted bull. But HERODOTUS* judiciously ascribes this sally of passion to a real madness or disorder of the brain: Otherwise, says the historian, he never would have openly affronted any established worship. For on that head, continues he, every nation are best satisfied with their own, and think they have the advantage over every other nation.

It must be allowed, that the ROMAN CATHOLICS are a very learned sect; and that no one communion, but that of the church of ENGLAND, can dispute their being the most learned of all the Christian churches: Yet AVERROES,* the famous ARABIAN, who, no doubt, had heard of the EGYPTIAN superstitions, declares, that, of all religions, the most absurd and nonsensical is that, whose votaries eat, after having created, their deity.

I believe, indeed, that there is no tenet in all paganism, which would give so fair a scope to ridicule as this of the *real presence*: For it is so absurd, that it eludes the force of all argument. There are even some pleasant stories of that kind, which, though somewhat profane, are commonly told by the Catholics themselves. One day, a priest, it is said, gave inadvertently, instead of the sacrament, a counter, which had by accident fallen among the holy wafers. The communicant waited patiently for some time, expecting it would dissolve on his tongue: But finding that it still remained entire, he took it off. *I wish*, cried he to the priest, *you have not committed some mistake: I wish you have not given me God the Father: He is so hard and tough there is no swallowing him.*

A famous general, at that time in the MUSCOVITE service, having come to PARIS for the recovery of his wounds, brought along with him a young TURK, whom he had taken prisoner. Some of the doctors of the SORBONNE (who are altogether as positive as the dervishes of CONSTANTINOPLE) thinking it a pity, that the poor TURK should be damned for want of instruction, solicited MUSTAPHA very hard to turn Christian, and promised him, for his encouragement, plenty of good wine in this world, and paradise in the next. These allurements were too powerful to be resisted; and therefore, having been well instructed and catechized, he at last agreed to receive the sacraments of baptism and the Lord's supper. The priest, however, to make every thing sure and solid, still continued his instructions, and began the next day with the usual question, *How many Gods are there? None at all*, replies BENEDICT; for that was his new name. *How! None at all!* cries the priest. *To be sure*, said the honest proselyte. *You have told me all along that there is but one God: And yesterday I eat him.*

Such are the doctrines of our brethren the Catholics. But to these doctrines we are so accustomed, that we never wonder at them: Though in a future age, it will probably become difficult to persuade some nations, that any human, two-legged creature could ever embrace such principles. And it is a thousand to one, but these nations themselves shall have something full as absurd in their own creed, to which they will give a most implicit and most religious assent.

I lodged once at PARIS in the same *hotel* with an ambassador from TUNIS, who, having passed some years at LONDON, was returning home that way. One day I observed his MOORISH excellency diverting himself under the porch, with surveying the splendid equipages that drove along; when there chanced to pass that way some *Capucin* friars, who had never seen a TURK; as he, on his part, though accustomed to the EUROPEAN dresses, had never seen the grotesque figure of a *Capucin*: And there is no expressing the mutual admiration, with which they inspired each other. Had the chaplain of the embassy entered into a dispute with these FRANCISCANS, their reciprocal surprize had been of the same nature. Thus all mankind stand staring at one another; and there is no beating it into their heads, that the turban of the AFRICAN is not just as good or as bad a fashion as the cowl of the EUROPEAN. *He is a very honest man*, said the prince of SALLEE, speaking of DE RUYTER. *It is a pity he were a Christian.*

How can you worship leeks and onions? we shall suppose a SORBONNIST to say to a priest of SAIS. If we worship them, replies the latter; at least, we do not, at the same time, eat them. But what strange objects or adoration are cats and monkeys? says the learned doctor. They are at least as good as the relics or rotten bones of martyrs, answers his no less learned antagonist. Are you not mad, insists the Catholic, to cut one another's throat about the preference of a cabbage or a cucumber? Yes, says the pagan; I allow it, if you will confess, that those are still madder, who fight about the preference among volumes of sophistry, ten thousand of which are not equal in value to one cabbage or cucumber.[1]

Every by-stander will easily judge (but unfortunately the by-standers are few) that, if nothing were requisite to establish any popular system, but exposing the absurdities of other systems, every voter of every superstition could give a sufficient reason for his blind and bigotted attachment to the principles in which he has been educated. But without so extensive a knowledge, on which to ground this assurance (and perhaps, better without it), there is not wanting a sufficient stock of religious zeal and faith among mankind. DIODORUS SICULUS[2] gives a remarkable instance to this purpose, of which he was himself an eye-witness. While EGYPT lay under the greatest terror of the ROMAN name, a legionary soldier having inadvertently been guilty of the sacrilegious impiety of killing a cat, the whole people rose upon him with the utmost fury; and all the efforts of the prince were not able to save him. The senate and people of ROME, I am persuaded, would not, then, have been so delicate with regard to their national deities. They very frankly, a little after that time, voted AUGUSTUS a place in the celestial mansions; and would have dethroned every god in heaven, for his sake, had he seemed to desire it. *Presens divus habebitur** AUGUSTUS, says HORACE. That is a very important point: And in other nations and other ages, the same circumstance has not been deemed altogether indifferent.[3]

Notwithstanding the sanctity of our holy religion, says TULLY,[4] no crime is more common with us than sacrilege: But was it ever heard of, that an EGYPTIAN violated the temple of a cat, an ibis, or

---

[1] [See Hume's Note E, p. 187.]

[2] Diodorus Siculus, bk. I, ch. 83, paras. 8–9 [Loeb, i. 283].

[3] When Louis the XIVth took on himself the protection of the Jesuit's College of Clermont, the society ordered the king's arms to be put up over the gate, and took down the cross in order to make way for it: Which gave occasion to the following epigram:

> Sustulit hinc Christi, posuitque insigna Regis:
> Impia gens, alium nescit habere Deum.

> [A wicked folk are they, and other God they have,
> That down the Christ and up the ensigns of the king.]

[4] Cicero, *De Natura Deorum*, bk. I, ch. 29 [Loeb, 79].

a crocodile? There is no torture, an EGYPTIAN would not undergo, says the same author in another place,[1] rather than injure an ibis, an aspic, a cat, a dog, or a crocodile. Thus it is strictly true, what DRYDEN observes,

> 'Of whatsoe'er descent their godhead be,
> 'Stock, stone, or other homely pedigree,
> 'In his defence his servants are as bold
> 'As if he had been born of beaten gold.'
>
> ABSALOM and ACHITOPHEL

Nay, the baser the materials are, of which the divinity is composed, the greater devotion is he likely to excite in the breasts of his deluded votaries. They exult in their shame and make a merit with their deity, in braving, for his sake, all the ridicule and contumely of his enemies. Ten thousand Crusaders inlist themselves under the holy banners; and even openly triumph in those parts of their religion, which their adversaries regard as the most reproachful.

There occurs, I own, a difficulty in the EGYPTIAN system of theology; as indeed, few systems of that kind are entirely free from difficulties. It is evident, from their method of propagation, that a couple of cats, in fifty years, would stock a whole kingdom; and if that religious veneration were still paid them, it would, in twenty more, not only be easier in EGYPT to find a god than a man, which PETRONIUS says* was the case in some parts of Italy; but the gods must at last entirely starve the men, and leave themselves neither priests nor votaries remaining. It is probable, therefore, that this wise nation, the most celebrated in antiquity for prudence and sound policy, foreseeing such dangerous consequences, reserved all their worship for the full-grown divinities, and used the freedom to drown the holy spawn or little sucking gods, without any scruple or remorse. And thus the practice of warping the tenets of religion, in order to serve temporal interests, is not, by any means, to be regarded as an invention of these later ages.

The learned, philosophical VARRO,* discoursing of religion, pretends not to deliver any thing beyond probabilities and appearances: Such was his good sense and moderation! But the passionate, the zealous AUGUSTIN, insults the noble ROMAN on his scepticism and reserve, and professes the most thorough belief and

---

[1] Cicero, *Tusculan Disputations*, bk. V, ch. 27 [Loeb, 507].

assurance.[1] A heathen poet, however, contemporary with the saint, absurdly esteems the religious system of the latter so false, that even the credulity of children, he says, could not engage to believe it.[2]

It is strange, when mistakes are so common, to find every one positive and dogmatical? And that the zeal often rises in proportion to the error? *Moverunt*, says SPARTIAN, & *ca tempestate, Judæi bellum quod vetabantur mutilare genitalia.*[3]

If ever there was a nation or a time, in which the public religion lost all authority over mankind, we might expect, that infidelity in ROME, during the CICERONIAN age, would openly have erected its throne, and that CICERO himself, in every speech and action, would have been its most declared abettor. But it appears, that, whatever sceptical liberties that great man might take, in his writings or in philosophical conversation; he yet avoided, in the common conduct of life, the imputation of deism and profaneness. Even in his own family, and to his wife TERENTIA, whom he highly trusted, he was willing to appear a devout religionist; and there remains a letter, addressed to her, in which he seriously desires her to offer sacrifice to APOLLO and ÆSCULAPIUS, in gratitude for the recovery of his health.[4]

POMPEY's devotion was much more sincere: In all his conduct, during the civil wars, he paid a great regard to augures, dreams, and prophesies.[5] AUGUSTUS was tainted with superstition of every kind. As it is reported of MILTON, that his poetical genius never flowed with ease and abundance in the spring; so AUGUSTUS observed, that his own genius for dreaming never was so perfect during that season, nor was so much to be relied on, as during the rest of the year. That great and able emperor was also extremely uneasy, when he happened to change his shoes, and put the right foot shoe on the left foot.[6] In short it cannot be doubted, but the

---

[1] Augustin, *City of God*, bk. III, ch. 17 [Loeb, i. 337].

[2] Claudius Rutilius Namatianus, *A Voyage Home to Gaul*, bk. I, l. 394 [Loeb, see *Minor Latin Poets*, 799].

[3] Aellius Spartianus, *Historia Augusta*, 'Life of Hadrian', bk. XIV, para. 2. [The Jews at this time initiated war because they were forbidden to mutilate their genitals.]

[4] Cicero, *Letters to his Friends*, bk. XIV, letter 7 [Loeb, iii. 205].

[5] Cicero, *On Divination*, bk. II, ch. 9 [Loeb, 397].

[6] Suetonius, *The Twelve Caesars*, 'The Deified Augustus', chs. 90–92 [Loeb, i. 261]. Pliny, *Natural History*, bk. II, ch. 5, para. 24 [Loeb, i. 185].

votaries of the established superstition of antiquity were as numerous in every state, as those of the modern religion are at present. Its influence was as universal; though it was not so great. As many people gave their assent to it; though that assent was not seemingly so strong, precise, and affirmative.

We may observe,* that, notwithstanding the dogmatical, imperious style of all superstition, the conviction of the religionists, in all ages, is more affected than real, and scarcely ever approaches, in any degree, to that solid belief and persuasion, which governs us in the common affairs of life. Men dare not avow, even to their own hearts, the doubts which they entertain on such subjects: They make a merit of implicit faith; and disguise to themselves their real infidelity, by the strongest asseverations and most positive bigotry. But nature is too hard for all their endeavours, and suffers not the obscure, glimmering light, afforded in those shadowy regions, to equal the strong impressions, made by common sense and by experience. The usual course of men's conduct belies their words, and shows, that their assent in these matters is some unaccountable operation of the mind between disbelief and conviction, but approaching much nearer to the former than to the latter.

Since, therefore, the mind of man appears of so loose and unsteady a texture, that, even at present, when so many persons find an interest in continually employing on it the chissel and the hammer, yet are they not able to engrave theological tenets with any lasting impression; how much more must this have been the case in ancient times, when the retainers to the holy function were so much fewer in comparison? No wonder, that the appearances were then very inconsistent, and that men, on some occasions, might seem determined infidels, and enemies to the established religion, without being so in reality; or at least, without knowing their own minds in that particular.

Another cause, which rendered the ancient religion much looser than the modern, is, that the former were *traditional* and the latter are *scriptural*; and the tradition in the former was complex, contradictory, and, on many occasions, doubtful; so that it could not possibly be reduced to any standard and canon, or afford any determinate articles of faith. The stories of the gods were numberless like the popish legends; and though every one, almost, believed a part of these stories, yet no one could believe or know the whole: While, at the same time, all must have acknowledged, that no one part stood on a better foundation than the rest. The traditions of different cities and nations were also, on many occasions, directly opposite; and no reason could be assigned for preferring one to the other. And as there was an infinite number of stories, with regard to which tradition was nowise positive; the gradation was insensible, from the most fundamental articles of faith, to those loose and precarious fictions. The pagan religion, therefore, seemed to vanish like a cloud, whenever one approached to it, and examined it piecemeal. It could never be ascertained by any fixed dogmas and principles. And though this did not convert the generality of mankind from so absurd a faith; for when will the people be reasonable? yet it made them faulter and hesitate more in maintaining their principles, and was even apt to produce, in certain dispositions of mind, some practices and opinions, which had the appearance of determined infidelity.

To which we may add, that the fables of the pagan religion were, of themselves, light, easy, and familiar; without devils, or seas of brimstone, or any object that could much terrify the imagination. Who could forbear smiling, when he thought of the loves of MARS and VENUS, or the amorous frolics of JUPITER and PAN? In this respect, it was a true poetical religion; if it had not rather too much levity for the graver kinds of poetry. We find that it has been adopted by modern bards; nor have these talked with greater freedom and irreverence of the gods, whom they regarded as fictions, than the ancients did of the real objects of their devotion.

The inference is by no means just, that, because a system of religion has made no deep impression on the minds of a people, it must therefore have been positively rejected by all men of common sense, and that opposite principles, in spite of the prejudices of education, were generally established by argument and reasoning. I know not, but a contrary inference may be more probable. The less importunate and assuming any species of superstition appears, the less will it provoke men's spleen and indignation, or engage them into enquiries concerning its foundation and origin. This in the mean time is obvious, that the empire of all religious faith over the understanding is wavering and uncertain, subject to every variety of humour, and dependent on the present incidents, which strike the imagination. The difference is only in the degrees. An ancient will place a stroke of impiety and one of superstition alternately, throughout a whole discourse;[1] A modern often thinks in the same way, though he may be more guarded in his expression.

LUCIAN tells us expressly,[2] that whoever believed not the most ridiculous fables of paganism was deemed by the people profane and impious. To what purpose, indeed, would that agreeable author have employed the whole force of his wit and satire against the national religion, had not that religion been generally believed by his country-men and contemporaries?

LIVY[3] acknowledges as frankly, as any divine would at present, the common incredulity of his age; but then he condemns it as severely. And who can imagine, that a national superstition, which could delude so ingenious a man, would not also impose on the generality of the people?

The STOICS bestowed many magnificent and even impious epithets on their sage; that he alone was rich, free, a king, and equal to the immortal gods. They forgot to add, that he was not inferior in prudence and understanding to an old woman. For surely nothing can be more pitiful than the sentiments, which that sect entertain with regard to religious matters; while they seriously agree with the common augurs, that, when a raven croaks from the left, it is a good omen; but a bad one, when a rook makes a noise from the same quarter. PANÆTIUS was the only STOIC, among the GREEKS, who so much as doubted with regard to auguries and divination.[4] MARCUS ANTONINUS[5] tells us, that he himself had received many admonitions from the gods in his sleep. It is true, EPICTETUS[6] forbids us to regard the language of rooks and ravens; but it is not, that they do not speak truth: It is only, because they can fortel nothing but the breaking of our neck or the forfeiture of our estate; which are circumstances, says he, that nowise concern us. Thus the STOICS join a philosophical enthusiasm to a religious

---

[1] [See Hume's Note F, p. 188.]
[2] Lucian, 'The Lover of Lies', para. 3 [Loeb, iii. 325].
[3] Livy, *History of Rome*, bk. X, ch. 40 [Loeb, iv. 515].
[4] Cicero, *On Divination*, bk. I, ch. 3 [Loeb, 231] and 7 [Loeb, 237].
[5] Marcus Aurelius, *The Meditations*, bk. I, para. 17 [Loeb, 25].
[6] Epictetus, *Encheiridion*, para. 18 [Loeb, ii. 497].

superstition. The force of their mind, being all turned to the side of morals, unbent itself in that of religion.[1]

PLATO[2] introduces SOCRATES affirming, that the accusation of impiety raised against him was owing entirely to his rejecting such fables, as those of SATURN's castrating his father URANUS, and JUPITER's dethroning SATURN: Yet in a subsequent dialogue,[3] SOCRATES confesses, that the doctrine of the mortality of the soul was the received opinion of the people. Is there here any contradiction? Yes, surely: But the contradiction is not in PLATO; it is in the people, whose religious principles in general are always composed of the most discordant parts; especially in an age, when superstition sate so easy and light upon them.[4]

The same CICERO, who affected, in his own family, to appear a devout religionist, makes no scruple, in a public court of judicature, of treating the doctrine of a future state as a ridiculous fable, to which no body could give any attention.[5] SALLUST[6] represents CÆSAR as speaking the same language in the open senate.[7]

But that all these freedoms implied not a total and universal infidelity and scepticism amongst the people, is too apparent to be denied. Though some parts of the national religion hung loose upon the minds of men, other parts adhered more closely to them: And it was the chief business of the sceptical philosophers to show, that there was no more foundation for one than for the other. This is the artifice of COTTA* in the dialogues concerning the *nature of the gods*. He refutes the whole system of mythology by leading the orthodox gradually, from the more momentous stories, which were believed, to the more frivolous, which every one ridiculed: From the gods to the goddesses; from the goddesses to the nymphs; from the nymphs to the fawns and satyrs. His master, CARNEADES, had employed the same method of reasoning.[8]

---

[1]   The Stoics, I own, were not quite orthodox in the established religion; but one may see, from these instances, that they went a great way: And the people undoubtedly went every length.

[2]   Plato, *Euthyphro*, 6 A–B.   [3]   Plato, *Phaedo*, 64 A, 65 A, 68 B.

[4]   [See Hume's Note G, p. 189.]

[5]   Cicero, 'On Behalf of Cluentius', ch. 61, para. 171 [Loeb, ix. 409].

[6]   Sallust, *On the War with Catilene*, ch. 51, para. 16 [Loeb, 93].

[7]   [See Hume's Note H, p. 190.]

[8]   Sextus Empiricus, *Against the Physicists*, bk. I, paras. 182–90 [Loeb, iii. 95. The latter part of Hume's paragraph is a paraphrase of Sextus.]

Upon the whole, the greatest and most observable differences between a *traditional, mythological* religion, and a *systematical, scholastic* one are two: The former is often more reasonable, as consisting only of a multitude of stories, which, however groundless, imply no express absurdity and demonstrative contradiction; and sits also so easy and light on men's minds, that, though it may be as universally received, it happily makes no such deep impression on the affections and understanding.

XIII   IMPIOUS CONCEPTIONS OF THE DIVINE NATURE IN POPULAR RELIGIONS OF BOTH KINDS

The primary religion of mankind arises chiefly from an anxious fear of future events; and what ideas will naturally be entertained of invisible, unknown powers, while men lie under dismal apprehensions of any kind, may easily be conceived. Every image of vengeance, severity, cruelty, and malice must occur, and must augment the ghastliness and horror, which oppresses the amazed religionist. A panic having once seized the mind, the active fancy still farther multiplies the objects of terror; while that profound darkness, or, what is worse, that glimmering light, with which we are environed, represents the spectres of divinity under the most dreadful appearances imaginable. And no idea of perverse wickedness can be framed, which those terrified devotees do not readily, without scruple, apply to their deity.

This appears the natural state of religion, when surveyed in one light. But if we consider, on the other hand, that spirit of praise and eulogy, which necessarily has place in all religions, and which is the consequence of these very terrors, we must expect a quite contrary system of theology to prevail. Every virtue, every excellence, must be ascribed to the divinity, and no exaggeration will be deemed sufficient to reach those perfections, with which he is endowed. Whatever strains of panegyric can be invented, are immediately embraced, without consulting any arguments of phænomena: It is esteemed a sufficient confirmation of them, that they give us more magnificent ideas of the divine objects of our worship and adoration.

Here therefore is a kind of contradiction between the different principles of human nature, which enter into religion. Our natural terrors present the notion of a devilish and malicious deity: Our propensity to adulation leads us to acknowledge an excellent and divine. And the influence of these opposite principles are various, according to the different situation of the human understanding.

In very barbarous and ignorant nations, such as the AFRICANS and INDIANS, nay even the JAPONESE, who can form no extensive ideas of power and knowledge, worship may be paid to a being, whom they confess to be wicked and detestable; though they may be cautious, perhaps, of pronouncing this judgment of him in public, or in his temple, where he may be supposed to hear their reproaches.

Such rude, imperfect ideas of the Divinity adhere long to all idolaters; and it may safely be affirmed, that the GREEKS themselves never got entirely rid of them. It is remarked by XENOPHON,[1] in praise of SOCRATES, that this philosopher assented not to the vulgar opinion, which supposed the gods to know some things, and be ignorant of others: He maintained, that they knew every thing; what was done, said, or even thought. But as this was a train of philosophy[2] much above the conception of his countrymen, we need not be surprised, if very frankly, in their books and conversation, they blamed the deities, whom they worshipped in their temples. It is observable, that HERODOTUS in particular scruples not, in many passages, to ascribe *envy* to the gods; a sentiment, of all others, the most suitable to a mean and devilish nature. The pagan hymns, however, sung in public worship, contained nothing but epithets of praise; even while the actions ascribed to the gods were the most barbarous and detestable. When TIMOTHEUS, the poet, recited a hymn to DIANA, in which he enumerated, with the greatest eulogies, all the actions and attributes of that cruel, capricious goddess: *May your daughter*, said one present, *become such as the deity whom you celebrate.*[3]

But as men farther exalt their idea of their divinity; it is their notion of his power and knowledge only, not of his goodness,

---

[1] *Memorabilia of Socrates*, bk. I, ch. 1 [Loeb, 7].

[2] It was considered among the ancients, as a very extraordinary, philosophical paradox, that the presence of the gods was not confined to the heavens, but was extended everywhere; as we learn from Lucian, 'Hermontimus or Concerning Sects', para. 81 [Loeb, vi. 409].

[3] Plutarch, *Concerning Superstition*, ch. 10 [Loeb, ii. 485].

which is improved. On the contrary, in proportion to the supposed extent of his science and authority, their terrors naturally augment; while they believe, that no secrecy can conceal them from his scrutiny, and that even the inmost recesses of their breast lie open before him. They must then be careful not to form expressly any sentiment of blame and disapprobation. All must be applause, ravishment, extacy. And while their gloomy apprehensions make them ascribe to him measures of conduct, which, in human creatures, would be highly blamed, they must still affect to praise and admire* that conduct in the object of their devotional addresses. Thus it may safely be affirmed, that popular religions are really, in the conception of their more vulgar votaries, a species of dæmonism; and the higher the deity is exalted in power and knowledge, the lower of course is he depressed in goodness and benevolence; whatever epithets of praise may be bestowed on him by his amazed adorers. Among idolaters, the words may be false, and belie the secret opinion: But among more exalted religionists, the opinion itself contracts a kind of falsehood, and belies the inward sentiment. The heart secretly detests such measures of cruel and implacable vengeance; but the judgment dares not but pronounce them perfect and adorable. And the additional misery of this inward struggle aggravates all the other terrors, by which these unhappy victims to superstition are for ever haunted.

LUCIAN[1] observes that a young man, who reads the history of the gods in HOMER or HESIOD, and finds their factions, wars, injustice, incest, adultery, and other immoralities so highly celebrated, is much surprised afterwards, when he comes into the world, to observe that punishments are by law inflicted on the same actions, which he had been taught to ascribe to superior beings. The contradiction is still perhaps stronger between the representations given us by some later religions and our natural ideas of generosity, lenity, impartiality, and justice; and in proportion to the multiplied terrors of these religions, the barbarous conceptions of the divinity are multiplied upon us.[2] Nothing can preserve untainted the genuine principles of morals in our judgment of human conduct, but the absolute necessity of these principles to the existence of society. If common conception can indulge princes in

---

[1] Lucian, 'Menippus or the Descent into Hades', para. 3 [Loeb, iv. 79].
[2] [See Hume's Note I, p. 190. This note is important—ed.]

a system of ethics, somewhat different from that which should regulate private persons; how much more those superior beings, whose attributes, views, and nature are so totally unknown to us? *Sunt superis sua jura.*[1] The gods have maxims of justice peculiar to themselves.*

XIV BAD INFLUENCE OF POPULAR RELIGIONS ON MORALITY*

Here I cannot forbear observing a fact, which may be worth the attention of such as make human nature the object of their enquiry. It is certain, that, in every religion, however sublime the verbal definition which it gives of its divinity, many of the votaries, perhaps the greatest number, will still seek the divine favour, not by virtue and good morals,* which alone can be acceptable to a perfect being, but either by frivolous observances, by intemperate zeal, by rapturous extasies, or by the belief of mysterious and absurd opinions. The least part of the *Sadder*,* as well as of the *Pentateuch*, consists in precepts of morality; and we may also be assured, that that part was always the least observed and regarded. When the old ROMANS were attacked with a pestilence, they never ascribed their sufferings to their vices, or dreamed of repentance and amendment. They never thought, that they were the general robbers of the world, whose ambition and avarice made desolate the earth, and reduced opulent nations to want and beggary. They only created a dictator,[2] in order to drive a nail into a door; and by that means, they thought that they had sufficiently appeased their incensed deity.

In ÆGINA, one faction forming a conspiracy, barbarously and treacherously assassinated seven hundred of their fellow-citizens; and carried their fury so far, that, one miserable fugitive having fled to the temple, they cut off his hands, by which he clung to the gates, and carrying him out of holy ground, immediately murdered him. *By this impiety*, says HERODOTUS,[3] (not by the other many cruel assassinations) *they offended the gods, and contracted an inexpiable guilt.*

---

[1] Ovid, *Metamorphoses*, bk. IX, ll. 499–500.

[2] Called 'Dictator clavis figendae causa', Livy, *History of Rome*, bk. VII, ch. 3 [Loeb, iii. 365].

[3] Herodotus, bk. VI, ch. 91 [Loeb, iii. 243].

Nay, if we should suppose, what never happens, that a popular religion were found, in which it was expressly declared, that nothing but morality could gain the divine favour; if an order of priests were instituted to inculcate this opinion, in daily sermons, and with all the arts of persuasion; yet so inveterate are the people's prejudices, that, for want of some other superstition, they would make the very attendance on these sermons the essentials of religion, rather than place them in virtue and good morals. The sublime prologue of ZALEUCUS's laws[1] inspired not the LOCRIANS, so far as we can learn, with any sounder notions of the measures of acceptance with the deity, than were familiar to the other GREEKS.

This observation, then, holds universally: But still one may be at some loss to account for it. It is not sufficient to observe, that the people, every where, degrade their deities into a similitude with themselves, and consider them merely as a species of human creatures, somewhat more potent and intelligent. This will not remove the difficulty. For there is no *man* so stupid, as that, judging by his natural reason, he would not esteem virtue and honesty the most valuable qualities, which any person could possess. Why not ascribe the same sentiment to his deity? Why not make all religion, or the chief part of it, to consist in these attainments?

Nor is it satisfactory to say, that the practice of morality is more difficult than that of superstition; and is therefore rejected. For, not to mention the excessive penances of the *Brachmans* and *Talapoins*; it is certain, that the *Rhamadan* of the TURKS, during which the poor wretches, for many days, often in the hottest months of the year, and in some of the hottest climates of the world, remain without eating or drinking from the rising to the setting sun; this *Rhamadan*, I say, must be more severe than the practice of any moral duty, even to the most vicious and depraved of mankind. The four lents of the MUSCOVITES, and the austerities of some *Roman Catholics*, appear more disagreeable than meekness and benevolence. In short, all virtue, when men are

_____

[1] To be found in Diodorus Siculus, bk. XII, chs. 20–21 [Loeb, iv. 415. If Diodorus, first century BC, reports Zaleucus, *c.*650 BC, correctly, then Zaleucus formulates as a condition of his constitution perhaps the oldest statement of the design argument: 'that gods exist, and that as [the people's] minds survey the heavens and its orderly scheme and arrangement, they should judge that these creations are not the result of chance or the works of men's hands . . .'—J. G.]

reconciled to it by ever so little practice, is agreeable: All superstition is for ever odious and burthensome.

Perhaps, the following account may be received as a true solution of the difficulty. The duties, which a man performs as a friend or parent, seem merely owing to his benefactor or children; nor can he be wanting to these duties, without breaking through all the ties of nature and morality. A strong inclination may prompt him to the performance: A sentiment of order and moral obligation joins its force to these natural ties: And the whole man, if truly virtuous, is drawn to his duty, without any effort or endeavour. Even with regard to the virtues, which are more austere, and more founded on reflection, such as public spirit, filial duty, temperance, or integrity; the moral obligation, in our apprehension, removes all pretension to religious merit; and the virtuous conduct is deemed no more than what we owe to society and to ourselves. In all this, a superstitious man finds nothing, which he has properly performed for the sake of his deity, or which can peculiarly recommend him to the divine favour and protection. He considers not, that the most genuine method of serving the divinity is by promoting the happiness of his creatures. He still looks out for some more immediate service of the supreme Being, in order to allay those terrors, with which he is haunted. And any practice, recommended to him, which either serves to no purpose in life, or offers the strongest violence to his natural inclinations; that practice he will the more readily embrace, on account of those very circumstances, which should make him absolutely reject it. It seems the more purely religious, because it proceeds from no mixture of any other motive or consideration. And if, for its sake, he sacrifices much of his ease and quiet, his claim of merit appears still to rise upon him, in proportion to the zeal and devotion which he discovers. In restoring a loan, or paying a debt, his divinity is nowise beholden to him; because these acts of justice are what he was bound to perform, and what many would have performed, were there no god in the universe. But if he fast a day, or give himself a sound whipping; this has a direct reference, in his opinion, to the service of God. No other motive could engage him to such austerities. By these distinguished marks of devotion, he has now acquired the divine favour; and may expect, in recompense, protection and safety in this world, and eternal happiness in the next.

Hence the greatest crimes have been found, in many instances, compatible with a superstitious piety and devotion; Hence, it is justly regarded as unsafe to draw any certain inference in favour of a man's morals, from the fervour or strictness of his religious exercises, even though he himself believe them sincere. Nay, it has been observed, that enormities of the blackest dye have been rather apt to produce superstitious terrors, and encrease the religious passion. BOMILCAR, having formed a conspiracy for assassinating at once the whole senate of CARTHAGE, and invading the liberties of his country, lost the opportunity, from a continual regard to omens and prophecies. *Those who undertake the most criminal and most dangerous enterprizes are commonly the most superstitious*; as an ancient historian[1] remarks on this occasion. Their devotion and spiritual faith rise with their fears. CATILINE was not contented with the established deities and received rites of the national religion: His anxious terrors made him seek new inventions of this kind;[2] which he never probably had dreamed of, had he remained a good citizen, and obedient to the laws of his country.

To which we may add, that, after the commission of crimes, there arise remorses and secret horrors, which give no rest to the mind, but make it have recourse to religious rites and ceremonies, as expiations of its offences. Whatever weakens or disorders the internal frame promotes the interests of superstition: And nothing is more destructive to them than a manly, steady virtue, which either preserves us from disastrous, melancholy accidents, or teaches us to bear them. During such calm sunshine of the mind, these spectres of false divinity never make their appearance. On the other hand, while we abandon ourselves to the natural undisciplined suggestions of our timid and anxious hearts, every kind of barbarity is ascribed to the supreme Being, from the terrors with which we are agitated; and every kind of caprice, from the methods which we embrace in order to appease him. *Barbarity, caprice*; these qualities, however nominally disguised, we may universally observe, form the ruling character of the deity in popular religions. Even priests, instead of correcting these depraved ideas of man-

[1] Diodorus Siculus, bk. XX, ch. 43 [Loeb, x. 257].

[2] Cicero, 'First Speech against Catiline'. [It is not clear to what part of the attack upon Catiline Hume is directing his readers.] Sallust, *The War with Catiline*, ch. 22 [Loeb, 41].

kind, have often been found ready to foster and encourage them. The more tremendous the divinity is represented, the more tame and submissive do men become his ministers: And the more unaccountable the measures of acceptance required by him, the more necessary does it become to abandon our natural reason, and yield to their ghostly guidance and direction. Thus it may be allowed, that the artifices of men aggravate our natural infirmities and follies of this kind, but never originally beget them. Their root strikes deeper into the mind, and springs from the essential and universal properties of human nature.

XV   GENERAL COROLLARY

Though the stupidity of men, barbarous and uninstructed, be so great, that they may not see a sovereign author in the more obvious works of nature, to which they are so much familiarized; yet it scarcely seems possible, that any one of good understanding should reject that idea, when once it is suggested to him. A purpose, an intention, a design is evident in every thing; and when our comprehension is so far enlarged as to contemplate the first rise of this visible system, we must adopt, with the strongest conviction, the idea of some intelligent cause or author. The uniform maxims, too, which prevail throughout the whole frame of the universe, naturally, if not necessarily, lead us to conceive this intelligence as single and undivided, where the prejudices of education oppose not so reasonable a theory. Even the contrarieties of nature, by discovering themselves every where, become proofs of some consistent plan, and establish one single purpose or intention, however inexplicable and incomprehensible.

Good and ill are universally intermingled and confounded; happiness and misery, wisdom and folly, virtue and vice. Nothing is pure and entirely of a piece. All advantages are attended with disadvantages. An universal compensation prevails in all conditions of being and existence. And it is not possible for us, by our most chimerical wishes, to form the idea of a station or situation altogether desirable. The draughts of life, according to the poet's fiction, are always mixed from the vessels on each hand of JUPITER: Or if any cup be presented altogether pure, it is drawn only, as the same poet tells us, from the left-handed vessel.

The more exquisite any good is, of which a small specimen is afforded us, the sharper is the evil, allied to it; and few exceptions are found to this uniform law of nature. The most sprightly wit borders on madness; the highest effusions of joy produce the deepest melancholy; the most ravishing pleasures are attended with the most cruel lassitude and disgust; the most flattering hopes make way for the severest disappointments. And, in general, no course of life has such safety (for happiness is not to be dreamed of) as the temperate and moderate, which maintains, as far as possible, a mediocrity, and a kind of insensibility, in every thing.

As the good, the great, the sublime, the ravishing are found eminently in the genuine principles of theism; it may be expected, from the analogy of nature, that the base, the absurd, the mean, the terrifying will be equally discovered in religious fictions and chimeras.

The universal propensity to believe in invisible, intelligent power, if not an original instinct, being at least a general attendant of human nature, may be considered as a kind of mark or stamp, which the divine workman has set upon his work; and nothing surely can more dignify mankind, than to be thus selected from all other parts of the creation, and to bear the image or impression of the universal Creator. But consult this image, as it appears in the popular religions of the world. How is the deity disfigured in our representations of him! How much is he degraded even below the character, which we should naturally, in common life, ascribe to a man of sense and virtue!

What a noble privilege is it of human reason to attain the knowledge of the supreme Being; and, from the visible works of nature, be enabled to infer so sublime a principle as its supreme Creator? But turn the reverse of the medal. Survey most nations and most ages. Examine the religious principles, which have, in fact, prevailed in the world. You will scarcely be persuaded, that they are any thing but sick men's dreams: Or perhaps will regard them more as the playsome whimsies of monkies in human shape, than the serious, positive, dogmatical asseverations of a being, who dignifies himself with the name of rational.

Hear the verbal protestations of all men: Nothing so certain as their religious tenets. Examine their lives: You will scarcely think that they repose the smallest confidence in them.

The greatest and truest zeal gives us no security against hypocrisy: The most open impiety is attended with a secret dread and compunction.

No theological absurdities so glaring that they have not, sometimes, been embraced by men of the greatest and most cultivated understanding. No religious precepts so rigorous that they have not been adopted by the most voluptuous and most abandoned of men.

Ignorance is the mother of Devotion: A maxim that is proverbial, and confirmed by general experience. Look out for a people, entirely destitute of religion: If you find them at all, be assured, that they are but a few degrees removed from brutes.

What so pure as some of the morals, included in some theological systems? What so corrupt as some of the practices, to which these systems give rise?

The comfortable views, exhibited by the belief of futurity, are ravishing and delightful. But how quickly vanish on the appearance of its terrors, which keep a more firm and durable possession of the human mind?

The whole is a riddle,* an ænigma, an inexplicable mystery. Doubt, uncertainty, suspence of judgment appear the only result of our most accurate scrutiny, concerning this subject. But such is the frailty of human reason, and such the irresistible contagion of opinion, that even this deliberate doubt could scarcely be upheld; did we not enlarge our view, and opposing one species of superstition to another, set them a quarrelling; while we ourselves, during their fury and contention, happily make our escape into the calm, though obscure, regions of philosophy.

HUME'S NOTES TO
THE NATURAL HISTORY

NOTE A (p. 140)

'Fragilis et laboriosa mortalitas in partes ista digessit, infirmitatis suae memor, ut portionibus quisquis coleret, quo maxime indigeret.' Pliny, *Natural History*, bk. II, ch. 5 [Frail, toiling mortality, remembering its own weakness, has divided such deities into groups, so as to worship in sections, each the deity he is most in need of. Loeb, i. 179]. So early as Hesiod's time there were 30,000 deities. *Works and Days*, l. 252. But the task to be performed by these seems still too great for their number. The provinces of the deities were so subdivided, that there was even a God of *Sneezing*. See Aristotle, *Problems*, bk. XXXIII, ch. 7 [Loeb, ii. 215]. The province of copulation, suitably to the importance and dignity of it, was divided among several deities.

NOTE B (p. 148)

It will be easy to give a reason, why Thales, Anaximander, and those early philosophers, who really were atheists, might be very orthodox in the pagan creed; and why Anaxagoras and Socrates, though real theists, must naturally, in ancient times, be esteemed impious. The blind, unguided powers of nature, if they could produce men, might also produce such beings as Jupiter and Neptune, who being the most powerful, intelligent existences in the world, would be proper objects of worship. But where a supreme intelligence, the first cause of all, is admitted, these capricious beings, if they exist at all, must appear very subordinate and dependent, and consequently be excluded from the rank of deities. Plato (*Laws*, bk. X, 886 A–E) assigns this reason for the imputation thrown on Anaxagoras, namely his denying the divinity of the stars, planets, and other created objects.

NOTE C (p. 160)

Verrius Flaccus, cited by Pliny, *Natural History*, bk. XXVIII, ch. 4 [Loeb, viii. 14 f.] affirmed, that it was usual for the Romans, before they laid siege to any town, to invocate the tutelar deity of the place, and by promising him greater honours than those he at present enjoyed, bribe him to betray his old friends and votaries. The name of the tutelar deity of Rome was for this reason kept a most religious mystery; lest the enemies of the republic should be able, in the same manner, to draw him over to their service. For without the name, they thought nothing of that kind could be practised. Pliny says, that the common form of invocation was preserved to his time in the ritual of the pontifs. And Macrobius has transmitted a copy of it from the secret things of Sammonicus Serenus.*

NOTE D (p. 163)

Most nations have fallen into this guilt of human sacrifices; though, perhaps, that impious superstition has never prevailed very much in any civilized nation, unless we except the Carthaginians. For the Tyrians soon abolished it. A sacrifice is conceived as a present; and any present is delivered to their deity by destroying it and rendering it useless to men; by burning what is solid, pouring out the liquid, and killing the animate. For want of a better way of doing him service, we do ourselves an injury; and fancy that we thereby express, at least, the heartiness of our good-will and adoration. Thus our mercenary devotion deceives ourselves, and imagines it deceives the deity.

NOTE E (p. 169)

It is strange that the Egyptian religion, though so absurd, should yet have borne so great a resemblance to the Jewish, that ancient writers even of the greatest genius were not able to observe any difference between them. For it is remarkable that both Tacitus and Suetonius, when they mention that decree of the senate, under Tiberius, by which the Egyptian and Jewish proselytes were banished from Rome expressly treat these religions as the same; and it appears, that even the decree itself was founded on that supposition. 'Actum et de sacris Egyptiis, Judaicisque pellendis; factumque patrum consultum, ut quatuor millia libertini generis *ea superstitione* infecta, quis idonea aetas, in insulam Sardiniam veherentur, coercendis illic latrociniis; et si ob gravitatem coeli interissent, *vile damnum*: Ceteri cederent Italia, nisi certam ante diem profanos ritus exuissent.' Tacitus, *Annals*, bk. II, ch. 85 [Another debate dealt with the prescription of the Egyptian and Jewish rites, and a senatorial edict directed that four thousand descendants of enfranchised slaves, tainted with that superstition and suitable in point of age, were to be shipped to Sardinia and there employed in suppressing brigandage: 'if they succumbed to the pestilential climate, it was a cheap loss.' The rest had orders to leave Italy, unless they had renounced their impious ceremonial by a given date. Loeb, 517]. 'Externas caeremonias, Egyptios, Judaicosque ritus compescuit; coactus qui *superstitione ea* tenebantur, religiosas vestes cum instrumento omni comburere, &c.' Suetonius, 'Tiberius', ch. 36 [He abolished foreign cults, especially the Egyptian and the Jewish rites, compelling all who were addicted to such superstitions to burn their religious vestments and all their paraphenalia. Loeb, i. 345]. These wise heathens, observing something in the general air, and genius, and spirit of the two religions to be the same, esteemed the differences of their dogmas too frivolous to deserve any attention.

NOTE F (p. 174)

Witness this remarkable passage of Tacitus: 'Præter multiplices rerum humanarum casus cœlo terraque prodigia, et fulminum monitus et futurorum præsagia, læta, tristia, ambigua, manifesta. Nec enim unquam atrocioribus populi Romani cladibus, magisque justis approbatum est, non esse curæ Diis securitatem nostram, esse ultionem.' *Histories* bk. I, ch. 3 [Besides the manifold misfortunes that befell mankind, there were prodigies in the sky and on the earth, warnings given by thunderbolts, and prophecies of the future, both joyful and gloomy, uncertain and clear. For never was it more fully proved by awful disasters of the Roman people or by indubitable signs that the gods care not for our safety, but for our punishment. Loeb, i. 7]. Augustus's quarrel with Neptune is an instance of the same kind. Had not the emperor believed Neptune to be a real being, and to have dominion over the sea, where had been the foundation of his anger? And if he believed it, what madness to provoke still farther that deity? The same observation may be made upon Quintilian's exclamation, on account of the death of his children, *Institutio Oratoria*, bk. VI, Preface [Loeb, ii. 375].

NOTE G (p. 175)

Xenophon's conduct, as related by himself, is, at once, an incontestable proof of the general credulity of mankind in those ages, and the incoherencies, in all ages, of men's opinions in religious matters. That great captain and philosopher, the disciple of Socrates, and one who has delivered some of the most refined sentiments with regard to a deity, gave all the following marks of vulgar, pagan superstition. By Socrates's advice, he consulted the oracle of Delphi, before he would engage in the expedition of Cyrus. *Anabasis*, bk. III, ch. 1, para. 5. Sees a dream the night after the generals were seized; which he pays great regard to, but thinks ambiguous. *Ibid.*, para. 11. He and the whole army regard sneezing as a very lucky omen. *Ibid.*, ch. 2, para. 9. Has another dream, when he comes to the river Centrites, which his fellow-general, Chirosophus, also pays great regard to. *Ibid.*, bk. IV, ch. 3, para. 8. The Greeks, suffering from a cold north wind, sacrifice to it; and the historian observes, that it immediately abated. *Ibid.*, ch. 5, paras. 3–5. Xenophon consults the sacrifices in secret, before he would form any resolution with himself about settling a colony. Bk. V, ch. 6, paras. 16–17. He was himself a very skilful augur. *Ibid.*, para. 29. Is determined by the victims to refuse the sole command of the army which was offered him. Bk. VI, ch. 1, paras. 22–24. Cleander, the Spartan, though very desirous of it, refuses it for the same reason. *Ibid.*, ch. 6, para. 36. Xenophon mentions an old dream with the interpretation given him, when he first joined Cyrus. *Ibid.*, ch. 1, para. 22. Mentions also the place of Hercules's descent into hell as believing it, and says the marks of it are still remaining. *Ibid.*, bk. VI, ch. 2, para. 2. Had almost starved the army, rather than lead them to the field against the suspices. *Ibid.*, ch. 4, paras. 12–16. His friend, Euclides, the augur, would not believe that he had brought no money from the expedition, till he (Euclides) sacrificed, and then he saw the matter clearly in the Exta.* Bk. VII, ch. 8, paras. 1–3. The same philosopher, proposing a project of mines for the encrease of the Athenian revenues, advises them first to consult the oracle. *Ways and Means*, ch. 6, paras. 2–7. That all this devotion was not a farce, in order to serve a political purpose, appears both from the facts themselves, and from the genius of that age, when little or nothing could be gained by hypocrisy. Besides, Xenophon, as appears from his Memorabilia, was a kind of heretic in those times, which no political devotee ever is. It is for the same reason, I maintain, that Newton, Locke, Clarke, &c. being *Arians* or *Socinians*,* were very sincere in the creed they professed: And I always oppose this argument to some libertines, who will needs have it, that it was impossible but that these philosophers must have been hypocrites.

NOTE H (p. 175)

Cicero, *Tusculan Disputations*, bk. I, chs. 5–6 [Loeb, 13–17], and Seneca *Moral Epistles*, 24 [Loeb, i. 177], as also Juvenal, *Satire* 2, ll. 149–52, maintain that there is no boy or old woman so ridiculous as to believe the poets in their accounts of a future state. Why then does Lucretius so highly exalt his master for freeing us from these terrors? Perhaps the generality of mankind were then in the disposition of Cephalus in Plato (*Republic*, bk. I, 330 D–331 A) who while he was young and healthful could ridicule these stories; but as soon as he became old and infirm, began to entertain apprehensions of their truth. This we may observe not to be unusual even at present.

NOTE I (p. 178)

Bacchus, a divine being, is represented by the heathen mythology as the inventor of dancing and the theatre. Plays were anciently even a part of public worship on the most solemn occasions, and often employed in times of pestilence, to appease the offended deities. But they have been zealously proscribed by the godly in later ages; and the play-house, according to a learned divine, is the porch of hell.

But in order to show more evidently, that it is possible for a religion to represent the divinity in still a more immoral and unamiable light than he was pictured by the ancients, we shall cite a long passage from an author of taste and imagination, who was surely no enemy to Christianity. It is the Chevalier Ramsay,* a writer, who had so laudable an inclination to be orthodox, that his reason never found any difficulty, even in the doctrines which free-thinkers scruple the most, the trinity, incarnation, and satisfaction: His humanity alone, of which he seems to have had a great stock, rebelled against the doctrines of eternal reprobation and predesti-nation. He expresses himself thus: 'What strange ideas,' says he, 'would an Indian or a Chinese philosopher have of our holy reli-gion, if they judged by the schemes given of it by our modern free-thinkers, and pharisaical doctors of all sects? According to the odious and too *vulgar* system of these incredulous scoffers and credulous scribblers, "The God of the Jews is a most cruel, unjust, partial, and fantastical being. He created, about 6000 years ago, a man and a woman, and placed them in a fine garden of Asia, of which there are no remains. This garden was furnished with all sorts of trees, fountains, and flowers. He allowed them the use of all the fruits of this beautiful garden, except one, that was planted in the midst thereof, and that had in it a secret virtue of preserving them in continual health and vigour of body and mind, of exalting their natural powers and making them wise. The devil entered into the body of a serpent, and solicited the first woman to eat of this forbidden fruit; she engaged her husband to do the same. To punish this slight curiosity and natural desire of life and knowledge, God not only threw our first parents out of paradise, but he condemned all their posterity to temporal misery, and the greatest part of them to eternal pains, though the souls of these innocent children have no more relation to that of Adam than to those of Nero and Mahomet; since, according to the scholastic drivellers, fabulists, and mythologists, all souls are created pure, and infused immedi-ately into mortal bodies, so soon as the foetus is formed. To accomplish the barbarous, partial decree of predestination and reprobation, God abandoned all nations to darkness, idolatry, and superstition, without any saving knowledge or salutary graces; unless it was one particular nation, whom he chose as his peculiar people. This chosen nation was, however, the most stupid, un-grateful, rebellious, and perfidious of all nations. After God had thus kept the far greater part of all the human species, during near 4000 years, in a reprobate state, he changed all of a sudden, and took a fancy for other nations besides the Jews. Then he sent his only begotten Son to the world, under a human form, to appease his wrath, satisfy his vindictive justice, and die for the pardon of sin. Very few nations, however, have heard of this gospel; and all the rest, though left in invincible ignorance, are damned without exception, or any possibility of remission. The greatest part of those who have heard of it, have changed only some speculative notions about God, and some external forms in worship: For, in other respects, the bulk of Christians have continued as corrupt as the rest of mankind in their morals; yea, so much the more perverse and criminal, that their lights were greater. Unless it be a very small select number, all other Christians, like the pagans, will be for ever damned; the great sacrifice offered up for them will become void and of no effect; God will take delight for ever, in their torments and blasphemies; and though he can, by one *fiat* change their hearts, yet they will remain for ever uncoverted and unconvertible, because he will be for ever unappeasable and irreconcileable. It is true, that all this makes God odious, a hater of souls, rather than a lover of them; a cruel, vindictive tyrant, an impotent or a wrathful daemon, rather than an all-powerful, beneficent father of spirits: Yet all this is a mystery. He has secret reasons for his conduct, that are impenetrable; and though he appears unjust and barbarous, yet we must believe the contrary, because what is injustice, crime, cruelty, and the blackest malice in us, is in him justice, mercy, and sovereign goodness." Thus the incredulous free-thinkers, the judaizing Christians, and the fatalistic doctors have disfigured and dishonoured the sublime mysteries of our holy faith; thus they have confounded the nature of good and evil; transformed the most monstrous passions into divine attributes, and surpassed the pagans in blasphemy, by ascribing to the eternal nature, as perfections, what makes the most horrid crimes amongst men. The grosser pagans contented themselves with divinizing lust, incest, and adultery; but the predestinarian doctors have divinized cruelty, wrath, fury, vengeance, and all the blackest vices.' See the Chevalier Ramsay's *Philosphical Principles of Natural and Revealed Religion*, Glasgow, 1748–9, Part II, p. 401.

The same author asserts, in other places, that the *Arminian* and *Molinist* schemes serve very little to mend the matter: And having thus thrown himself out of all received sects of Christianity, he is obliged to advance a system of his own, which is a kind of *Origenism*, and supposes the pre-existence of the souls both of men and beasts, and the eternal salvation and conversion of all men, beasts, and devils. But this notion, being quite peculiar to himself, we need not treat of. I thought the opinions of this ingenious author very curious; but I pretend not to warrant the justness of them.

AN ABSTRACT OF
THE NATURAL HISTORY

I. That polytheism is the original religion of mankind, (*a*) because of the overwhelming evidence of ancient authorities and the evidence of more recent geographical explorations, and (*b*) because it is implausible to suppose that very primitive man first arrived at the sophisticated notion of a single God and then lost it as civilization and understanding progressed.

II. Contemplation of the structure of nature suggests a single governing power. The vicissitudes of human life suggest many and diverse powers influencing human weal and woe.

III. The 'unknown causes' of human fortune and misfortune appear as malevolent or benevolent or capricious agents, and are thus given human characteristics. Moreover, people who are weakest and most vulnerable to capricious fortune are most superstitious.

IV. Elves and fairies and pagan gods have much in common. All are products of the natural world, not creators of it. As such their powers are much greater than those of human beings but of the same kind.

V. That polytheism draws its extreme anthropomorphism from, among other things, allegory and the worship of human beings as heroes.

VI. That monotheism evolved from polytheism, not by reasoning, but by comparison with the development of human societies where one leader tends to predominate and become ever more powerful. Once this process has started, the leading god receives greater and greater attention until the rest become relatively insignificant. But the vulgar conception of the leading god remains anthropomorphic.

VII. The absurd results of the conjunction of sublime powers and gross anthropomorphism are exemplified in ancient, Roman Catholic and Mahometan practices.

VIII. The first conception of gods as powerful but limited beings, who are themselves subject to destiny and are parts of nature, gives way by fear and flattery of the supposed chief of these beings to a conception of deity as 'unity and infinity, simplicity and spirituality'. But these conceptions in turn prove too remote for ordinary human nature, and demi-gods or other intermediaries are introduced until they again become too much the objects of worship. So there is a flux and reflux of polytheism and monotheism.

IX. That polytheism, claiming no single truth about a unique god, is more tolerant than monotheism. 'It naturally admits the gods of other sects and nations to a share of divinity.' This is verified by historical and contemporary observations and is evident in the history of Christianity.

X. That polytheism, because of the nearness of gods to human heroes, engenders courage and upstanding character; monotheism engenders abasement and 'monkish virtues'.

XI. Polytheism is easily supposable and 'natural', but it is ill adapted to defence by argument and philosophy. Monotheism readily attracts philosophical defence but in turn makes philosophy its bondsman, all natural possibilities which differ from the approved religion being branded heretical.

XII. Actual religions (ancient and modern) contain many beliefs which appear absurd to anyone not committed to the religion. But modern religion, being scriptural, is more determined in its articles of faith than former traditional religions where no one was expected to believe or know all the inconsistent stories. [This long section is much illustrated from Hume's very extensive reading of classical sources.]

XIII. That both theism and polytheism have conceptions of deity which combine what is admirable with what is malicious. Thus great (or even infinite) power is attributed to entities of mixed moral character. The result is the moral confusion which concedes that 'the gods have maxims of justice peculiar to themselves'. [In Note I (see p. 190), Hume artfully shows that Christianity is not exempt from this defect.]

XIV. That religious devotion tends less to enhance morality than to engender superstitious observances, dogmatic zeal and the embracing of absurd beliefs. This may well be because morality is natural 'and what many would have performed, were there no god in the universe', whereas austerities and acts of special devotion can only relate to god since they manifestly have no other use or reason to be.

XV. Aphoristic and rhetorically expressed conclusions. These contrast the apparent reasons for belief in a single designer-intelligence, and what that belief would lead us to expect of religion and to do, with the actual practices and real results of religion. The final result of our investigations is that 'the whole is a riddle, an ænigma, an inexplicable mystery' leading to 'doubt, uncertainty, suspense of judgment'.

EXPLANATORY NOTES

An Enquiry concerning Human Understanding, Section XI

11   *a particular providence*: in the first edition of the *Enquiry* (1748)
      Hume called Section XI 'Of the Practical Consequences of Natural
      Theology' thus drawing attention to its challenge to the supposed
      moral and social dimension of philosophical religion. The title he
      substituted in 1751, and subsequently retained, draws more attention
      to his thesis that the design argument fails to establish God's 'provi-
      dence'. A *provident* God is one concerned with us and active (or
      immanent) in his creation. Thus God as normally spoken of and to
      in the Jewish, Christian, and Islamic religions is a provident God.
      For a full discussion of Section XI, see *Hume's Enquiry concerning
      Human Understanding*, ed. P. Millican (Oxford, forthcoming).

      Protagoras: Greek teacher-philosopher or 'sophist', very roughly
      485–415 BC, whose main thesis seems to have been the relativity of
      knowledge, 'Man is the measure of all things'. Diogenes Laertius,
      writing 600 years later, says that Protagoras began one book ' "As to
      the gods, I have no means of knowing either that they exist or that
      they do not exist . . ." For this introduction to his book the Athenians
      expelled him; and they burnt his works in the market place.' (bk. IX,
      ch. 8.) Plato, who might have been expected to mention this, does
      not do so even in the *Theaetetus* or *Protagoras* and the story may be
      a later invention or attached to the wrong name.

      Socrates: Athenian philosopher, 469–399 BC, teacher of Plato and
      the main character in many of his dialogues, was charged before a
      large democratic jury (the 'dicastery' of 501 men) with corrupting
      the minds of the young and introducing strange gods. As Hume says,
      there were other (political) motives, and Socrates, like Bertrand
      Russell, must have been for long an exceptionally irritating 'gadfly'
      to those in authority. For his defence, see Plato's *Apology*. Socrates
      was condemned to death by a majority vote and spurned all oppor-
      tunities of escape.

      Epicurus: Athenian philosopher, 341–270 BC, founder of the school
      of the Epicureans who, along with the Stoics, largely dominated later
      classical philosophy. Epicurean writings were the main channel
      through which the ideas of ancient atomism (that the universe con-
      sists of infinite void space and an infinite number of eternally exist-
      ing minimum physical particles) were conveyed to seventeenth-

century Europe. Hume makes his sceptical friend a quasi-Epicurean because (*a*) Epicurus flatly rejected the possibility of an afterlife and (*b*) although the Epicureans did not demur at observing conventional religious 'superstitions', their gods were a refined and elusive product of the natural world, and were to man no more than examples of blessedness who did nothing, created nothing, promised nothing to him, and required nothing from him. Thus Epicurean gods exercised no *providence*.

12   *or disputation*: for the toleration associated with religion in 'early ages', see Hume's *Natural History of Religion*, particularly Part IX.

13   *fill all the urn . . . my adversaries*: voting in Athenian courts was conducted by placing a black or a white bean in a jar: a white one for 'in favour' or 'innocent'; a black one for 'against' or 'guilty'.

    principles of reason: Hume is alluding to the eighteenth-century intellectual fashion for rationalized defences of Christianity. Conspicuous examples are Samuel Clarke's Boyle Lectures of 1704 and 1705 published as *A Discourse concerning the Being and Attributes of God* (1705 and many later editions) and Joseph Butler's *The Analogy of Religion* (1736 and many later editions)

    They paint . . . admire: for other statements of the design argument, see *Dialogues*, Parts II and III, p. 45 and p. 56 below.

14   *chance, or . . . unguided force*: this was the actual Epicurean view, much criticized in antiquity. See, for example, Cicero's *De Natura Deorum*, bk. II, ch. 37. For Hume's brilliant variation of this view, see *Dialogues*, Part VIII.

15   *Zeuxis*: Athenian painter who flourished about 430 BC, mentioned in Plato's *Protagoras*. It was said of him that his painting of grapes 'deceived the birds'.

    Jupiter: the chief Roman god, here used as a conveniently discreet cover for what most of Hume's readers would construe as God the Father.

16   *If they tell me . . . present world*: for a discussion of the above argument to and from a cause, see J. C. A. Gaskin, *Hume's Philosophy of Religion*, 2nd edn. (London, 1988), 17–21.

    unhappy: for Hume's full discussion of these matters, see *Dialogues*, Parts X and XI.

17   *The religious hypothesis*: for a discussion of 'the religious hypotheses', see Antony Flew, *Hume's Philosophy of Belief* (London, 1961), ch. 9.

19 *in the school, or in the closet*: in the lecture room in public or in one's own apartments in private.

20 *art*: skilled workmanship.

22 *analogy*: points of similarity. One of Hume's main themes in the *Dialogues* is to show the remoteness of the analogy upon which the design argument depends. See in particular Part II.

23 *enthusiasm*: very strong, emotionally aroused confidence in some belief, in eighteenth-century usage almost always *religious* belief. Hume is not entirely correct in saying there is no enthusiasm among philosophers. But such as there is is usually reserved for minute arguments without practical application.

Hume's Letter concerning the Dialogues

25 *Had it been my good Fortune . . . that of Cleanthes*: cf. Cicero's letter of July, 45 BC, to M. T. Varro referring to Cicero's dialogues in the *Academica*: 'I have given you the part of Antiochus which I think I understand you to approve of, while I have taken to myself the character of Philo.' (See Cicero, *Letters to Friends*, Loeb, III. 209). See my Introduction for Hume's relation to Cicero, pp. xxi–xxii.

26 *a profest Atheist, & . . . an Epicurean, which is little or nothing different*: for the Epicureans, the gods are a refined part of the natural universe, not its external cause or its creators. They exist in self-sufficient blessedness, inactive and unrelated to man and the processes of the world. See Lucretius, *The Nature of the Universe*, iii. 18–24. Thus Hume concludes that the Epicureans might just as well say there are no gods: at least the gods *matter* no more for the Epicurean than for the atheist.

si quid novisti rectius, &c.: Horace, *Epistles*, I. vi. 67–8. In full:

> Vive, vale! Si quid novisti rectius istis,
> Candidus imperti; si nil his utere mecum.

'Live long, farewell. If you know something better than these precepts, pass it on, my good fellow. If not, join me in following these.' (Loeb, 29.)

You ask me . . . which you argue: Hume inadvertently confuses who is for and against what in this sentence. Read: 'You question my suggestion that the idea of cause and effect is nothing but constant conjunction. I would gladly know whence is that farther Idea of Causation *for* which you argue [or against which *I* argue]?'

27 *my Petition*: a piece of minor writing by Hume entitled 'The Bellman's Petition', designed to ridicule the claim of the Scottish clergy for increased stipends.

Dialogues concerning Natural Religion

30 *natural religion*: in eighteenth-century usage this phrase is usually preferred to its synonym 'natural theology' (which Hume in fact uses on p. 129). Both phrases indicate the system of conclusions about God's (or the gods') existence and nature that are supposedly attainable from evidence and by reasoning accessible to any thinking person irrespective of special revelations conveyed by the Bible, Koran, or other privileged source. Do *not* confuse references to natural religion with ideas of nature worship or pantheism which are entirely different.

34 *inexplicable*: much of Philo's speech is a summary of the sceptical doubts concerning human understanding which Hume had himself developed in *A Treatise of Human Nature* (1739–40). 'Coherence of parts', etc. are 'inexplicable' because we cannot say, ultimately, *why* things are as the best science finds them to be. See 'Hume on Causation' by G. J. Warnock in *David Hume: A Symposium*, ed. D. F. Pears (London, 1963).

35 *Pyrrhonians*: excessive sceptics concerning knowledge and certainty first associated with Pyrrho of Elis (*c*.365–275 BC). The main vehicle of scepticism from the ancient world is the writings of Sextus Empiricus (second century AD) which first became generally available in modern Europe in 1569. In Section XII of *An Enquiry concerning Human Understanding* (1748), Hume distinguished between excessive (Pyrrhonian) scepticism and mitigated (Academic) scepticism or scepticism consequential upon a proper understanding of our limitations. See Introduction, p. xiv. In Part I of the *Dialogues*, Philo expresses mitigated scepticism while Cleanthes chides him with excessive scepticism. The distinction becomes important again in Part XII. For an exceptionally informative working out of the relations between scepticism and religion, and Hume's part in this process, see Terence Penelhum, *God and Skepticism* (Dordrecht, 1983).

Stoics: followers of Zeno of Citium (335–263 BC), Chrysippus (*c*.280–207 BC), and others in the rigorous analytic and metaphysical system of logic, ethics, and physics which, in rivalry to Epicureanism, dominated the classical world between the third century BC and the second century AD.

The bent of his mind relaxes: Hume is here writing from vivid personal experience in his earlier days. See *A Treatise of Human Nature*, the final section of Book I, 'Conclusion of this book'.

36 *common life*: for a book-length development of this theme, see D. W. Livingston, *Hume's Philosophy of Common Life* (Chicago, 1984).

38 *scepticism*: for a full discussion of the immensely important balance between legitimate scepticism with regard to reason, when reason is applied to 'remote and abstruse' subjects, and the practical need to trust reason and the senses in common life, see J. C. A. Gaskin, *Hume's Philosophy of Religion*, 2nd edn. (London, 1988), 104–21.

rainbow: for Newton (1642–1727) on the rainbow etc., see his paper to the Royal Society, 1672, reproduced in *Newton's Philosophy of Nature*, ed. H. S. Thayer and J. H. Randall (New York, 1953), 68–81.

Copernicus and Galilæo: Copernicus (1473–1543) and Galileo (1564–1642) both held that the sun was fixed and that the Earth and other planets moved about it. Copernicus may have held the theory only as a convenience of calculation, but Galileo certainly held it as a true description of the way things really are. Thus the ancient suggestion of the eminent mathematician and astronomer of Alexandria, Aristarchus of Samos, *c*.280 BC, was revived as 'the Copernican System'.

39 *evidence*: in *An Enquiry concerning Human Understanding*, Section X, a very critical discussion of miracles, Hume remarks that 'a wise man . . . proportions his belief to the evidence'. This is the enterprise undertaken, and differently resolved, by Cleanthes and Philo in their discussion of the nature of God in Parts II to XI of the *Dialogues*.

40 *contrary . . . to our very senses*: Cleanthes means that to all common sense appearances it is the sun that moves and the Earth that remains at rest.

popular religion: Cleanthes is speaking in very broad generalizations here. Christianity took from classical philosophy some of the means for articulating, ordering, and understanding what it believed. But it also assimilated from Greek philosophical monotheism such arguments as were of use to the new religion. Thus reasons and evidence beyond that of the biblical revelation were incorporated into Christianity as the 'natural religion' which Philo attacks and Cleanthes defends in the *Dialogues*, and which Hume attacks in *An Enquiry concerning Human Understanding*, particularly in Sections I, XI, and XII.

40 *Academics*: it is not immediately clear whether Hume is referring here to the Academics as the exponents of Plato's two-world philosophy (a philosophy potentially useful to Christianity) or to the Academics in the period when they were associated with scepticism with regard to knowledge in general and rival philosophies in particular. The context suggests the latter. This is confirmed at the top of p. 42.

Reformers: Protestant Reformers.

Locke: John Locke (1632–1704). See his *An Essay concerning Human Understanding* (1690), particularly bk. IV, chs. 10 and 18, and *The Reasonableness of Christianity* (1695).

41 *Bayle*: Pierre Bayle (1647–1706), author of the vast *Dictionnaire historique et critique* (1696), an invaluable source for sceptical arguments against philosophy and theology, used by Hume (here and elsewhere in the *Dialogues*, notably in Part XI), Voltaire, and others.

Lord Bacon: Francis Bacon (1561–1626), first of the great line of British empiricist philosophers. The much quoted dictum in Hume's text is from the essay 'Of Atheism' (1597).

David's fool: 'The fool hath said in his heart, there is no God.' (Psalms 14: 1.)

the dissolution of the ancient schools: the last surviving schools of ancient philosophy in Athens were shut down by the Christian Emperor Justinian in AD 529.

deism: the word was commonly if somewhat vaguely used in the eighteenth century to indicate belief in a single deity, as manifested to reason by the natural world, *without* the additional information supposed to be provided by a particular revelation such as that contained in the Bible. Thus, typically, the deist would accept and rely heavily on the design argument but reject the Trinitarian revelation that God is 'three persons in one substance'. The word had strong depreciatory overtones (note, for example, Hume's use of it in relation to Cicero, p. 171) and Hume strongly resisted its application to himself. (See Günter, Gawlick, 'Hume and the Deists: a Reconsideration' in *David Hume*, ed. G. P. Morice (Edinburgh, 1977), and J. C. A. Gaskin, 'Hume's Attenuated Deism', in *Archiv für Geschichte der Philosophie*, 1983.) Hume's refusal to be called a deist probably resulted from his real rejection of deism's typical appeal to *reasons* for belief in a designer or creator God, and a wish to avoid the odium of the appellation.

42 *Peripatetics*: followers of Aristotle.

43 *to conceive them*: see 1 Corinthians 2: 9.

Malebranche: theologian and Cartesian philosopher (1638–1715). His *Recherche de la vérité* (1675) influenced both Berkeley and Hume. See C. J. McCracken, *Malebranche and British Philosophy* (Oxford, 1983).

44 *anthropomorphites*: those who profess to understand the Deity as one to whom can be applied language which draws its meaning from human attributes and activities. Physical anthropomorphism is readily rejected by any religion that does not regard its god as a physical object. Mental or moral anthropomorphism is more difficult to reject as it is not clear how, for example, such a word as 'mercy' in 'God's mercy is everlasting' can be understood at all if it is totally detached from its anthropomorphic sense.

whatever it be: compare this initial claim of Philo's with his final conclusion, Part XII, p. 129.

ideas: the conclusion of Hume's syllogism, 'We have no ideas of divine attributes and operations', is understandable in non-technical language, but note that by 'idea' Hume means the thought or image associated with a term by means of an actual experience or 'impression'. See Hume's *Treatise*, I. i. 1 and *An Enquiry concerning Human Understanding*, Section II.

45 *argument* a posteriori . . . *proofs* a priori: Demea's version of the 'proof *a priori*' is given later in Part IX. Demea is complaining in Part II that the design argument, an 'argument *a posteriori*', provides at best only a 'probable' conclusion by comparison with the 'certain' conclusion of a valid *a priori* proof. What is worse, according to Demea, better according to Cleanthes, is that the *a posteriori* argument both depends upon and seeks to establish a certain anthropomorphic similarity between God and man which the *a priori* proof does not. Demea, in whom extreme rationalism and quasi-mysticism combine, rejects the anthropomorphism as offensive; Philo rejects it because God is incomprehensibly different from man. Arguments are *a priori* or *a posteriori* in the terms used by Hume and his contemporaries depending mainly upon whether they employ *a priori* or *a posteriori* propositions. 'An *a priori* proposition is one that can be known to be true, or false, without reference to experience, except in

so far as experience is necessary for understanding its terms. An *a posteriori* proposition can be known to be true, or false, only by reference to how, as a matter of contingent fact, things have been, are, or will be.' (*A Dictionary of Philosophy*, ed. A. Flew (London, 1979), entry '*a priori*'.)

47   *a contradition*: cf. *Enquiry*, Section IV, Part I and Cleanthes' argument against Demea in *Dialogues*, Part IX.

49   *phlegm*: coolness or calmness.

   blowing: blossoming or growing to its full potential.

50   *agitation of the brain which we call thought*: such radical reduction of Descartes's soul/body (or thinking substance/material substance) dualism is seldom *explicitly* suggested by Hume.

   animalcule: minute animal. It was thought that sperm contained such entities.

51   *argument from experience*: see also the final paragraph of Section XI of the *Enquiry*, p. 23 f. above.

52   *Dialogues*: Galileo's *Dialogue concerning the Two Chief World Systems* (1632). See the translation by S. Drake (Berkeley, Calif., 1953).

53   *The schools*: in general, in medieval Europe, the divisions of subjects taught in universities, and the buildings where such teaching was carried on. In particular, in the present context, the Scholastic and Aristotelian schools of philosophy which Galileo opposed.

56   *a force like that of sensation*: this is Cleanthes' statement of the 'irregular' design argument. It no longer invites the discussion of analogy undertaken in Part II, but claims that the 'idea of a contriver' is not a result of argument. It is more like a direct perception (and as such immune from all but the most excessive scepticism). The source of the passage could well be Colin Maclaurin, *An Account of Sir Isaac Newton's Philosophical Discoveries* (1748). See R. H. Hurlbutt, *Hume, Newton and the Design Argument* (Lincoln, Nebr., 1965), 40–2.

58   *mysterious self-annihilation*: Plotinus (AD 205–270) was the main exponent of a system of metaphysically enhanced Platonism known as Neoplatonism. Apart from postulating at least three orders of being, it tended at times towards what would now be called mysticism. See, for example, Plotinus *The Enneads*, VI. ix. 2: 'There were not two, beholder was one with beheld . . .'

61   *What is the soul of man? . . . distinct from each other*: for Hume's

attempted account of the self, see *Treatise*, I. iv. 6, 'Of Personal Identity'.

62 *the universal consent of mankind*: argument to the real existence of a divine entity from the fact of almost universal belief in *some* sort of divinity. See, for example, Cicero, *De Natura Deorum*, Book I, ch. 44; II, ch. 5; II, chs. 8–10; or Sextus Empiricus, *Against the Physicists*, Book I, ch. 61. See also Hume's Introduction to *The Natural History of Religion*, p. 134 below.

63 *his elephant*: see John Locke, *An Essay concerning Human Understanding*, II. xiii. 19: 'Had the poor Indian philosopher (who imagined that the earth also wanted something to bear it up) but thought of this word "substance", he needed not to have been at the trouble to find an elephant to support it, and a tortoise to support his elephant . . .'

66 *Naturalists indeed . . . totally inexplicable*: cf. Hume's *Enquiry concerning Human Understanding*, Section IV, Part I: 'It is confessed, that the utmost effort of human reason is to reduce the principles, productive of natural phenomena, to a greater simplicity, and to resolve the many particular effects into a few general causes . . . But as to the causes of these general causes, we should in vain attempt their discovery . . . these are probably the ultimate causes and principles which we shall ever discover in nature.'

67 *Lucretius*: Roman poet (*c*.99–55 BC) whose massive and influential *On the Nature of the Universe* is the most extensive account of the Epicurean atomist system that has survived from antiquity.

Tully: the preferred eighteenth-century name for M. T. Cicero (106–43 BC) whose work on the philosophy of religion, *De Natura Deorum* (*On the Nature of the Gods*) provided Hume with the form he follows in the *Dialogues*. See Introduction, p. xx.

69 *seeming difficulties*: see Parts X and XI where the difficulties are treated as very real.

70 *Dæmons*: from the Greek '*daimon*', a word originally synonymous with '*theos*' (god) but later used of a being intermediary between gods and men: demigod.

to multiply causes: the methodological principle known as Occam's Razor, 'don't multiply explanatory entities without need', had for Hume been reinforced by Newton in 'Rule I' of Book III of *Principia Mathematica*: 'We are to admit no more causes of natural things than such as are both true and sufficient to explain their appearance.'

70 *theogony*: an account of the genealogy of gods associated with attempts to account for phenomena on earth. See in particular the early Greek poem *Theogony* by Hesiod, who flourished about 735 BC. Hume later refers to Hesiod explicitly. See *Dialogues*, p. 77 and p. 82.

this argument: see Cicero's *De Natura Deorum*, bk. I, ch. 18 (Loeb, 49) where Velleius, the Epicurean, states the argument. The ridicule is undertaken by Cotta, the Sceptic, bk. I, chs. 25–8.

73 *theists of antiquity*: Hume could have been thinking of Plato in, for example, *Laws*, x. 895–9, where 'soul' or 'life' is associated with what is self-moving ('thus all things are full of gods'), or with Plato in the *Timaeus*; or Hume could have been thinking of the general Stoic thesis that 'reason, law or God' permeates all base matter.

final causes: whatever may be the final end, object or purpose of the working of anything, or of what is done.

75 *Constantinople*: capital of the Byzantine (Eastern Roman) Empire until taken by the Turks in 1453. The Turkish occupation dispersed Greek scholarship from its ancient stronghold to the eventual enlightenment of western Europe.

Lucullus: Roman general who carried on a war against Mithridates in Asia Minor, 74–67 BC. Cherry trees apart, Lucullus became exquisitely rich as a result of his campaigns.

80 *principles*: compare *An Enquiry concerning Human Understanding*, Section IV, Part I: 'Elasticity, gravity, cohesion of parts, communication of motion by impulse; these are probably the ultimate causes and principles which we shall ever discover in nature.' Here the word 'principle' means the origin, or fundamental source of change or operation of a system.

82 *Timæus*: Plato's main work on cosmology, heavily influenced by Pythagorean views about the world (universe) being a living creature endowed with soul and intelligence. Not a few students of Plato would sympathize with Hume's 'so far as he is intelligible' in relation to this notoriously obscure dialogue.

84 *matter infinite*: the Epicureans argued that the universe consisted in an infinite number of indestructible particles distributed in infinite space. Compare Hume's supposition with Lucretius, *De Rerum Natura*, i. 1021–37, e.g. 'being many and shifted in many ways, [the primary particles] are harried and set in motion with blows through-

out the universe from infinity, thus by trying every kind of motion and combination, at length they fall into such arrangements as the sum of things consists of; and this being also preserved through many great cycles of years, when once it has been cast together into convenient motions, brings it about that . . .' (Loeb, 85.)

85 *The beginning of motion*: that motion ever 'began' is precisely the supposition that the Epicureans (and Philo himself in the next paragraph) do not hold. In their view, matter and its movement are one, not two: they are co-eternal, and neither are such as require or can be given any separate explanation. Matter in motion is the ultimate way the universe eternally is.

87 *order*: note that in the preceding paragraph Hume anticipates the formal structure of a theory of natural selection: the well-adaptedness of, for example, animals to their environment is not to be accounted for in terms of the purposes of a guiding intelligence, but in terms of accidental features which enable the animals to survive within the given environment.

88 *ectypal, not archetypal*: of the nature of a copy, not of a prototype.

90 *The argument*: what follows is Hume's paraphrase of the *a priori* argument for God's existence set out by Samuel Clarke in the Boyle Lectures for 1704 and 1705 and subsequently published as *A Discourse concerning the Being and Attributes of God*. For an analysis of Clarke's argument, see W. L. Rowe, *The Cosmological Argument* (Princeton, NJ, 1975). For an assessment of Hume's representation of Clarke's argument, see M. A. Stewart, '*Hume and the "Metaphysical Argument a Priori"*' in *Philosophy, Its History and Historiography* (The Hague, 1985).

91 *Nothing is demonstrable . . . contradiction*: cf. Hume's *Enquiry concerning Human Understanding*, Section IV, Part I and Section XII, Part III.

92 *Dr. Clarke*: see *A Discourse concerning the Being and Attributes of God*, 9th edn. (1736), pp. 22 f. where the *sense* of the words Hume apparently quotes may be found, but not the words themselves or anything like them.

95 *It is my opinion . . . agitated and tormented*: compare this paragraph with *The Natural History of Religion*, Part III.

Dr. Young: Edward Young (1683–1765), author of *Night Thoughts* of which Johnson remarked, 'The excellence of this work is not exactness but copiousness'.

96 *Leibnitz has denied it*: the *Theodicy* (1710) contains a somewhat

repetitive argument to the effect that all possible worlds contain some evil and that the present is the best of possible worlds. For additional comments by Hume, see *An Enquiry concerning Human Understanding*, Section VIII, Part II (Oxford, 1975), 101.

96　*Dr. King*: William King (1650–1729), Archbishop of Dublin. Hume's wording in the paragraph beginning 'And why should man . . .' is similar to King's as translated in *An Essay on the Origin of Evil* (1739), 104.

98　*afraid of death*: this is not precisely a quotation from Lucretius, but most of Book III of *The Nature of the Universe* is an attempt to counter fear of death. For Hume's discussion of the deliberate breaking of 'the secret chain', see his essay 'Of Suicide'.

99　*that the greatest prosperities . . . contentment*: Hume is quoting from vol. II of Bayle's *A General Dictionary, Historical and Critical* (London, 1735), the article 'Charles V'.

　　And suitably to . . . reject the present: see Cicero's *Cato Major de Senectute* (*Cato Major: Of Old Age*).

100　*whence then is evil?*: no such terse and effective sequence of questions occurs in any extant work of Epicurus. The immediate source for Hume is very probably Bayle's *Dictionary* (which he is using extensively in this part of the *Dialogues*), the article on Paulicians, note E or (for both Bayle and Hume) *On the Anger of God*, ch. 13, by Lactantius (AD 260–340), for which see *The Works of* Lactantius, trans. W. Fletcher (Edinburgh, 1871; or London, 1951). A somewhat similar form of words occurs in Sextus Empiricus (second century AD), but there is no attribution to Epicurus. See his *Outlines of Pyrrhonism*, III. iii.

101　*natural attributes . . . uncertain*: to what purpose establish that the Deity is, for example, the cause of the universe or intelligent, or the designer, while leaving it uncertain whether the Deity is good in an understandable sense, or exercises providence: cf. Cicero, *De Natura Deorum*, bk. III, chs. 35 and 37.

107　*only the inference*: the inference to a provident God is scrutinized by Hume in *An Enquiry concerning Human Understanding*, Section XI. See p. 16 above. For a discussion of Hume's differentiation between the 'inference' problem caused by evil in the world (a problem for the design argument) and the 'consistency' problem (the problem for someone who believes in a benevolent God and needs to account for evil in the world), see J. C. A. Gaskin, *Hume's Philosophy of Religion*, 2nd edn. (London, 1988), ch. 3.

108 *particular volitions*: decisions (by the Deity) arrived at for each particular occasion.

112 *natural evil*: (or 'physical evil') suffering caused by the working of the natural world independently of any human agent's free actions. Natural evil is contrasted by Hume later in Part XI with 'moral evil'—suffering resulting from a human agent's free actions.

113 *the Manichæan system*: an adaptation (by the Parthian prophet Mani, AD 216–277) of the Zoroastrian religion's belief in an opposition of good and evil deities in the world; cf. Hume's remark in *An Enquiry concerning the Principles of Morals*, Section V, Part II, 'Could we admit the two principles of the Manicheans, it is an infallible consequence, that their sentiments of human actions, as well as of everything else, must be totally opposite, and that every instance of justice and humanity, from its necessary tendency, must please the one deity and displease the other.' (Oxford, 1975, 227.)

114 *the ultimate cause of all things*: for Hume's development of the idea that moral guilt attaches to God as the 'ultimate cause and author' of man's actions, see *An Enquiry concerning Human Understanding*, Section VIII, Part II.

116 *I must confess . . . profess that intention*: this paragraph is the core of Philo's apparent retraction of the outcome of his earlier arguments. Its status is much disputed by various interpreters. See Introduction.

121 *My inclination . . . eternal*: compare this paragraph and the argument of the following two pages with *An Enquiry concerning Human Understanding*, Section XI, p. 23 above.

The above note . . . the manuscript: despite N. Kemp Smith's editorial note, it is not entirely clear when one looks at the manuscript whether Hume intends this as a note written in his own person, i.e. a *comment* on Philo's speech, or as a *part* of Philo's speech. The reasons for taking it as a part of the speech are set out in *The Natural History of Religion and Dialogues concerning Natural Religion*, ed. A. Wayne Colver and J. V. Price (Oxford, 1976), 250 n. 5.

122 *vulgar superstition*: a phrase Hume is inclined to use as a way of referring to what on examination turns out to be religion as ordinarily understood in the world. Note, for example, his remark in a letter of 1764; 'It is putting too great a Respect on the Vulgar, and on their Superstitions, to pique one'self on Sincerity with regard to them.' *New Letters of David Hume*, ed. R. Klibansky and E. C. Mossner (Oxford, 1954), 83.

122   *The proper office of religion*: cf. Hume in the first edition of the *History of England* (London, 1757), ii. 449 n.: 'The proper office of religion is to reform men's lives, to purify their hearts, to inforce all moral duties, and to secure obedience to the laws and civil magistrate.' See also E. C. Mossner, *The Life of David Hume* (Edinburgh, 1954; 2nd edn. Oxford, 1970), 306–7.

124   *superstition or enthusiasm*: for Hume's attempt to characterize these 'corruptions' of religion, see his essay of 1741 'Of Superstition and Enthusiasm'.

frivolous species of merit: Hume is referring to those 'merits' created by religion within their own belief systems which have no reference to the natural good of mankind. See, for example, *An Enquiry concerning the Principles of Morals*, Section III, Part II (Oxford, 1975), 199 and Section IX, Part I, 270.

125   fasces *and* axes: the bundle of rods with an axe projecting carried before the chief Roman magistrates as an indication of their authority to punish.

But we must treat . . . in the world: cf. *The Natural History of Religion*, p. 184.

126   *Iphigenia in Tauride*: Hume does not point out to us the passage. It could be ll. 1157–233 in which Iphigenia warns her hearer about Greek deceptions while she herself is actually deceiving her hearer.

128   *all devout people*: Hume's examination of the psychology of religion is greatly extended in *The Natural History of Religion*, a work written at the same time as, or not long after, the first draft of the *Dialogues* here ending.

To know God, *says Seneca,* is to worship him: this is not quite what Seneca wrote in the *Moral Epistles*, 95. 50: 'Primus est deorum cultus deos credere', which is to say, 'The first step in divine worship is to believe in the Gods'. (See Loeb, iii. 88–9.)

130   *nearer to the truth*: Hume owes a great deal both in the structure of the *Dialogues* and in some of his particular arguments, to Cicero's *De Natura Deorum* (*On the Nature of the Gods*). This is strikingly evident in the conclusion where Cicero wrote, also criss-crossing the approvals and obscuring his own position, 'Here the conversation ended, and we parted, Velleius thinking Cotta's discourse to be the truer, while I felt that that of Balbus approximated more nearly to a semblance of the truth'. Velleius is the Epicurean, Balbus the Stoic, and Cotta (cf. Philo) the academic or sceptical critic of both. For a general survey of Hume's use of Cicero, see Peter Jones, *Hume's*

Sentiments: Their Ciceronian and French Context (Edinburgh, 1982), 29–42.

The Natural History of Religion

134 *in all places and in all ages*: see note to p. 62 above.

136 *that perfect Being, who bestowed order on the whole frame of nature*: here and in other places in the *Natural History* (see pp. 138, 150, 154, and 184) Hume apparently takes for granted the design argument he had so damaged in the *Dialogues* and elsewhere. See Introduction, pp. xxiii–xxvi above.

Milton: see *Paradise Lost*, iv. 205–357.

138 *One design prevails throughout the whole*: cf. *Dialogues*, Part V, p. 70.

141 *armies in the clouds*: cf. Hume in the letter of 1751 to Gilbert Elliot, printed in full above p. 26.

144 *The leaders . . . are the women*: before Strabo and Hume should attract the anachronistic epithet 'sexist', consider the relative proportions of men and women still usually seen in churches.

145 *Now, suppose . . . same denomination*: in this complex paragraph, Hume is arguing that there is less difference between a believer in minor spirits of the earth and an atheist, than betwwen such a believer and a theist. Hence the believer in spirits is 'a kind of superstitious atheist'.

146 *Amphitrion*: play by Plautus (*c.*254–184 BC) in which, among other excitements, Jupiter contrives the amalgamation of two nights to prolong his amours.

148 *physiologers*: students or teachers of natural science.

Thales, Anaximenes, Heraclitus . . . Anaxagoras: all Presocratic philosophers. Hume's main point is that the Homeric gods were originally conceived and long regarded as a product of the natural world, not as creators of it.

149 Stoics *and* Academics: see notes to p. xv and p. 35 above. Hume is using the terms very loosely here. Marcus Aurelius was indeed a Stoic; Plutarch neither a Stoic nor an Academic in any obvious sense.

152 *Heliogabalus*: according to Herodian, in the source to which Hume directs us, the sun god worshipped under his Phoenician name.

152 *Areopagites*: the advisory body of chief men in Athens.

154 *Many theists ... have denied a* particular *providence*: by any dictionary definition (eighteenth century or now) of the word 'theist', what Hume appears to be saying here is at the very least confusing. Theists are by definition those who believe (on whatever grounds) in a single omnipotent God exerting particular providence, that is to say, exerting control, guidance, or forethought in the moral and personal affairs of mankind and in the physical processes of the world. To deny a particular providence is one of the characteristics of a deist. See note to p. 41 above. In the present paragraph, Hume could be saying that theists are just like deists in that they both appeal to the design argument 'the chief or sole argument for a divine existence' (see p. 14 above) or he could be anticipating the usage which becomes evident later in the *Natural History* (e.g. p. 160) in which 'theist' operates as a synonym for 'monotheist'. In this usage, the deist who denied providence and the theist who affirmed it would still both be 'theists', i.e. *mono*theists, as contrasted with *poly*theists.

idolatrous: here and elsewhere in the *Natural History* (note especially the first sentence of Part IX), Hume uses 'polytheism' and 'idolatrous worship' as synonyms. But it is not the case that, for example, all ancient pagans worshipped idols as such, any more than a Roman Catholic praying to a saintly image thinks the image itself *is* the saint.

156 *Thus, the God of Abraham ... of the Jews*: the sentence in square brackets read, in the proof sheets now lost but seen by Grosse and Green in 1874 when preparing their edition of Hume's works: 'Thus the deity, whom the vulgar Jews conceived only as the God of Abraham, Isaac, and Jacob, became their Jehovah and Creator of the world.' In a letter to Adam Smith dated February or March 1757, Hume had written: 'You have read all the Dissertations in Manuscript; but you will find that on the natural History of Religion somewhat amended in point of Prudence.' Both the present amendment and the one noted below look like prudence.

The Jacobins: orginally a name for the French friars of the order of St Dominic.

Cordeliers: a name sometimes used in France for the Franciscans.

157 *sometimes painted ... powers and faculties*: in the proof sheets, the words within square brackets read 'sometimes degraded him so far to a level with human creatures as to represent him wrestling with a man, walking in the cool of the evening, showing his back parts, and

descending from Heaven to inform himself of what passes on earth'.

Magians: a priestly cast among the ancient Medes (western Iran), a main source of the Zoroastrian religion.

160 *compatible*: this difference between polytheism and monotheism (of, for example, the Christian type) provides the occasion for Hume's contrary miracles argument in *An Enquiry concerning Human Understanding*, Section X, Part II. See J. C. A. Gaskin, 'Contrary Miracles Concluded', in *Hume Studies*, 1985.

163 *the fatal vengeance of inquisitors*: it is easy to overlook the radical and risky opinion Hume is here expressing. In effect he is saying that the mass executions of heretics and the suppression of opposition by Christians is far *worse* than the practice of religions which overtly give occasional human sacrifices to their gods.

monkish virtues: for Hume on this theme, see *An Enquiry concerning the Principles of Morals*, Section IX, Part I.

166 *Arian, Pelagian . . . Protestant*: all save the last (and even that from one point of view) are well-documented Christian heresies. Information concerning them can be found, for example, in the *Oxford Dictionary of the Christian Church*, ed. F. L. Cross, (Oxford, 1958; 2nd edn. 1974).

the destruction of philosophers: for more on the relation of religion and philosophy, see *An Enquiry concerning Human Understanding*, Section I.

167 *Herodotus*: see *History*, bk. III, chs. 29 and 38.

Averroes: Islamic judge and philosopher, *c*.1126–98. His magisterial commentaries on Aristotle helped reintroduce the latter to medieval Europe. In this sentence and the next paragraph, Hume is alluding to the Roman Catholic doctrine of the real presence whereby the bread and wine used in the mass somehow become the body and blood of 'their deity'.

169 Presens divus habebitur *Augustus*: 'a god on earth Augustus shall be held', Horace, *Odes*, bk. III, ode 5.

170 *Petronius says*: *Satyricon*, para. 17 (Loeb, 23).

Varro: *On the Latin Language*, bk. V, ch. 10 (paras. 57–74).

172 *We may observe*: this paragraph is important if one asks whether Hume held that belief in a god (of some sort) is so fundamental a part of our understanding of the world that we cannot do without it. Compare *Dialogues*, pp. 36 f. and for discussions, see T. Penelhum 'Natural Belief and Religious Belief in Hume's Philosophy', *The*

Philosophical Quarterly, 1983; and J. C. A. Gaskin, *Hume's Philosophy of Religion* (London, 1988), ch. 7.

175   *This is the artifice of Cotta*: *De Natura Deorum*, bk. iii.

178   *affect to praise and admire*: the distortion which 'popular religion' imposes on morality is a theme returned to many times by Hume. His main complaints are that religion (*a*) creates 'frivolous species of merits', (*b*) creates false species of crimes (e.g. suicide), (*c*) involves praising the Almighty for his apparent responsibility for deeds which in humans would be real crimes, and (*d*) results in a variety of hypocritical affirmations of belief or conduct (see the note on the character of the clergy attached to Hume's essay 'Of National Characters', 1748).

179   *The gods have maxims of justice peculiar to themselves*: Hume's mild sarcasm is apparent when read, for example, against the much quoted verse Isaiah 55: 8: 'For my thoughts are not your thoughts, neither are your ways my ways, says the Lord.'

XIV: this whole section is of the first importance in understanding Hume's arguments and opinions concerning the relation of morality and religion. See also *Dialogues*, Part XII; *An Enquiry concerning Human Understanding*, Section, XI; and the account of secular morality developed in *An Enquiry concerning the Principles of Morals*, Sections I–V and IX.

not by virtue and good morals: if Hume concedes any function to 'true religion' it is the enhancement of natural morality. See note to p. 122 above.

the Sadder: almost certainly Hume's spelling for the *Seder* or *Siddur*, the Jewish book of prayer and worship.

185   *The whole is a riddle*: cf. the penultimate paragraph of the *Dialogues*. Note also Hume's sentiments in a letter to Andrew Millar, 3 September 1757; 'As to my Opinions, you know I defend none of them positively: I only propose my Doubts, where I am so unhappy as not to receive the same Conviction with the rest of Mankind.' In *An Enquiry concerning Human Understanding*, Hume in effect gives a philosophical structure to his 'doubts' about religion. Confident conclusions should be rejected, he maintains, and our arguments are unreliable because human understanding 'is by no means fitted for such remote and abstruse subjects'.

187   *And Macrobius . . . Sammonicus Serenus*: striking evidence of the remarkable range of Hume's classical reading as seen throughout the *Natural History*. Macrobius was an early fifth century AD eclectic

writer on literature, antiquities, etc. His large extant work, *The Saturnalia*, mentions, in Book III, Serenus' only known writing, *Res Reconditae*. Serenus died in AD 212.

189 *Exta*: 'the vitals of the sacrificial victim'. Throughout these references to Xenophon, Hume gives page references to an eighteenth-century edition of the Greek text which had an accompanying Latin translation.

190 Arians *or* Socinians: Christian heresies; the former after Arius (fourth century) the latter after Socinus (sixteenth century). Both tend to emphasize the unity and eternity of God, and doubt the eternity and divinity of Jesus, thus questioning Trinitarian doctrines. It would perhaps be fairer to speak of Locke and Newton as 'so-called' Arians as they never accepted these terms in application to themselves.

191 *the Chevalier Ramsay*: Andrew Michael Ramsay (1686–1743), born in Ayr, spent most of his life on the Continent; eccentric; converted to Roman Catholicism in 1710. Ramsay's sketch of Christian theology is, to Hume's evident relish, much more damaging than its innocent author intended. Comparable sketches, where the intention to damage Christianity is unambiguous, may be found in Bertrand Russell's 'A Free Man's Worship' in *Mysticism and Logic*, and in Mark Twain's *No. 44, The Mysterious Stranger*, ch. 34.

DESCRIPTIVE INDEX OF
CLASSICAL NAMES IN HUME'S TEXTS

ANAXAGORAS (*c.*500–*c.*427 BC) influential Presocratic Athenian philosopher prosecuted for impiety.

ANAXIMANDER (first half of 6th cent. BC) Ionian Greek philosopher or scientist of Miletus responsible for very daring physical and cosmological speculations.

ANAXIMENES (middle 6th cent. BC) successor of Anaximander in Miletus.

ARISTOPHANES (*c.*444–*c.*380 BC) Athenian comic playwright of great distinction.

ARISTOTLE (348–322 BC) magisterially important Greek philosopher many of whose writings are still extant. Pupil of Plato, tutor of Alexander the Great.

ARNOBIUS (late 2nd cent. AD) Latin author of an extant work chiefly valuable for its accounts of Greek and Roman customs and rituals.

ARRIAN (AD *c.*90–*c.*175) Greek author of a history of the Asiatic expedition of Alexander the Great.

AUGUSTINE (AD 354–430) prolific Latin Christian theologian, author of *The City of God.*

CAESAR, JULIUS (*c.*102–44 BC) the Dictator, general, author of the *Gallic War, et al..*

CHRYSIPPUS (*c.*280–207 BC) third and most important head of the School of Stoic Philosophy (the Stoa) in Athens; prolific author, none of whose works survive.

CICERO, MARCUS TULLIUS (106–43 BC) Roman statesman and author of numerous extant works in the finest Latin including eight on philosophy.

CURTIUS, RUFUS (early 1st cent. AD) Latin author of a history of Alexander the Great, occasionally known by his full name Quintus Curtius Rufus.

DIO CASSIUS (AD *c.*155–*c.*235) Greek historian of Rome from the beginnings to AD 229.

DIODORUS SICULUS (late 1st cent. BC to early 1st cent. AD) Greek world historian, only a fraction of whose monumental work survives.

DIOGENES LAERTIUS (2nd cent. AD) author of ten books of *Lives of the Philosophers* which happens to incorporate almost all the extant writings of Epicurus.

DIONYSIUS OF HALICARNASSUS (late 1st cent. BC) Greek rhetor and historian of Rome down to 264 BC, in which year the history of Polybius begins.

EPICTETUS (AD *c.*55–135) Stoic philosopher and moralist who taught in Rome; his *Discourses* survive written in Greek by Arrian.

and almost mystical metaphysical system survives in the *Enneads* and represents the last original development of classical philosophy.

PLUTARCH (AD *c*.46–*c*.120) Roman administrator and immensely prolific author of biographies and general works on morality and any other subject that caught his attention.

POLYBIUS (*c*.203–*c*.120 BC) Greek historian of Rome.

QUINTILIAN (AD *c*.37–before 100) Latin writer on oratory.

SALLUST (86–*c*.34 BC) Roman politician and author of a number of monographs on Roman history.

SENECA (*c*.5 BC–AD 65) senior Roman administrator richly endowed with literary ability and worldly goods, eventually a victim of undue proximity to Nero; author of tragedies and very fine letters and essays commending and applying Stoicism.

SEXTUS EMPIRICUS (late 2nd cent. AD) unoriginal compiler of enormously influential works on ancient scepticism whose writings have survived when his sources have been lost.

SOCRATES (469–399 BC) paragon of Greek philosophy known through writings of Plato, Xenophon, and others.

SPARTIANUS (early 4th cent. AD) one of the writers of the histories of the Caesars.

STRABO (63 BC–AD *c*.21) Greek geographer.

SUETONIUS (AD *c*.69–*c*.140) Roman biographer best known for his lives of the Roman emperors from Julius Caesar to Domitian.

TACITUS (AD *c*.55–after 115) most vivid, accurate, ironical, and readable of Roman historians, a contemporary of much of what he relates.

THALES (early 6th cent. BC) of Miletus, generally spoken of as the first philosopher; a competent astronomer and statesman.

THUCYDIDES (*c*.457–*c*.400 BC) historian of the war between Sparta and Athens, 431–404 BC, renowned for his clear, cool, concise style; his consistency and detachment.

VARRO (116–27 BC) Latin grammarian and polymath.

XENOPHON (*c*.430–*c*.369 BC) Greek general, adventurer, and author of diverse works of great interest including accounts of Socrates and of his own extraordinary escape from Persia with Greek mercenaries.

ZENO (335–263 BC) founder of the School of Stoic Philosophy in Athens.

Classical Literary Criticism

Greek Lyric Poetry

Myths from Mesopotamia

APOLLODORUS   The Library of Greek Mythology

APOLLONIUS OF RHODES   Jason and the Golden Fleece

APULEIUS   The Golden Ass

ARISTOTLE   The Nicomachean Ethics
                       Physics
                       Politics

CAESAR   The Civil War
                       The Gallic War

CATULLUS   The Poems of Catullus

CICERO   The Nature of the Gods

EURIPIDES   Medea, Hippolytus, Electra, and Helen

GALEN   Selected Works

HERODOTUS   The Histories

HESIOD   Theogony and Works and Days

HOMER   The Iliad
                       The Odyssey

HORACE   The Complete Odes and Epodes

JUVENAL   The Satires

LIVY   The Rise of Rome

LUCAN   The Civil War

MARCUS AURELIUS   The Meditations

OVID   The Love Poems
                       Metamorphoses
                       Sorrows of an Exile

The Oxford World's Classics Website

www.worldsclassics.co.uk

- Information about new titles
- Explore the full range of Oxford World's Classics
- Links to other literary sites and the main OUP webpage
- Imaginative competitions, with bookish prizes
- Peruse *Compass*, the Oxford World's Classics magazine
- Articles by editors
- Extracts from Introductions
- A forum for discussion and feedback on the series
- Special information for teachers and lecturers

www.worldsclassics.co.uk

American Literature

British and Irish Literature

Children's Literature

Classics and Ancient Literature

Colonial Literature

Eastern Literature

European Literature

History

Medieval Literature

Oxford English Drama

Poetry

Philosophy

Politics

Religion

The Oxford Shakespeare

A complete list of Oxford Paperbacks, including Oxford World's Classics, OPUS, Past Masters, Oxford Authors, Oxford Shakespeare, Oxford Drama, and Oxford Paperback Reference, is available in the UK from the Academic Division Publicity Department, Oxford University Press, Great Clarendon Street, Oxford OX2 6DP.

In the USA, complete lists are available from the Paperbacks Marketing Manager, Oxford University Press, 198 Madison Avenue, New York, NY 10016.

Oxford Paperbacks are available from all good bookshops. In case of difficulty, customers in the UK can order direct from Oxford University Press Bookshop, Freepost, 116 High Street, Oxford OX1 4BR, enclosing full payment. Please add 10 per cent of published price for postage and packing.